# Farewell to
# HIGHBURY

In memory of my father

© Norman Fox 2006
Published by The Bluecoat Press, Liverpool
Printed and bound by Compass Press Ltd of London
Book design by MARCH Graphic Design Studio, Liverpool

Cover photograph: Sam Bartram of Charlton saves at the feet of Ted Drake
(photograph courtesy of Getty Images).
All the pictures in the photo section of the book are courtesy of Empics except for
the picture of Thierry Henry on page 15 of the photo section which is courtesy of
David Ashdown of *The Independent*.

ISBN 1 904438 36 9

# Farewell to
# HIGHBURY
## The Arsenal Story

Norman Fox

**The Bluecoat Press**

# CONTENTS

# WHY LEAVE HOME?

HIGHBURY. Go to any part of the world where people talk about football and that word evokes instant recognition. When the Arsenal Stadium, as it is correctly but rarely called, was finally condemned to its distinguished history by a decision to build a new stadium, there was a widespread nostalgic and real sense of impending loss. Highbury will be remembered for being a place of rare interest: a football ground of genuine architectural importance and, at the same time, one that created a distinctive atmosphere. The 'visitors', whether players or fans, felt that it was neither alarmingly intimidating nor warmly welcoming. It was ... Highbury.

The stadium's two most recognisable grandstands were the fashionable symbols of the 1930s era of Herbert Chapman. In more recent times, Highbury was up-dated and made more comfortable, yet it gave the impression of being a fading old stage to which Arsenal's greatness of the past might never return, at least in any lasting way. But return it did, which is why, rightly or wrongly, Arsenal concluded that they had outgrown this monument to the magnetism of their name and the devotion of Gunners fans the world over.

It was resolved that Highbury could no longer be considered a viable home for a revived and thrusting club. 'Viable' – a word favoured by accountants; a word that pays no respect to history, personal memories, the loyalty of fans to their club and their appreciation of a meeting place that was a home from home. Certainly Highbury was too small to contain all of the multitudes that wanted to see Arsene Wenger's champions, but Arsenal also claimed that in the era of multi-million pound transfer fees and ludicrously high wages, income from a stadium with a capacity of only 38,500 was insufficient. However, the need for a highly successful Premiership club to place such emphasis on increased gate receipts at a time when television money and sponsorship had become such huge sources of income was not accepted without some scepticism. And when it was announced that the new £357m project at nearby Ashburton Grove was to be called the 'Emirates Stadium', rather than, say, 'New Highbury' or even 'Emirates Highbury', there was an understandable argument that the famous old home was being replaced by somewhere that, even before it had been opened, was already dedicated to an all-powerful master called the 'sponsor'. Those doubts were given additional worrying impetus.

The club's decision to pitch up somewhere else was a venture that came before somebody moved football's financial goalposts. That person was, of course, Roman Abramovich, the Russian oil billionaire who bought Chelsea, bought every player who wanted to accept his money and was in the business of buying success. In the past, that accusation had often been directed at Arsenal. The difference was that, traditionally, they bought with the money that came out of football itself. It had been generated by 'football people' or the club's share of television income that had not been directed at them alone.

Chelsea had been adopted by an individual who took spending into a different league. That may or may not result in long-term success, but it must have made Arsenal less comfortable about their move away from a ground that held such a distinguished place in the development of the game. Not that the accountancy company Deloitte and Touche, which each year reports on the financial health of clubs throughout Europe, was pessimistic about the future of Arsenal in particular. Looking back at the remarkable 2003-04 season, when the team were unbeaten in League matches, and even taking into account the club's long failure to win the ultimate prize of the European Champions' League, the company still reported that Arsenal had moved up the European money league from seventh to sixth. The report went as far as to say: "With Chelsea's success and Arsenal's Emirates Stadium development, we can foresee a scenario where English clubs fill the top three places in the 2006-07 money league".

Arsenal's own prediction is that the move will add £30m to annual profits. However, they will have a huge on-going debt that will make it imperative that the move to the new stadium is a success, which in turn will depend on investment in the future strength of the team. Obviously, this is a precarious tightrope.

In the cold terms of profit or loss, the financial experts may well be right. Whether the Emirates Stadium will ever replace Highbury in the affection of the fans is another matter.

Highbury could never be compared with the majority of other significant football grounds in Britain, most of which are easily found. Look for the floodlight pylons, or, in recent years, the vast new stands and, even from a distance, it would be difficult to miss them. Highbury was not like that. Anyone unfamiliar with the area in north London could come out of Arsenal tube station, only a few yards from the stadium's nearest entrance, and still need to ask directions. As Arsenal reawakened under the guidance of Arsene Wenger, other clubs in the forefront of the game (most conspicuously Manchester United) expanded their grounds ever upward.

Highbury remained concealed within residential streets, hemmed in by houses, many of which had gone from elegant prosperity to crumbling neglect and, in the 1990s, back to become 'desirable' and expensive.

Three sides of the stadium were always obscured, but the East Stand rose like a meticulously sculptured cliff: the most famous frontage of any club football stadium in the world. That aspect will remain after Arsenal have taken up residence a goalkeeper's long kick away in the new stadium. For more than seventy years, the façade of that unmistakably 1930s-style stand, with its entrance to the marble-clad reception area, represented the uniqueness of Arsenal.

During many of those years, people called them the 'Bank of England Club'. Highbury was the visual proof of prosperity. It was not always so; not at the beginning of the club's life nor in many subsequent years. Whether Arsenal's riches in the twenty-first century will be increased by a move to a new, bigger and expensive stadium and sustain them for as long as Highbury has been their home, who knows? Could the leaving of Highbury be like the failed experiment of playing European matches at Wembley, which was neither home nor away, or be a turning point in the effort to become a consistently major player in Europe rather than simply being a club capable of doing remarkable things within the confines of domestic competition?

# CHAPTER 1
# RED DAWN AT DIAL SQUARE

THE CLUB THAT GREW TO BECOME ARSENAL came into existence in the 1880s. It had a lowly upbringing on the southern outskirts of London where employees of the Woolwich munitions factory, particularly those football enthusiasts who had come from Scotland and the Midlands to seek employment, had already formed several other teams. The one they called Dial Square, after an area between Woolwich and Plumstead where there was a sundial over the entrance to a workshop, was the first root of what would develop into the world famous Arsenal.

Football itself was pulling away from the days when it was the preserve of the public schools. It was nurtured and spread by men like those at Woolwich; hard-working people in need of diversion and recreation. Not that the other residents of the area were waiting with avid enthusiasm to have as new neighbours a football club keen to be compared with those that had already begun to prosper in the midlands, the north and, primarily, in Scotland. Woolwich was essentially a rugby/cricket area in which the 1885 decision by the Football Association to legalise professionalism was viewed as tantamount to a liaison with the Devil. Most of the residents were not sorry when, in 1888, the Football League was formed without a southern club being involved.

David Danskin came from Fife to find work at Woolwich. For him football was not simply a hobby. A fiery enthusiast, he more than anyone campaigned to establish the professional game in the south of England through the foundation of the embryo Arsenal. Although there were plenty of football enthusiasts from the North and Midlands in the workshops, he knew that the real requirement was a core of players that was more than just enthusiastic. Fred Beardsley and Morris Bates, both former members of the Nottingham Forest club, had also come south to take employment at Woolwich and wanted to continue playing football. They, together with three workmates, John (known as Jack) Humble, Richard Pearce and Elijah Watkins (who became the club's first secretary) joined Danskin as founding fathers of a club that was slow to prosper.

The founders searched the factory to find like-minded men who wanted to share their ambition. Spare cash was short. Even buying the first ball required everyone to chip in. But Beardsley, who had been in goal for Forest in the FA Cup semi-final of 1885, was relentless in his determination and had some previous administrative experience in helping to set up Woolwich Union, one of the other clubs based at the factory.

In all probability there were at least half a dozen Woolwich teams in existence in the years before 1890. No exact date can be suggested for the official meeting that marked the formation of Arsenal's infant club, but the first match for Dial Square was against Eastern Wanderers on 11 December 1886. It was played on muddy, uneven ground on the Isle of Dogs. Records are scarce and unreliable. Dial Square certainly won, and 6-0 is said to have been the score. Elijah Watkins admitted that he was unsure of the outcome because "when the ball was not in the back gardens, it was in the ditch; and that was full of the loveliest material that could possibly be". The team was probably: Beardsley; Danskin, Porteous, Gregory, Bee, Wolfe, Smith, Moy, Whitehead, Morris, Duggan.

Encouraged by that win, though not by the experience of playing on a mud-patch next to that evil-smelling ditch, the players got together on Christmas Day, 1886 to discuss future plans. One thing was clear. If they were to be successful and attract paying spectators in greater numbers, they needed to find a better ground and change the club's name from Dial Square to something more imposing. The grand title Royal Arsenal was chosen, though perhaps not for any pretentious reason. The meeting was held at the Royal Oak pub, so in all probability the players simply combined the 'Royal' with the 'Arsenal' where they worked.

Over the years, the club's name changed several times. It remained Royal Arsenal until 1891 when it became Woolwich Arsenal, though in reality the club never actually played matches in the borough of Woolwich. Obviously a later move to north London meant that the 'Woolwich' was even less an accurate description of the club's home, so that was dropped and so emerged simply Arsenal, although 'The Arsenal' has been a colloquial title lasting for generations.

Royal Arsenal's first match was played against Erith at Plumstead Common on 8 January 1887. The team was: Beardsley; Danskin, Porteous, Gregory, Price, Wells, Smith, Moy, Whitehead, Crighton, Bee.

In the early games the players wore whatever colour shirt they could provide. Finally red was chosen, partly because at least two of the founder members of the team wore old Forest shirts, but mainly as a result of Forest being persuaded by Beardsley to donate a whole set and a ball. As a result, most people called the club the Woolwich Reds. It was all very well having new shirts but the club was still without a regular home.

The Sportsman Ground on Plumstead Common was often waterlogged and unusable. As a result, the team sometimes appeared at Manor Field, which was conveniently close to the Railway Tavern, where they were allowed to change, wash and be 'refreshed'. In their first full season, when gates usually numbered about 500, they played ten games, won seven and lost two. They conceded only eight goals, though whether in those early days anyone suggested they were boring who knows!

As the club grew in stature, they won the Kent Senior Cup, Kent Junior Cup and London Charity Cup, before entering the country's most important competition, the FA Cup, for the first time in 1889-90. Meantime, the need to find a more permanent and better site became obvious. Nevertheless, they stayed in the Plumstead area. Between 1890 and 1893 they played at the Invicta Ground, just behind the High Street. There they had a home that did at least look more like a real football ground, with some terraces and a stand. Even in those infant years, they were attracting crowds of several thousands. However, their status nationally was still so low that they had to battle through preliminary Cup games before they faced the Swifts, who had several internationals in their side and won comfortably 5-1.

The Cup defeat was not unexpected yet no less humiliating because it emphasised that there was a substantial difference between being able to achieve success in the Kent and south London area and making inroads nationally. The answer then, as it has remained to this day, was the raising of money to provide the incentives to attract the best players. Arsenal were not the first and far from the last at home or abroad to realise that if they could find good jobs outside football for the players they wanted, the magnet would be irresistible. Sure enough, the side was strengthened by players brought in from all over England and, importantly, Scotland, where the game was thriving. However, in the following season they were still not strong enough to overcome the powerful Derby County in the FA Cup and, as a result, Jack Humble realised that the only way forward was to persuade the club to espouse total professionalism. The difficult decision was taken. It proved far less painful than the outcome.

The south of England was still firmly against professionalism. Having taken the plunge, the club's members realised that while they seemed to have no other option, at the same time they had acted provocatively. The London Football Association openly reviled 'northern' professionalism, which was attracting southern players. They banned the club from playing in all of their competitions, leaving only the FA Cup and friendly games, which were not attractive to spectators. The only answer was to lead a campaign to have a southern area professional league that would have twelve clubs. Relations with Tottenham were already tense because Spurs considered that they were competing for the same support. They were not improved when Tottenham failed to be elected. Several of the clubs began to have misgivings, especially after a threat by the London FA to ban them all.

Woolwich Arsenal, alone, refused to buckle. They applied to the Football League to become members of the newly formed Second Division for the season 1893-94. It was a decision not without risk since the club had not done well against teams from the Midlands and North and now they were committing themselves to play against them on a league basis. In addition, the cost would be demanding.

Their home was still the Invicta Ground, owned by the Weaver Mineral Water Company that had been charging them a rent of £200 a year. Seeing that their tenants were moving into the higher circles of football's establishment, the company demanded a further £150, an impossible amount to raise. As a result, the club moved back to the Manor Field, which had to be up-dated for Second Division football and became known as the Manor Ground. The bulk of the work was carried out by supporters, who also helped financially. Arsenal's first League match was played on 2 September, 1893 when they drew 2-2 with Newcastle United. The team was: Williams; Powell, Jeffrey, Devine, Buist, Howat, Gemmell, Henderson, Shaw, Elliott, Booth. The scorers were Shaw and Elliott. By the end of the season Arsenal were ninth.

In those early years, under the guidance of Sam Hollis (the first official manager), the team had moderate success. They improved to eighth in 1894-5 and seventh in the next season. Hollis was in charge when, in 1896, they produced such curious League results as beating Newcastle United 5-1 yet losing 8-0 to Loughborough Town. Oddly enough, while that became Arsenal's record League defeat, their record League victory (12-0) was produced against Loughborough in 1900. Hollis was succeeded by Tom Mitchell, who, from 1884 to 1896, had been in charge of Blackburn Rovers. Then came George Elcoat, who, in 1898 and 1899, made a significant improvement by bringing in virtually a whole team of Scots. However, the turn of the century saw more problems because men were called away for duty in the Boer War in South Africa (1899-1902). Work at Woolwich producing armaments involved long hours, including Saturdays. The club barely survived the pressures. Financially there was little in reserve.

The tide turned under the guidance of the first fully professional manager, Harry Bradshaw, who knew that because of the club's precarious financial position he had to find players locally. Amongst his discoveries was Jimmy Ashcroft, who had been keeping goal for nearby Gravesend. In 1906, Ashcroft became the club's first international when he played for England against Northern Ireland. Before that, however, in 1904, the club added another feather to their own cap by becoming the first southern side to win promotion to the First Division when, needing one point from their last match of the season, at home to Port Vale, they played out a goalless draw to finish second behind Preston. Achieving the negative and turning it into the positive was to become a theme that stuck.

In that early part of the twentieth century, Woolwich Arsenal began to realise that, in the future, competition between clubs from different countries could become attractive to the supporters, perhaps financially profitable and a useful test of ability outside the usual run of domestic games. They invited a team made up of players from several clubs in Paris (plus Hodges, an Arsenal reserve whom the French had to borrow to complete their team) to play at the Manor Ground. The Continental visitors were neither impressed by the weather nor impressive in their football.

The game took place on a dank December Monday afternoon. A crowd of about 3,000 turned up, more out of curiosity than expectancy. Woolwich Arsenal scored 26, Paris 1. The *Daily Express* reported: "Football as played at Plumstead yesterday, although highly amusing, serves no good purpose beyond the fact that it proves to our friends from across the Channel that they still have a lot to learn before they can hope to compete with our best Association clubs". The writer added: "Such farces are seldom seen on English grounds, and it is to be hoped that in future fixtures of this kind will not be encouraged. Any one of our school XIs would easily have given the Paris team of yesterday a beating".

The 'superiority complex' that was so blatant in this early report was probably justified at the time. Unfortunately it remained within the English game up until and even after Hungary (who in that country's formative footballing years had been given a solid grounding by the English coach Jimmy Hogan) came to Wembley in 1953 and humiliated England 6-3. With some special exceptions, British-born players of the past half-century have tended to lack the natural technique and sense of adventure of their foreign brothers. In 2005, Arsenal were roundly criticised for naming a team and all the substitutes without a single home-produced player. Undoubtedly a huge influx of foreign imports throughout British football has had a

13

damaging effect on the number of home produced players achieving first team status in the Premiership, but there is no avoiding the fact that the majority of players brought in from around the world have been technically superior.

Arsenal cannot be accused of failing to embrace the idea of playing against foreign opposition long before it became fashionable. At the end of the 1906-07 season they went on a sixteen-day tour of Europe during which they played eight matches, winning seven including a 9-1 victory in Berlin and a 9-0 win in Budapest.

Once he had taken the club into the First Division, Bradshaw felt he had achieved all he could and accepted a substantial wage increase to become the first manager of Fulham. Phil Kelso, a tough Scot, took over at a good time, building on Bradshaw's work. Gates improved, and so did the finances. In the 1906-07 season, the team took fifteen points from their opening nine games and became the first southern club ever to head the First Division. They also reached the FA Cup semi-final for the second year (they lost to Newcastle in 1905-06 and then Sheffield Wednesday). They failed to maintain their early season League form, however, but still finished a creditable seventh, generally impressing with their well-organised play. When results began to go wrong, the whole situation changed. Woolwich was not an easy place to reach and other London clubs were more accessible. There was plenty of football to watch, including matches in the expanding Southern League.

In 1908, Kelso was attracted away to take over from Bradshaw at Fulham and was followed by George Morrell, another Scot, who had managed Rangers but soon found that his new job was far more difficult than he expected. The club had to make money by selling off most of the team that had reached the last FA Cup semi-final, including four forwards and the outstanding Ashcroft. At least they clung on to Joe Shaw, a reliable full back on the field and a stalwart supporter of the club in the background. Later he would become assistant manager. And in Andy Ducat they discovered a constructive half-back who became the first of several footballer-cricketers that over the years the club had on their books, most famously the outstanding exponent of both games, Denis Compton. Ducat played for Surrey and England.

# CHAPTER 2
## ARRIVAL OF THE 'DICTATOR'

IN 1910, RELEGATION WAS NARROWLY AVOIDED when finishing just ahead of Chelsea and Bolton Wanderers. Crowds dwindled and, at the same time, a debt of £3,000 was accumulated. The club had no choice but to make it known that a wealthy purchaser or patron would be welcome. Along came Henry Norris, certainly wealthy, often controversial, brilliant and sometimes devious. He was the man without whom Woolwich Arsenal would not have become the celebrated Arsenal FC or made their all-important move to Highbury.

Early in the twentieth century, Norris held the position of Mayor of Fulham. He had also been Chairman of Fulham FC. His riches had come from his work as an estate agent and property developer, building over 2,000 houses in and around Fulham. He helped finance the local football club's building of Craven Cottage, which allowed them to move into the Football League. Bernard Joy, a fine amateur player for Arsenal and later respected journalist, described Norris as "nothing less than a dictator". Norris himself would not have denied that he was dictatorial and ambitious. He had the feeling that Fulham would never become one of the country's truly important clubs. With proper respect to their longevity, occasional success and likeable character, he was right in the short and long term. He was also aware of Arsenal's financial problems but saw a potential and rescued them from likely oblivion.

His original proposal was to combine Fulham and Arsenal under a ground-sharing arrangement at Craven Cottage. This met with the disapproval of the Football Association and the Football League. As a result, Arsenal remained at Plumstead and Fulham further developed the Cottage. Norris remained convinced that Arsenal were in the wrong place and that they should move, leaving south London to Millwall and Charlton Athletic who were beginning to come to prominence. This time he was not going to be diverted from his objective. He had already made enemies within the game's authorities but the club recognised him as their saviour.

In their desperation to attract bigger gates, they signed Alf Common, the goalscoring inside-forward or centre-forward who, in 1905, had become the first £1,000 player when he moved from Sunderland to Middlesbrough. Now, though, in 1910, he was thirty-years-old and restrictively overweight. Arsenal simply believed that his name alone would draw in the crowds and, briefly, they were right. After a while it became obvious that Common was no substitute for the popular Ducat, who had been sold to Aston Villa for £1,500. Ducat, a right-half, had scored three goals on his first appearance for Arsenal back in 1905 and had gone on to play six times for England over a period of eleven years.

The 1912-13 season proved a terrible term for Arsenal. Elsewhere, and in spite of the growing certainty of a future war (or perhaps because of it), there was a defiant, almost carefree mood. The music halls were packed and successful football clubs were drawing big crowds. Arsenal were relegated for the first and only time in their history. The signing of Common was transparently a publicity gimmick that backfired. He was unfit and no longer a real threat to opposing defences. The weak team won only one home game, scored just eleven goals on their own ground and finished bottom, five points behind Notts County who were also relegated. The financial situation was again perilous. Their bank balance was only just in the black and income from gates averaged only £200.

Norris was even more convinced that if survival was to be guaranteed the club had to move nearer to the centre of the capital. He said attendances would automatically rise and the whole financial situation be improved. Easier said than done. He examined the requirements and came to the conclusion that the first priority was to find a site that was in a residential area that had a large population living within walking distance of the ground. He felt sure that those people would become the bedrock supporters, but he was keen to tap into the potential of having a stadium that was also easily reached from central London. Additionally, it would not make sense to move anywhere too close to a rival club. He travelled around the London area looking for possible locations. Harringay and Battersea were suitable in terms of population but no ideal space was available. He even went back south of the Thames in search of what was needed, without success.

The club's officials then discovered that St. John's College of Divinity, at Highbury, might be willing to dispense with its playing fields. Norris and his partner, William Hall, saw an end to their search. Gillespie Road underground station was close by and, at the same time, the area around had a large residential population. Not that the locals were much pleased by rumours of a football club coming to their doorsteps. Norris worked on various schemes to make the approach more attractive to the powerful site owners, the Ecclesiastical Commissioners, who were far from convinced that they should be seen to encourage a football club. On the other hand, they were attracted by the thought of the money they would receive if they did sell.

Gradually Arsenal increased the amount they were prepared to pay and, eventually, a section of the estate (some six acres) was offered to them on a twenty-one year lease at a cost of £20,000, an awful lot of money in those days. Norris still had to convince the shareholders who were asked to attend a meeting at the Connaught Rooms, in central London, in March, 1913. There, in dramatic terms, he made his case. Unless the club moved to an area in which they could attract better attendances they would almost certainly die. He told them about the site he had seen and said that it was not possible to pay their way in Plumstead because they were no longer the only League club in London. He said that Highbury was the apex of an equilateral triangle, with a line drawn from Clapton Orient and Tottenham Hotspur grounds as the base.

He stressed that the club had been in the Football League for longer than the others in London but had forfeited patronage by being in the wrong place. On the following morning the *Daily Mirror* commented: "It would be a thousand pities if a club like The Arsenal had to put up its shutters for lack of support, seeing that for twelve years they were the only members in town of the Football League, and most people will wish The Arsenal good luck in their plucky endeavour to keep the flag flying under the most disastrous conditions in years".

The area that the club decided they wanted included two cricket pitches, two football pitches and several tennis courts. The Archbishop of Canterbury himself had to sign the deed of transfer, together with members of the Bench of Bishops, who insisted that no matches would be played on Good Friday or Christmas Day. That edict remained in force until 1925, when the club bought the whole of the estate, about ten acres, for £47,000 and paid £17,000 for some additional land. The original college was on the site that later accommodated a large block of flats. The college continued as tenants of the club until a fire during the Second World War destroyed the buildings.

Locally, the arrival of an ambitious football club was resented. Residents in what was a quiet spot out of the centre of London spoke about the imposition of "undesirable elements of professional football". In the meantime, other London clubs were also unhappy. Tottenham were particularly upset because they had invested some £40,000 in ground improvements, while Clapton Orient, based at Homerton, also feared competition for spectators. In spite of being miles away on the west of

London, Chelsea joined the objectors. Tottenham and Clapton Orient issued a joint statement saying that if "The Arsenal" moved to the Islington area "No club will be safe".

The Islington Borough Council took the side of the opposition. They raised a petition protesting that football clubs were in the business of exploiting players in order to raise share values. They also maintained that property prices in the area would fall. What these days would be called the NIMBY factor was a considerable barrier to the club's plans. You could see the point. There was a considerable difference between having students at a college of divinity as your neighbours and the noisy fans of a professional football club.

A meeting was called by the League Management Committee to allow all interested parties to air their views on the newcomers. William Hall represented Arsenal, C.D. Roberts spoke for Tottenham and G. Arbor for Clapton Orient. After a long debate, the following resolution was adopted. "In view of the fact that a considerable number of clubs in the League have changed their ground without application to, or consent from, the League, this Committee is unanimously of the opinion that they have no right to interfere with the proposal of Woolwich Arsenal to remove its ground to Gillespie Road. The Committee are of the opinion that there is ample population and opportunity for three League clubs within the area from which the crowds for the three clubs will be drawn; and for those reasons they decline to convene a special meeting of the League, and are of the opinion that under the rules and practice of the League there is no right to interfere".

Of paramount importance to the success of the proposed new ground was, as Norris had recognised, the fact that Gillespie Road underground station, which had opened in 1906, was only a few steps from Highbury. As a result, people in central London would be more likely to attend Arsenal matches than those being played further afield. So the last game at the Manor Ground took place on 28 April 1913. During that final forlorn season in south London, the club obtained Jock Rutherford from Newcastle. He had been known as a clever England international inside-forward but, at Arsenal, he established himself on the right wing and served the club well for more than a decade. In the future, many players brought to the club after having made their names elsewhere would be asked to change positions, with considerable success.

Once the final negotiations for the purchase of the land at Highbury had been completed, there was optimism about the club's ability to exist for years to come. For the moment, however, there was not a lot of hope on the pitch itself. In 1913-14, promotion to Division One was missed, though only by goal average, and war-time football would not see crowds large enough to cover costs. In spite of that, one of the most up-to-date stadiums in the world was beginning to take shape ... not the Highbury of the modern era, nevertheless an arena much to be envied.

The choice of designer for the new ground was Archibald Leitch, a Scottish engineer and architect, who had worked on the new Hampden Park as well as Ibrox and Parkhead (Celtic Park). His perception of a perfect stadium was a full-length, two-tier stand on one side of the pitch and open terracing on the other three. The first clubs to appreciate his work south of the border were Chelsea, Fulham, Blackburn Rovers and Tottenham. He also produced Everton's classic Goodison Park.

Leitch planned that his two-tier stand at Highbury would be built on the eastern side with a capacity of nine thousand, mainly seated, though standing room would be available at one end. This, the largest stand in London, would have a multi-span roof. The fascia of each gable would contain a letter from ARSENAL FC. On the other three sides of the pitch there would be standing room only, and all open to the elements. Leitch cut costs by discovering that much of the banking could be made out of the rubble from the underground railway excavations.

Opening day (6 September, 1913) found a pitch that was not properly prepared because there was still a considerable slope. The first match for what had become known as 'The Arsenal' was against Leicester Fosse who were beaten 2-1. The players had no warm water in which to wash. One player who was injured could not struggle to the dressing room and had to be carried off on a milk cart.

Arsenal went on to finish third in Division Two, thus ending the season fairly satisfactorily in the eyes of most people – not so Norris. The outlay on the new ground to him personally was in the region of £125,000, but any ideas he may have had of recouping his investment were removed by the outbreak of World War I. The total cost of the move from Plumstead was about £50,000, while the new stand involved spending another £50,000. Norris personally guaranteed a bank overdraft of £10,000 and loaned the club an unsecured £15,000. Not surprisingly, when the war ended the overall debt was still £60,000. By then, Norris had received a knighthood and he might have been forgiven for abandoning what seemed to be a seriously ailing club. That would have underestimated his defiance and determination.

# CHAPTER 3
## PROMOTION SCANDAL

NORRIS HAD ALREADY SHOWN HIMSELF TO BE SHREWD, persuasive and ruthless. Arsenal badly needed to gain prestige and improve gate receipts. First Norris worked to improve the playing side. In 1919, he appointed the experienced Leslie Knighton as manager. Knighton, who had done good work behind the scenes at Huddersfield and Manchester City, was immediately told that he was not to pay more than £1,000 in transfer fees and that, ideally, he should produce his own players from local sources. At the same time, he was more or less ordered to get the club back into the First Division pronto (a situation that many a manager over the years would recognise).

In the same year, it was decided that because of the growth in the public's post-war appetite for football entertainment, the First and Second Divisions should be made larger by two clubs, making twenty-two in each. The results of the last full season before the war stopped League competition (1914-15) were taken into account. In that period Derby and Preston had finished at the top of Division Two while Chelsea and Tottenham Hotspur had occupied the last two places in Division One. Norris talked to anyone who would listen and whipped up support for Arsenal, who had finished only sixth in the Second Division in 1915, and, to all intents and purposes, had no case for promotion. After all, Birmingham, Wolves and Barnsley had finished ahead of them and behind the two leaders.

Somehow Norris persuaded a sufficient number of influential people on the League Management Committee that his club should take one of the two promotion places. This despite the fact that the committee members had earlier indicated that they were inclined to re-elect Chelsea and Tottenham and allow Derby and Preston to have promotion, which would have been perfectly logical. Norris continued to talk at length to all of the members of the Management Committee. Finally, he won the support of the committee's president, John McKenna, who was also Chairman of Liverpool.

The decision itself had to be taken at the annual meeting. There, McKenna first proposed that Chelsea should take one of the places on merit. The proposal went through without being opposed. He then made a strong, passionate speech in favour of Arsenal. Anyone looking at his argument on the basis of fair play would have interpreted it as nonsense. Why should Arsenal be given priority over Barnsley, Wolves and Birmingham let alone Spurs? McKenna talked about Arsenal's service to the League cause, which was also a spurious argument since Wolves and Birmingham had been in the League longer. Amazingly, his recommendation was accepted. Lucky Arsenal indeed!

They were voted to membership of the First Division (which they never relinquished) along with Chelsea, Derby and Preston. Tottenham were enraged. Norris was accused of being deeply involved in an outrageous scandal ... Arsenal never looked back. Although Spurs won promotion to the First Division in the 1919-20 season and scored over one hundred goals in the process, it took a long time for them to forgive and they never forgot. Indeed, in September, 1922, when the teams met at White Hart Lane, the match was so ill-disciplined that an FA Commission of Inquiry was called and Spurs were warned that if spectator violence was repeated their ground would be closed.

So, in 1919, Arsenal had become controversial new members of the top division. Of course, anyone wishing to cite the scandal could justifiably claim that history showed that the club never actually won the right to be there and remain there. Be that as it may, Norris's audacity and dubious tactics ensured that they would become the most popular club in the capital. A feeling for Highbury of those days can be taken from a report by 'Spectator', who began his article on a match against Newcastle by saying: "The excellently-appointed new ground of Arsenal was packed by a huge crowd estimated at 60,000. Both teams had to run the gauntlet of an army of press photographers and cinematographic operators. McCracken lost the toss and Arsenal elected to play with the sun behind their backs. They immediately pressed, feeding Rutherford, the ex-Novocastrian winger, assiduously". Reporting changes! Newcastle won but McCracken was several years away from being the defender who forced the change in the offside law.

The stadium's location close to the centre of London made it attractive when it came to arranging international fixtures. The first was held on 15 March 1920 when Wales beat England 2-1. Three years later, on 19 March 1923, the ground held the first England game against foreign opposition when Belgium visited and lost 6-1. However, the prestige of becoming London's first international venue (ahead of the Empire Stadium, Wembley) did little to help the club financially.

Leslie Knighton's time as manager up to 1925 was hard work. A few of the pre-war team remained, including Shaw and Rutherford, but new talent was not easy to find. Knighton had to rely on being tipped off by friends and former colleagues at other clubs. Indeed, it was a friend who suggested that he took a look at a wing half who was playing in Army teams. The name was Tom Whittaker who, after long deliberation about whether he would be better off becoming a marine engineer, signed as a professional in 1920. Whittaker was later to become one of the club's most eminent trainers and managers.

One of Knighton's best discoveries was Bob John, who had been playing in South Wales and had seemed on the verge of signing for Cardiff City. Knighton persuaded him that his career would be better served by moving to London rather than staying in Wales. He was right. John became one of the most versatile players of his generation and an essential part of the great Arsenal team that would evolve in the 1930s.

Norris continued to worry about the effect that ever increasing transfer fees would have not only on Arsenal but the game as a whole. He tried to persuade the League that there should be an upper limit of £1,650. This was one of the few occasions on which he was unable to get his own way. There was self-interest in his campaign since he knew that while other clubs would be prepared to raise the fees well above his suggested maximum figure, at Arsenal that was the most the club would pay. Consequently, Knighton had to get along with what he had, which often meant experimenting by moving players from position to position. Norris was not satisfied with the outcome.

This was a period in football's history in which a considerable amount of faith was being put in strange, allegedly strength (physical and mental) building 'medicines'. Knighton recalled that when he was faced with an important Cup tie which Arsenal badly needed to win, he sat in his office with his head in his hands "wondering how on earth we were going to put West Ham out of the Cup". Then somebody handed him a card on which was the name of 'a distinguished West End doctor' whom he visited. The doctor told him: "What the boys require is something in the nature of a courage-pill. Occasionally we administer such things to patients requiring abnormal stamina or resistance for a particular purpose. They do no harm but simply tone up the nervous reflexes to produce the maximum effort, and they leave no serious after-effects".

In his desperation, Knighton was ready to try anything. He explained: "When we went to Upton Park, I talked the matter over and, as a sign of good faith to the boys, I had offered to take my pill when they took theirs. And I needed it! One hour before play began we sat solemnly round, each swallowing his silver pill. Alf Baker suddenly guffawed and we all saw the comic side of it but every man did his duty and swallowed his pill. Then we sat around nervously awaiting the results".

Shortly before the kick-off, it was clear that the players were eager to get into action. Knighton remarked: "So was I. I felt I needed to run, jump, shout. There was something in those pills. I felt I could push down a wall with my fists". Sitting in the dressing room, what none of them could have known was that a London fog had come down. The match was called off and the players were left with a raging thirst which they said they could not quench no matter how much they drank. Some of their successors of the 1990s often had the same problem!

When the game was finally played, Knighton again gave the players what he called their "pluck pills" and, he said, they "seemed like giants – supercharged". In spite of that they only drew and it was decided that the pills would not be taken before the replay, which resulted in another draw before, eventually, they lost the second replay. What the doctor ordered nobody really knows, although a mixture of strychnine and other chemicals was mentioned.

The Knighton teams sometimes came dangerously close to relegation, and the Cup brought no respite. Inevitably, the manger took the blame and was sacked. The club was again on the edge of bankruptcy and desperately needed a man who knew his football, had an excellent record and ambition. All very well, but Norris was still adamant that the new manager would not be given *carte-blanche* to spend as much as he wished in the transfer market. He was about to meet his match.

# CHAPTER 4
## CHAPMAN AND HIS MONUMENT

T HE MOST SIGNIFICANT MOMENT IN THE WHOLE HISTORY of Arsenal came in May, 1925 when Herbert Chapman was appointed manager. The importance of Chapman to football, the club and to Highbury itself cannot be over-stressed. He came from a Yorkshire mining area. His father could neither read nor write but the young Chapman was clever enough to take his place at a technical college in Sheffield, where he studied Mining Engineering. In fact, he followed a career in engineering until, in 1921, he took a job as full-time manager of Huddersfield Town.

His own playing career was distinguished more by the number of clubs for which he appeared than the quality of his play. He represented ten different ones, including Spurs, before, in 1907, becoming player-manager of Northampton Town. His wide experience both as a player and in industry prepared him well for club management and he quickly took Northampton from bottom of the Southern League to the top (1909) and brought them several good Cup runs. He then went back to Yorkshire to manage Leeds City, of the Second Division, who were struggling. Under his guidance, by 1914 they had become good enough to come close to gaining promotion, taking fourth place, two points behind Arsenal who had missed out on promotion behind Notts County and Bradford.

In the war years, Chapman was in charge of running a munitions factory, which was a strange coincidence in view of his later work with Arsenal. At the same time, he remained in charge of the depleted though successful Leeds team. He was astute, opportunistic and, like Norris, not beyond bending the rules. He had been in trouble with the League over alleged illegal payments and, in 1919, again found himself accused when Leeds were told to appear before a League commission to defend themselves against accusations that similar offences occurred between 1916 and 1918. When the club refused to show their financial records, they were expelled. Chapman could argue that he was not actively involved with the club during the time in question but there is little doubt that he must have known about the situation.

The demise of Leeds City led to the rise of Huddersfield Town, who decided that it was an opportunity to move their club out of the Rugby League stronghold where they were based and into the Leeds ground. The idea was firmly rejected by a small, dedicated group of supporters but the shock of realising that they had come so close to being moved out of Huddersfield spurred them into earnest work to ensure that the club not only survived but prospered as never before.

By the time Chapman was asked to become assistant to Ambrose Langley at Huddersfield, the team had already gained promotion to the first division and appeared in the 1920 FA Cup Final. Having not been involved in football for some four years, Chapman had been released from his suspension. In any case, the League probably thought that he would be too out of touch to have much of a future in the game. How wrong they were.

Langley was not popular with the supporters who blamed him for the proposal to move to Leeds. As a result, it was not long before he was replaced by Chapman, who remained until 1925 when he departed for Arsenal. Huddersfield dominated that period, becoming League champions twice before he left, and again in 1926. His drive and depth of knowledge was envied by many other clubs. Norris, never slow to poach a talent or two, approached him and suggested that he join Arsenal for a salary of £2,000 a year (considerably more than any other manager was receiving at the time). As far as is known, Chapman did not need any further enticement. Having spent some of his playing career in north London with Spurs, he was in accord with Norris, who emphasised to him that Arsenal had many advantages, not least being closer to the centre of London and within a few yards of an underground station. Not only that, the idea of raising the club out of their considerable difficulties to their full potential appealed to Chapman, who enthusiastically accepted the challenge. Huddersfield were furious.

After his appointment, Chapman told Arsenal supporters that the club needed a five-year plan and he asked them not to expect too much too rapidly. Most managers then and now make much the same vague plea, knowing that even if money is offered to assist them, time is likely to be the one thing that will not be on their side. Chapman was not naïve enough to believe that he would be given five years to pull the club round. Indeed, he acted quickly, bringing in the players he believed Arsenal needed. He seemed to ignore Norris's edict about not spending too much money. First he got the players, then he developed his tactics around them.

The purchase of Charlie Buchan, a player of such talent that he had a reputation for being 'too clever' for those who played with him, was full of intrigue. Buchan knew that if he moved south from Sunderland he would have to give up his shop. He asked for compensation. Quite how a deal was struck is not clear but it certainly caused bad feeling between Norris and Chapman. There is little doubt that Norris was what, in later years, would be called a 'wheeler-dealer' and Chapman's problems at Leeds sustained a lingering doubt about his own probity as far as financial matters were concerned.

Although thirty-four, Buchan was high on Chapman's list of priorities, which was ironic because this brilliant, ball-playing, goalscoring inside-forward for a renowned Sunderland side in the pre-First World War years, was actually born in south London. He had even played for Woolwich Arsenal as an amateur until the club disputed his claim for eleven shillings expenses and he left them to join Leyton. Arsenal had to pay a lot more to get him back: £2,000 as well as £100 a goal in the first season. He scored nineteen, which suited both clubs. Arsenal considered that he was a bargain and Sunderland were happy with the money.

Chapman had made a forceful impression and it would last for the all-too-brief period of his career at Highbury. He moved the players he had inherited into positions in which he thought they would improve. As an example, he turned Jimmy Brain from being a creative inside-forward into a goalscorer. In the 1925-26 season, Brain scored thirty-one goals, establishing a club record. When there were injuries, Chapman acted quickly to find replacements, thus Joe Hulme, the fastest winger of the time, was brought in, to good effect. Even so, from one personal point of view, Chapman had a frustrating first season (1925-26) in that his old club, Huddersfield, were again champions, but at least Arsenal finished second and they were back in profit.

Chapman was far from satisfied, especially as he felt some of the players were of the opinion that second best after the years of struggle was virtually the height of achievement. Early results in the new season (1926-27) confirmed his view. He knew that the defence needed a stronger, steadier influence. So he signed Tom Parker from Southampton and made him captain. Parker was to play one hundred and fifty five consecutive League games and become the rock of the defence in the manner of an early Tony Adams.

Although League results were variable and Highbury was not a ground much feared by opponents, Chapman's team rebuilding paid off in the FA Cup. They finally overcame their semi-final hoodoo (they had been in two before and lost both) by beating Southampton on a muddy Stamford Bridge pitch and so had to face Cardiff City in the 1927 Final at Wembley. Cardiff had played in the 1925 Final, losing to Sheffield United, but of the

Arsenal players only Buchan had previously appeared at the new national stadium (in international matches), although he had played in a Final for Sunderland way back in 1913 when it was held at Crystal Palace. He was now nearing retirement and suffering from an injury that made him a doubtful starter until the day before the match.

This was to be one of the game's many disappointing Cup Finals in terms of exciting incident but the outcome was historic. Arsenal were firm in defence, which pleased Chapman, though not everyone else. Buchan was clearly the most talented player on the pitch but could not quite spark the rest of the team. Hulme, who had been injured, was lethargic. Even George Allison, the BBC commentator (and Arsenal director) sounded bored.

With seventeen minutes left, Cardiff's rugged captain, Fred Keenor, took a throw-in to Hugh Ferguson who attempted a long shot. Dan Lewis, in the Arsenal goal, seemed untroubled, going on one knee to hold the ball. However, Ferguson chased down his own shot. Lewis caught sight of him but lost sight of the ball, which slipped away. He made another grab but it bounced off his elbow and journeyed slowly over the line. Ironically, Lewis was Welsh and his error gave Cardiff the trophy. He threw his losers medal on to the pitch. Bob John tried to say the right thing by promising Lewis that he would have another chance. He was wrong. When, three years later, Arsenal reached another Cup Final, Lewis was injured and unable to play. His mistake meant that, for the first and only time, the FA Cup was taken out of England.

# CHAPTER 5
# RECOGNITION AT LAST

THE SIGNIFICANCE OF ARSENAL'S FIRST CUP FINAL was less in the result than in the fact that, at last, the club had to be taken seriously throughout the land. Chapman was assembling probably the most efficient club grouping of players there had ever been. They were still guided on the pitch by the veteran yet still illustriously skilful Buchan. However, youth was moving in. Cliff 'Boy' Bastin, who had joined from Exeter City at the age of only seventeen, was to form an almost uncanny understanding with Alex James, Joe Hulme and the tall, graceful David Jack, who was one of so many gifted players who, over the years, have received less international recognition than they deserved (in his case only nine caps for England). This triumvirate formed the foundation of the 1930s triumphs.

For those players who were already moving toward the end of their careers, Chapman gave encouragement and so wrung out many more valuable performances in much the same way that Arsene Wenger extended the careers of several thirty-somethings when he arrived and gave himself a transitional period before the foreign legion arrived. In return, Chapman's players got the best out of financial 'arrangements', some of which would not have got past serious scrutiny by the football authorities of the time.

Of all the players in the dressing room in the period of Chapman's introductory work, it was Buchan in whom he most regularly confided. Buchan was thoughtful and had been on hand when, in the year of Chapman's arrival, the manager had put his mind to the effects of the change in the offside law. Prior to 1925, an attacking player had to have at least three opponents between himself and the goal. The new law changed that to two and had been forced upon the authorities because Bill McCracken, a quick and artful Newcastle full back, would organise the defence so that one player would remain upfield and wait until the opposing forwards attacked, then move forward to catch one of them offside. Others soon adopted the tactic and the game rapidly turned into a farce, with the referees stopping games so frequently that spectators began to give up going to matches.

Chapman and Buchan discussed Arsenal's reaction to the change.

There has always been debate as to whether it was Chapman or Buchan who actually came up with the 'third back' tactic. Buchan maintained that he was the one who invented it, which was probably right. He claimed that he put forward the defensive centre-half system during a talk in the dressing room before a match against Tottenham early in the 1925-26 season. Seemingly, the other players, and presumably Chapman himself, were still uncertain and had no intention of experimenting in a game against their geographically nearest rivals. But Chapman, Joe Shaw and Tom Whittaker (the assistant-trainer, later first team trainer, who was several years younger than some of the players but was to transform the treatment of injuries from cold sponge to the use of electrical equipment) all added their opinions in preparation for the new challenge offered by changing tactics. Incidentally, the opening day of the 1925-26 season, with the new rules in place, had seen Aston Villa score ten against Burnley. Arsenal later lost to Newcastle by 7-0, sparking a lively discussion between Buchan and Chapman about the need to counter the new threat.

Chapman transformed Herbie Roberts into one of the most effective centre halves the game would ever see. Opposing crowds thought they were being disparaging when they called him a 'stopper'. He was not concerned and the phrase 'stopper centre-half' became part of football's accepted language. Chapman continued to make refinements, including turning Jack Lambert from an inside-forward to centre-forward. He also decided that Charlie Jones was not quick enough to remain on the wing and moved him to half-back. Equally important, though, was his concern that he badly needed to reduce the average age of the side, which was why he gave nineteen-years-old Eddie Hapgood, a former milkman, a place at left-back. Hapgood became one of the most devastating tacklers in the game. He made up for his lack of weight with instinctive timing and he devotedly remained working at Highbury until 1945.

Tactically, Chapman was a master of the counter-attacking game. He was keen on having quick wingers but told the half-backs not to spend too much of the game rushing forward into the space they left behind. His idea was that if they allowed the other team's forwards to come at them and then won the ball they could counter at the moment of the opposition's greatest vulnerability. He advocated the notion that, when defending, all eleven players became defenders but when attacking ten of them were potential attackers. The plan, which many years later was so cleverly developed by the Dutch, became known as 'Total Football'. The effectiveness of Chapman's tactics inevitably led to the phrase 'Lucky

Arsenal' because fans of opposing clubs were under the impression that when Arsenal broke down their team's attacks and sped forward in numbers they were somehow benefiting from some lucky interception. On the contrary, it was planned that way and became a deftly deployed tactic.

Henry Norris's link with the club he had done so much to bring out of obscurity finally came to an end in the 1927-28 season. He had worked diligently to secure Arsenal's future but though now 'Sir Henry', he was still not above reproach in his dealings. He and William Hall (director) were suspended by the Football Association who had looked into Norris's actions and found him guilty of, amongst other things, hiring a chauffeur. His suspension from football for 'financial irregularities' imposed a stigma on the club that was difficult to erase. Norris later went to the High Court to appeal against the decision but that was refused and he had to give up all association with the club and the game. He died in 1934.

The great Arsenal teams of 1929 to 1935 were both fast and dangerous. Wingers would sweep inside at every opportunity and become goalscorers as well as providers. They benefited from the clever passing of James, while Lambert led the attack with power and was supported in a more subtle, deep-lying way by Jack, who began his time at Arsenal under the pressure of having become the first £10,000 transfer (it was actually £11,500). Chapman saw him as Buchan's likely replacement. So, in October, 1928, he had persuaded Bolton Wanderers to let him go.

The fee caused considerable controversy. Only the previous week, the Football Association's President, Sir Charles Clegg, had said that no player in the world was worth £10,000. Realistically, if anyone was going to command such a fee it was Jack. He was the finest English inside-right in the country, had won two FA Cup winners' medals and scored the very first goal at Wembley. Chapman was sure he would be an able replacement for Buchan and he was proved right.

The story goes that Bolton wanted £13,000 for Jack. In other words, they had no intention of selling him and, as a result, demanded what was, in those days, an absurdly high price. Chapman invited the Bolton directors to meet him in a hotel bar. Beforehand, he had told the waiter that whenever he ordered a gin and tonic for himself he did not want the gin. Whenever the Bolton directors asked for a drink they were to have double measures of whatever spirit they wanted. The ploy worked because the Bolton representatives mellowed considerably and the fee came down by £1,500.

Jack appeared in two further Cup Finals and was instrumental in Arsenal winning their sequence of League Championships. He also won five more England caps. In all, he played two hundred times for the club in an era in which there were far fewer games than in modern times. It was Arsenal's ability to pay the high fee for him that instigated the nickname the 'Bank of England Club'. Critics pointed out that in Jack's first season (1928-29) Arsenal finished only ninth and were beaten in the FA Cup sixth round by Aston Villa.

There was still more development required. Chapman knew he needed another scheming, clever organiser behind the attack to link with the half-backs. In all probability he was searching for a player in the mould of Clem Stephenson, who had done that job so admirably from inside-left at Huddersfield. He could hardly believe his ears when Preston announced that twenty-seven-years-old Scottish international Alex James had been placed on the transfer list at £9,000. James was stubbornly opinionated and determined to secure his future. He was not going to move unless it was financially attractive. Arsenal avoided accusations of illegal payments by making arrangements for him to have a job as a 'sports demonstrator' in Selfridges, the big London store. Since Arsenal were not directly involved, only topping up his salary, technically they could not be accused of making any under-the-counter payments.

The Football League committee members made it clear that they were not happy about the situation but there was nothing they could do, especially as James conveniently signed up for the store job before putting his name to a contract with Arsenal. The fans were not totally convinced of his worth. James had been a member of the 'Wembley Wizards' Scotland team that had scored five goals against England at Wembley the previous year (1928). So his perceived talent was that of a brilliant goalscorer. The fans were dubious when Chapman said he wanted to convert him into the play-maker, a creator of goals for others. James himself was far from convinced. Not for the first or last time, Chapman knew more about the potential of a player than the player knew about himself.

Of remarkable irony in view of the Francophile nature of Arsene Wenger's teams of the 1990s and early 2000s is the fact that, about this period in the 1930s, it was thought scandalous that, after professionalism had been adopted in France, some of that country's clubs attempted to bribe top English players into joining them. It was said that Nimes tried to get two Chelsea players, Hughie Gallacher and Tommy Law, by offering them more money than they could have received under the English maximum wage system. Nimes suggested that Gallacher and Law acted as player-coaches, thus being paid for having two jobs (which, in fact, was nothing more than clubs in England, including Arsenal, had been doing anyway). The French club denied the report but it sparked a worried response from the Football League. There was even a headline in the *Topical Times* warning : 'Grapple with the French Menace Now!'

A League official said that he was aware of approaches made to Alex James and David Jack, adding that a ban on all English clubs visiting France should be considered (Arsenal were in the forefront of Continental excursions for profitable and amicable friendly matches). He attempted to play down the attractions of French football but several established British players did join French clubs, some of whom had English managers or coaches (a former Arsenal player, Charlie Bell, managed Marseilles).

Without doubt, James had been tempted to play abroad. Writing in the *Sunday Graphic* he said that once professionalism had spread throughout the Continent, he could see a time when many British players would be tempted because "... we are professionals, not amateurs. The game is our only livelihood. How long does it take the average professional footballer (married) with an income of less that £8 a week to save £1,000? A good deal longer than the average footballer's career, believe me. Supposing, then, someone comes along with £1,000 in cold cash and says, 'Yours, if you sign'. Well not many players are going to refuse that temptation. No, I'm not saying the French 'menace' has arrived, but it's on its way". All in all, his remarks emphasised that footballers in the League were not being looked upon as the great entertainers that they undoubtedly were, nor rewarded accordingly.

# CHAPTER 6
# CHAPMAN TRIUMPHANT

## 1930 FA CUP WINNERS

ALTHOUGH HERBERT CHAPMAN BELIEVED that his capture of Alex James was the crucial act in his building of a team of potential champions, by midway through the 1929-30 season relegation looked more likely than the winning of the title. As for team selection, the manager seemed to be without a policy. In the opening fourteen matches of the season, he selected twelve different forwards. Joe Hulme was not at his best and there was little evidence that Arsenal were going to appear in what would be portrayed as Chapman's personal FA Cup Final; one that would not only give Arsenal their first trophy under his guidance but be a victory over the club he had taken to two League championship titles and an FA Cup win.

Fluctuating League results forced him to accept that he faced a crisis of form amongst several players who seemed to have lost their drive. He decided that the only way forward was to spend more money. He bought David Halliday from Sunderland for £6,000. Halliday had scored one hundred and fifty five times in four seasons and Chapman saw him as the ideal replacement for Jack Lambert. But goals still proved elusive. James had not settled and was failing to distribute the ball in the way that his colleagues wanted. He became increasingly criticised by the fans who gave him the 'get rid of it' treatment as soon as he got possession.

James himself felt that he was a victim of Arsenal's experiments with the new tactics that would later become so effective. He was being asked to begin attacks from deep in his own half, which did not appeal to him and, in any case, was too arduous. On the other hand, another side to the story was that the other players found him difficult to 'read'. He was astonishingly quick both physically and mentally. He was also unpredictable and more often than not probably had no idea what he was going to do until he had done it.

As a result of indifferent results, any chance of winning the League title had to be forgotten and everything possible done to have a good Cup run. In desperation, before a third round match against Chelsea at

Highbury Chapman dropped James, who had played poorly in the previous League game. The fans' reaction was that of 'told you so'. James, they thought, was not the man for the job. A re-arranged side won 2-0 in pouring rain.

In the fourth round, Birmingham, who were 2-0 down at one point, scrambled back for a 2-2 draw at Highbury and Arsenal's season, perhaps even their whole future, was on the line. If Chapman had failed to organise his team to win the replay at St Andrews, who knows whether the successes of the next few years and the international fame of the club would have come about. As it was, controversially, he decided that James, far from not being man enough for the job, should be the manager's choice as the man for the significant moment. It was a doubly curious decision because, during the week before the replay, Chapman had told James that he should remain in bed in the hope of finding some relief from the pain of rheumatism and long-term injuries to his ankles. James had a history of injury problems. Tom Whittaker had examined him shortly after the new player arrived at Arsenal and went straight to Chapman, more or less telling him he had bought somebody who would never be fully fit. Had the crowds known the pain James often endured, they would have been a little more forgiving.

On the Sunday morning before the replay, which was to be on the Wednesday, Chapman called on James at his home and ordered him to get up and go training at Brighton. James was baffled, asking why he should bother. Chapman said: "Because you're going to win the match for us". The truth was that he was unsure whether there was any chance that James would be declared fit enough to appear at all.

There was always something of the showman about James. The idea of coming off his sick bed to rescue Arsenal appealed to his sense of drama. Not only did he appear but, tactically, he played in exactly the way Chapman had always envisaged, not holding the ball for too long and, in spite of feeling dreadful, distributing it with care and precision. The forwards responded well. Even so, Arsenal won only by way of a penalty scored by Alf Baker. James was far from convinced that he had contributed anything at all. Chapman had realised that, in previous appearances, too much had been expected of him in terms of creative and defensive football. That had been leaving the attack short of a crucial supply line.

Chapman then made a crucial decision to switch Bastin from inside-forward to the left wing. Bastin was hesitant but agreed, although his partnership with James was slow to come into effect because James continued to be troubled by injuries. When they did play together it was an unlikely masterpiece of mutual understanding that became the heart of the team's successes. Off the field they could not abide each other. Indeed, Brian Glanville, in his autobiography *Football Memories*, recalled his only meeting with Alex James who told him: "You're the one that wrote that Bastin book! He wasn't such a great player!" That conclusion was surely wrong. Bastin was a quiet Devonian, though not lacking in self-esteem. His goalscoring feats were remarkable. In the 1931-32 season he scored thirty-three League goals yet had been playing as a winger. His five League Championship medals were testimony to his enduring talent.

Middlesbrough and West Ham were beaten away in the next two rounds of the Cup, leaving Hull City to be overcome in the club's fifth semi-final. Bearing in mind the fact that Hull were at the foot of the Second Division and would later be relegated, that game seemed likely to be the easiest so far. It was not. Their manager was Bill McCracken, the defender who in his playing days (as we have seen) had exploited the old offside definition and caught so many attackers in his trap that the law had to be changed.

Hull turned out to be stubborn opposition and Arsenal probably underestimated them. After only fifteen minutes, they capitalised on a mistake by Lewis to take the lead, Harrison lobbing the ball over the goalkeeper's head. Then Hapgood tried to clear a loose ball, only to divert it into his own goal. Arsenal grew more and more nervous and it was not until ten minutes from the end that Jack headed in from Hulme. With eight minutes left, Bastin rushed through the defence to equalise and force a dour replay which Arsenal won with one goal from Jack.

The Cup Final itself was a suitable tribute to Chapman and contained a personal duel between two of the stars of the game, James and Huddersfield's Alec Jackson, who had scored three goals for Scotland's 'Wembley Wizards'. Never before had the teams taken the field together. Huddersfield were led out by Tom Wilson, their centre-half, and Arsenal by Tom Parker. The afternoon was made all the more memorable by the fact that the German airship *Graf Zeppelin* flew over the stadium. The noise of the engines caused the crowd to divert their attention from the game. Some of the players were also unable to concentrate on what they were supposed to be doing. The fans were unsure whether to cheer or jeer the brooding monster. Then it dipped its nose as if in salute. Only then did the crowd feel obliged to cheer.

Basically, Huddersfield were still the team Chapman had formed. They were clear favourites, partly because they had seven internationals in their side but also as a result of coming through a much tougher series of earlier round matches. On the other hand, Chapman knew just about all there was to know about them. He planned his tactics with insider knowledge. Hapgood was told to shadow the supremely confident Jackson, whom Chapman knew had the ability to change the course of any match. The veteran Bob John was to keep a close watch on the dangerous Bob Kelly.

In the dressing room before the game, Chapman instigated yet another original form of motivation that many years later would become popular with players – especially if they were with Wimbledon. He decided that music would both spur and soothe them and so had a gramophone set up.

James was still seething after playing for Scotland on this same pitch three weeks earlier, when England got their revenge for the Wembley Wizards defeat by winning 5-2. That had hurt him personally because it seemed to add fuel to the arguments of the doubters who said that he was never going to succeed at Arsenal. On his return to Wembley, he urgently wanted to respond to his critics. On the other hand, this was not a fully formed team. Bastin was still inexperienced, as was Hapgood. It was also known that David Jack had not fully recovered from an injury. In spite of that, Arsenal imposed themselves on the game from the start, with Lambert and Bastin both having chances that they missed by inches.

Huddersfield took ten minutes to gather their thoughts. Then Jackson sent a diving header just past the post. James certainly did make an impression, scoring the crucial first goal in the sixteenth minute with a typically clever move and finish that may well have been one of the finest ever seen in a Cup Final. It seemed like a wonderful piece of improvisation or, alternatively, a brilliantly well-planned strike. James later admitted that on the way to the stadium, he had talked with Bastin about just such a move. The simple idea was that if Arsenal had a free-kick in Huddersfield's half, Bastin would quickly peel away to the wing. James would play the ball to him and set out for the penalty area, take the return pass and shoot. When Goodall fouled James, the move was put into action and it worked perfectly.

James admitted that he had not heard the referee whistle for the free-kick to be taken but took it anyway. After the goal the Huddersfield players protested that they too had failed to hear a whistle. The referee pointed out that all he was obliged to do under the Laws of the game was give a signal to indicate that the kick could be taken. He said that he had done that with a wave of his hand. Strangely, after previous matches in which James had played a quick free-kick, Chapman had given the impression that he did not consider it to be within the spirit of the game. On this occasion James ignored him, which was a brave thing to do. As far as is known, this time Chapman did not complain.

Huddersfield forced forward and kept Arsenal under pressure. Jack was obviously struggling and James had to orchestrate the whole performance. At the same time, Jackson was not getting his own way for Huddersfield. John and Hapgood were giving him a rough time. On the way to the match, the often-criticised Arsenal goalkeeper, Charlie Preedy, had said to the rest of the players: "I know you think I'm the worst goalkeeper in the world. I probably am, but today I'm going to play like the best". And he was not far wrong.

Parker then ensured that the advantage was maintained. His authority was an example to his team-mates, nine of whom had been brought to the club by Chapman, but the erratic goalkeeping of Preedy had the fans' hearts in their mouths as Huddersfield pressed with seemingly unrelenting strength.

The second goal came almost at the end, as a result of Lambert collecting the ball from James's clearance and making a long run more or less on his own. He easily went past a couple of tired defenders and beat the goalkeeper from several yards out. He turned and applauded James, as if sending a 'told you so' message back to the critics in the crowd.

Huddersfield had put up a stout defence but were the victims of Arsenal's developing power that was to bring the club world-wide celebrity and an upturn in their financial fortunes. Some people may have remembered that when he had taken over at Highbury, Chapman was asked how long he thought it would be before the Arsenal fans could expect to enjoy the same sort of success he had achieved with Huddersfield. He had said five years. It was almost five years to the day that Parker climbed the thirty-nine steps to the Royal Box and received the Cup from King George V. The scene was again being described on the radio by a commentator who may, or may not, have been entirely impartial: George Allison, still a significant Arsenal shareholder. Little did he know that soon, in tragic circumstances, he would become Chapman's successor.

The result of the Final meant that football in the south of the country was now able to hold its head high and Arsenal were established amongst the nobles of the game. In the evening, both teams and the clubs' officials gathered together for dinner at the Café Royal. It marked the drawing to a close of Huddersfield's era and the beginning of Arsenal's. Among the Arsenal supporters there that day were Messrs Danskin, Humble, Beardsley and Brown, four of the founder members of the club. None could have believed that their early work would harvest such a reward.

## FA CUP FINAL
(26 April 1930, Wembley)

### Arsenal 2 (James, Lambert) Huddersfield Town 0

*Arsenal:* Preedy; Parker, Hapgood, Baker, Seddon, John, Hulme, Jack, Lambert, James, Bastin.

*Huddersfield Town:* Turner; Goodall, Spence, Naylor, Wilson, Campbell, Jackson, Kelly, Davies, Raw, Smith.

*Referee:* T. Crew

# Chapter 7
# The New Highbury

## 1930-31 FIRST DIVISION CHAMPIONS

WITH THE MEMORY OF THE PREVIOUS TERM'S CUP win still vivid and encouraging, Arsenal tackled the next season confidently, knowing that, at last, Alex James was proving to be the player of Chapman's hopes and the key to his producing one of the most effective and innovative teams in the history of the game. Whereas earlier he had struggled to bring together the players necessary to achieve that efficiency, now he had the men he needed. He made few changes from the side that won the Cup, apart from the consequential replacement of Bill Seddon by Herbie Roberts at centre-half.

The new Arsenal tore into their early season opponents yet were hungry to improve. Fourteen goals were scored in their first four matches. They went nine games before losing to Derby County but, significantly, beat the leaders, Aston Villa, at Highbury in November. After Christmas, Villa responded with a run in which they dropped only six points out of a possible thirty-four and beat Arsenal 5-1 at Villa Park, where the wonderfully named Pongo Waring could never be completely controlled. Arsenal recovered and Jack scored four against Grimsby in a remarkable 9-1 win.

The title, which had never been won by a team from the South, was finally taken at Highbury. Liverpool were the visitors. Nerves were ragged. Only three minutes had gone when Roberts deflected the ball into his own net. In the end, though, Arsenal won 3-1 to finish seven points ahead of Villa. They had a record points total of sixty-six, losing only four games in all. They scored sixty goals away from home and a total home and away of one hundred and twenty seven, which Aston Villa (runners-up) beat by one. Sheffield Wednesday, who had been hoping to win their third consecutive Championship title, were third, fourteen points behind Arsenal who failed to score in only one match (predictably, perhaps, against Huddersfield) and scored four goals or more in seventeen. Lambert accumulated thirty-eight goals. He was expected to play an important part in the coaching of the clubs' young players after he retired but was killed in a car crash.

The season had been a resounding success, not just for the fans of Arsenal but for the prestige of the club as a whole. Attendances were greatly improved, partly because so many people who had never before followed any particular club were coming to Highbury (as Norris had always said, the easy journey from Central London was a bonus for the club). But mainly they came to watch a team that was totally 'modern'. The players seemed to read each other's thoughts, and there was mutual respect and support. The tactic of the rapid counter-attack was ahead of its time. At the back, Parker and Hapgood had the confidence that was built on seeing so many forwards come under their control. Roberts played the 'stopper' role with almost ruthless efficiency. No bruised centre forward enjoyed sharing the same pitch. Bob John and, in spite of Chapman's earlier doubts, Charlie Jones were new-style half-backs with the speed of wingers, so they could go forward quickly in support of the attack or keep pace with opposing forwards.

Bastin, on the left flank, would chase back like a modern wide midfield player, win the ball and get forward again before the opposition could recover. On the other wing, Hulme's speed was formidable. Jack, at inside right, was a natural goalscorer but also a sly creator. Lambert was tough and effective as the main goalscorer at centre-forward and then, of course, there was James, the general of the whole side. Giving him a more or less free role made it almost impossible for opposing teams to subdue him. He always seemed to have all the time in the world, which made it unnecessary to have much in the way of pace.

The increasingly fruitful Chapman years were making it obvious that Highbury needed to be upgraded. Success allowed the club to buy the whole Highbury site outright at a cost of £64,000. Also, the irritating clause that stopped matches being played on Good Friday and Christmas Day was removed, by permission of the Ecclesiastical Commissioners.

Highbury in the late 1920s was far less grand than it was to become in the 1930s. The tube station was still called Gillespie Road (the name can still be found on the wall tiles) and the North Bank remained under the name of the Laundry End. Even in March, 1935, when a club record crowd of 73,295 attended a match against Sunderland, it could hardly be claimed that they watched in comfort or that all could see much more than the hat or cap of the spectator in front. Work on improvements had begun four years earlier with a request to local people to dump all of their rubbish at the ground to help raise the levels of the banking. A coal merchant arrived with his horse and cart and attempted to back towards a large hole into which the rubbish was being discharged. Horse and cart fell in. The horse was too badly injured to be rescued and was shot. The body remained under the terracing.

The West side of the ground had never been covered, so the club decided it should become the site of the most modern stand ever built in Britain. Claude Waterlow Ferrier was employed as the architect, with assistance from Major W.B. Binnie. They had a reputation for designing elegant buildings, among them Trafalgar House and the Army and Navy Club in Pall Mall. Clearly the board of Arsenal had a high regard for the aesthetic appearance of the developing ground and so ensured that, over many years, Highbury would be regarded as a special edifice rather than simply another football arena.

In November, 1932, some six weeks ahead of schedule, the West Stand, with its four thousand one hundred seats and standing room for twenty-one thousand underneath, was completed, though at a cost of £45,000, which was far more than any other club had ever spent. It contained seven hundred tons of steel. Spectators going to their seats, which had shaped backs and arm-rests, were even provided with a lift. A two-and-half inch thick wooden rail was built into the back of the seats to stop excited spectators kicking directly at the seats in front. Rubber buffers were placed under the tip-up seats to stop the noise as spectators left. Quite what the fans of those days would have made of the high-decibel announcements and music that drown all other noise at modern games, who knows?

There was not another grandstand like it at any other ground in Britain. It signalled Arsenal's intention to reflect the glorious days of the Chapman era in the architecture of the stage on which his distinguished team played with such dynamic success. The stand was officially opened on 10 December by the Prince of Wales (who became the Duke of Windsor) before a match against Chelsea.

Chapman led the way when it came to recognising that football was a mass entertainment rather than simply a sport that happened to be popular. Not only did he work on building the team, he did all in his power to raise the profile of the club. It was Chapman who persuaded the London Electric Railway, which ran the underground system, to change the name of the nearby tube station from Gillespie Road to Arsenal. That was a masterstroke of publicity. With perfect timing, the name change occurred on 5 November, 1932, shortly before the official opening of the new stand.

At about this time, the board agreed to change the name of the ground from 'Highbury', which reflected the area in which it was housed, to

'Arsenal Stadium'. From the time of the proposal to the moment of Arsenal's leaving, early in the twenty-first century, the name 'Highbury' would remain the preferred choice of fans throughout the world.

Chapman continued to look for ways to make the stadium unique. He ordered a huge clock to be placed on top of the North Bank. It was twelve feet in diameter and recorded 45 minutes. The Football Association considered that it undermined the authority of the referee. Chapman would have none of it, saying that it was a service to the spectators, but he agreed to change its face to record sixty minutes.

Until Chapman's arrival, Arsenal had played in all red shirts, but in keeping with his determination to make his club different, in 1933, he arranged for them to have red shirts with white sleeves. But perhaps his most important and forward-looking idea was floodlit football. The first match played under lights at Highbury was held in November, 1932. On the evening of the game, there had been a conference at London's Great Eastern Hotel during which several club representatives spoke of the possibility that, in future, matches under lights would become commonplace. Not for the last time, the committee of the FA refused to accept innovation and rejected the whole idea. Ridiculously, Arsenal were unable to use floodlights for officially sanctioned matches until 1951.

# CHAPTER 8
# GET DOWN TO BRIGHTON!

## 1932-33 FIRST DIVISION CHAMPIONS
### ... AND THE WALSALL FIASCO

IN THE MIDDLE OF THE 1931-32 SEASON, Alex James suffered a serious knee injury and, because of his importance to the team, there seemed little chance of retaining the Championship title. The FA Cup became the more realistic target. The Final against Newcastle was reached and, surprisingly, the Double came into sight. In the matches running up to the time of the Final, fourteen out of fifteen League and Cup games were won. Then came James's knee injury in a match against West Ham. After that, results suddenly changed. In their next five games, they gained only one win. When it came to the Final, they were six points behind Everton and Joe Hulme had joined James on the injury list.

Chapman decided that neither player was in any condition to appear, but James, who always enjoyed a good argument, was furious because he felt he was fit enough. Hulme was not quite so certain about his own readiness but went along with James's plan to get in touch with a journalist and tell him that they were both fit and ready to play in the Final. The *Daily Sketch* sent a photographer to Highbury and the paper contained a picture of both players running round the perimeter track. Chapman phoned John Peters, the club's assistant secretary, and blamed him for allowing the Press into Highbury. He then called James and Hulme and told them to get down to Brighton, where the team were in preparation for the Final.

Characteristically, Chapman seized the momentum, letting it be known that on the following morning, the two players would have fitness tests. This time, photographers were welcome. Both players passed their rigorous examinations. That was not the end of the story, although there are various versions. James claimed that he had already changed when Chapman demanded his reappearance on the pitch, telling him to go in for a tackle with Tom Whittaker. Whittaker said that James had volunteered to go for one last tackle before the fitness tests was over because one of the photographers had arrived late and needed to get a picture. Either way, James collapsed in the tackle. His previously injured knee had buckled.

So Chapman, who in hindsight probably regretted ever allowing James and Hulme to goad him into the fitness tests, had to sit down and draw up another team. To compensate for the absence of James, he moved John into the attack. Bastin went inside and George Male was brought in from the Reserves to play at half-back. They were about to appear in one of the most controversial Finals of all time.

Arsenal grasped the lead when John took advantage of confusion in the goalmouth to head into an empty goal. They seemed in control until shortly before half-time, when Newcastle's Jimmy Richardson broke away, chasing a long pass out of defence towards the goal-line just inside the penalty area. The ball appeared to go out of play. The Arsenal players stood still, convinced it had and waited for the linesman to confirm their view. He did not. Richardson sent over a good centre and Jack Allen headed in. The Arsenal players protested but Newcastle rode their good fortune and Allen scored the winner after Jack missed an open goal.

The referee, who had been more than twenty yards from the 'over the line' incident, absurdly claimed he was only eight away and was sure that the ball had been in play. British Movietone News later showed that he was badly mistaken (probably the first time that technology had drawn attention to a refereeing error). Seventy-five years later, in the days of instant replays, football was still resisting the notion that technology could avoid just such problems. Curiously, Arsenal had become the first club to score first in a Cup Final at Wembley and lose. The over-the-line incident was pictured on the front pages of some newspapers. On those same pages was the story that the Nazi party had won in the German elections.

In the stands that day was G.H. Leavey who, just before the First World War when the club had been in severe financial trouble, was visited at his outfitters shop in Woolwich by the club's secretary who asked whether he would care to become a director. Leavey agreed and on the following Saturday was surprised to be asked to advance the team's wages. He kindly agreed to pay £60 and continued to subsidise the players throughout the season. Without him, the club would probably have gone out of existence.

After the Cup Final, all Arsenal could do was attempt to finish the season with heads high in the Championship, which they did, reaping nine points from their last five matches. However, newly-promoted Everton still finished the season two ahead, thanks in particular to Dixie Dean, who scored forty-four goals out of a total of one hundred and sixteen.

By the following season, the average age of an Arsenal player had again crept up, this time to around thirty. The loyal Parker retired mid-season after two hundred and fifty eight games. The player being groomed to take his place was Leslie Compton who was clearly a talented full-back but not yet reliable enough. So Chapman productively turned the reluctant George Male into a defender. With Hapgood on one side and Male the other, there was no better full-back pairing for club or country.

League results offered hope of winning the Championship and the crowds were thoroughly entertained. There was a 9-2 win over Sheffield United at Highbury on Christmas Eve but also a remarkable 5-3 defeat by Aston Villa at Villa Park – many witnesses said that was the finest game played between the wars.

In the middle of the quest for the title came one the most extraordinary FA Cup results in the competition's long history of surprises: defeat by Third Division Walsall, who became the champions of those many people who had no time for this expensively assembled Arsenal team, with what was interpreted as their mean, counter-attacking style. The Arsenal side included seven internationals, among them Bastin, James and Jack. Admittedly, several other regulars, including Lambert, John, Hapgood and Tim Coleman were injured, ill with 'flu or perhaps had not been chosen because Chapman thought they were surplus to the needs of the day. He could have recalled Hulme, who had not been at his best. He decided against. That was one of his few uncharacteristically poor tactical decisions.

He chose to bring in left-back Tommy Black, who had limited experience, mainly in Scottish junior football, left-half Norman Sidey, outside-right Billy Warnes and centre-forward Charlie Walsh. Of those, only Sidey had ever played in the first team. Reportedly, Walsh was so nervous that he put on one of his boots before his sock. Once he got on the field, he almost immediately missed an open goal and then whipped the ball off the feet of Jack, just as his famous senior was about to shoot.

To put Walsall's achievement in perspective, you have to place yourself in the minds of their players. They were about to face men who, by and large, were not only of high international standing but part of a team on the way to regaining the Championship. Most were household names. Walsall had a proud history, having been formed out of an amalgamation of the renowned Walsall Swifts and Walsall Town, but they had failed to establish themselves and had to seek re-election to the League a record seven times in the days of the Third Divisions North and South (nobody seemed to know in which area they should be included). Despite that, if there had been a straw poll of football fans country-wide, no doubt Walsall would have got most of the support. Arsenal were widely considered a team that had taken advantage of the offside rule change and simply grabbed victories like sneak thieves. In some quarters, they were also still considered newcomers to the old establishment, a club getting above themselves. They were particularly unpopular in the Midlands where unemployment was rampant.

Walsall ripped into them with their rugged, lower-division style and won 2-0. Roberts knew what sort of game it would be almost from the start when he was cut over the eye in his first challenge for the ball. Alsop headed in from a corner and Sheppard scored from the penalty spot. To make matters even more uncomfortable for Arsenal, a factory chimney began belching smoke across the pitch.

Chapman was severely criticised for failing to give Walsall respect. On the other hand, his mistake was understandable. In Walsall's previous four games, they had drawn three and lost one by 5-0. Their team had cost sixty-nine pounds. Arsenal's outlay had been about £30,000. Bastin came over as the worst of the losers when suggesting that at least five of the Walsall players could have been sent off in the first fifteen minutes. He said they had acted like steamrollers not footballers.

Several of Arsenal's inexperienced players were soon transferred. There was a strong feeling that they paid the penalty for Chapman's over-confidence. As for the Championship, surprisingly, the embarrassment at Walsall had no damaging effect. In fact, it gave the team a sound reason to redeem themselves. Even though James was again injured, they went on a long unbeaten run, then found themselves losing at home to teams beneath them. The decisive games saw them beat challengers Sheffield Wednesday 4-2 and Villa 5-0, both at Highbury. Bastin and Hulme were dynamic on the wings and the scourge of almost every goalkeeper they faced. Bastin scored thirty-three goals and Hulme twenty, while James probably laid on the majority. The title was won with fifty-eight points. Villa were four behind.

# CHAPTER 9
# DEATH OF THE GREAT PIONEER

## 1933-34 FIRST DIVISION CHAMPIONS

THE CHAMPIONSHIP WAS RETAINED, sadly as an appropriate but premature memorial to Herbert Chapman who, in January, 1934, died from pneumonia. His dedication to Arsenal's cause almost certainly brought about his death at the age of only fifty-nine. The previous weekend he had watched Arsenal draw at Birmingham. In spite of being unwell, he decided to go to Bury for a midweek game. He had been told about a player who might make the grade with Arsenal. He then travelled on to Hillsborough to watch Sheffield Wednesday, who were looking dangerous challengers for the title and were Arsenal's next opponents.

On both days, the weather had been dank. Chapman picked up a cold. The club's doctor suggested that he stay at home. Chapman insisted on going to watch the third team play at Guildford. The cold developed into pneumonia and in the early hours of the Saturday morning, he died at his home in Hendon. The funeral was held four days later with a huge assembly of friends, colleagues and players. The pall-bearers were Bastin, Hapgood, Hulme, James and Lambert. On the day of his death (January 6) the match against Sheffield Wednesday had gone ahead. Cliff Bastin said that, when he reached the ground, he could hear the newspaper sellers shouting the news. "It seemed just too bad to be true". Four trumpeters played the last post and Chapman's place on the bench remained empty. Over fifty-thousand fans, many of whom had not known of his death until they reached the ground, stood in silence. The match was drawn.

Chapman is acknowledged as the first real football manager and a pioneer of the game. In his career, he was involved in the winning of nine trophies, which may not seem remarkable in these days of a Continental game. Bear in mind, though, that, discounting the Charity Shield, in his era there were only ever two to seek in each season. The *Daily Express*, for which he wrote a column, claimed that he probably died "a poor man".

A lot has been written about Chapman. Much of it was summed up by Tony Pawson, a fine amateur player who appeared in the First Division and became an astute writer. He said: "In one respect Chapman was before his time. He recognised that professional football was an entertainment as well as a sport. His most important legacy was to establish the Manager as the man who mattered in a football club. If the players were to call him 'boss' he must be seen to be so. There was never any doubt about this with Chapman. George Hardy, the Chief Trainer, was sacked in public in the middle of a Cup replay for daring to shout to a player to move up-field, unwittingly interfering with a tactical plan".

Pawson also pointed out that before Chapman's era "the Manager was rarely the dominant figure in the club, his authority with the players all too easily undermined by the Directors or the Secretary in control of the selection and the pay. Thereafter, any Manager of character could ensure the proper relationship. The dapper, smiling Herbert Chapman, with his polished phrases, his shrewd publicity, made the point by example". For many years after his death, it was said that Chapman's footsteps could still be heard walking through the corridors of Highbury.

No manager past or present has ever been so full of original ideas, among them: numbered shirts, the development of floodlit football and the ten-yard 'D' at the edge of the penalty area. He also campaigned for the England team to have a single manager. On many occasions the football establishment resisted him but, in almost all cases, they were wrong and he was right.

As for the season itself, Chapman had known that it would have to be one of change. It had begun with James and Hulme both being injured. Hulme never really regained full fitness. Bastin, still a power, was moved from one position to another. The forwards were not as effective as they had been in previous seasons. Indeed, at the end of it, David Jack left to become manager of Southend. Only seventy-five goals were scored, the smallest number since Chapman had become manager in 1925. At least the defence, under the influence of Roberts, remained solid.

In an effort to improve the attack, players were again moved around and new ones brought in but the experiments were not a success. Chapman had fought his way through the problems and the team revived. They went back to the top of the table in November, ahead of Tottenham, and performed magnificently against a Vienna XI, who were the Austrian national team in all but name. Under the guidance of Jimmy Hogan, Austria had earlier visited Stamford Bridge and shocked England who scraped an undeserved 4-3 success. So for Arsenal to win 4-2 was a notable result.

Over the Christmas period, they held a four-point lead, ahead of Tottenham who were captained by Arthur Rowe, later to become that club's gifted manager. Then came the death of Chapman. Not surprisingly, the next three games were lost and Derby County took over the lead.

George Allison, director and journalist, was asked to become managing director, an appointment that although surprising brought back stability. He had at his side Tom Whittaker, whose healing hands were so important to the players, and Joe Shaw who continued to be an assistant rather in the way that, many years later, Pat Rice became a thread of continuity behind the scenes.

There were over two hundred applicants for the job of taking over from Chapman as manager. Many of them would probably have had a far better knowledge than Allison of footballers and the game itself. It was Whittaker in whom the players confided, not Allison. But it was Allison who was going to be mainly responsible for rebuilding the team.

Shortly after Allison's appointment, James was told that the club had agreed to let him join Derby County in a complicated cash and players transfer deal. Allison had looked at his squad and identified James, Charlie Jones, Bob John, Jack Lambert and David Jack as the ones of Chapman's days who needed to be replaced, though not all at the same time. James was furious, partly because he felt he was being poorly treated for the amount he had contributed to the great times, also because he was sure he could return after his injuries and continue to be a valuable member of the team. He was right. The transfer proposal was dropped and James linked up with new signing Ted Drake, a powerful centre-forward from Southampton, who later managed Chelsea when they won the Championship in 1955.

Although there was a 7-0 win over Crystal Palace in the fourth round of the FA Cup, the club departed the competition in the sixth, beaten by Aston Villa at Highbury. Once the initial shock of Chapman's death had gone, League performances improved, with eleven victories in the last fifteen games, including a 3-1 beating of Chapman's old club, Huddersfield, at Highbury. They then took to Liverpool a side weakened by international calls on their England players and still won 3-2. The turning point could easily be identified as the moment that the obstinate James refused to leave and started to play in unison with Drake.

The season could not have ended in a greater tribute to Chapman: 1. Arsenal (59pts); 2. Huddersfield Town (56pts). In addition Arsenal won the Charity Shield (beating Everton 3-0) and the Reserves took the London Challenge Cup and the London Combination trophy.

# CHAPTER 10
# THE HAT-TRICK OF TITLES

## 1934-35 FIRST DIVISION CHAMPIONS

IF WINNING THE CHAMPIONSHIP THE PREVIOUS SEASON paid homage to Herbert Chapman, there was an irony in achieving a third successive title because it equalled Huddersfield's record. Chapman had been the guiding light of both clubs. George Allison remained in overall charge of Arsenal as a club but team affairs were now organised by Joe Shaw and Tom Whittaker. However, Allison had been instrumental in the signing of Drake, who had been happily playing for Southampton and working as a gas meter inspector.

Drake was shy and not really interested in moving away from his home town. When he did, however, it proved a master-stroke for Allison who had already called him "the best centre-forward in the world". Drake was an uncompromising striker. Perhaps his nearest equivalent in the modern English game would be Alan Shearer. He used his weight well, made space for other players and was a fine header of the ball. Unhappily, his career was cut short by injury.

He had joined the club at a time of change. Two other new faces were in the dressing room: the comparatively frail Jack Crayston, signed from Bradford, and the fearsomely physical Wilf Copping, from Leeds. In the first home game of the season, Drake scored three goals in an 8-1 home win over Liverpool. He helped himself to four against Birmingham at Highbury and captured another three against Tottenham. The big scores continued. There was a 7-0 home win over Wolves, with Drake scoring four, an 8-0 victory over Middlesbrough (Drake again scored four) and poor Leicester had thirteen scored against them in their two meetings with this now thriving, regenerated side.

Drake finished the season with forty-two goals scored in only forty-one appearances. He obviously relished the service that was provided by Bastin and James and they enjoyed the fact that while opposing defenders were spending so much of their energy marking him, the goal would open up ahead of them. In November, the in-form Manchester City, with Matt Busby in the half-back line and, in goal, the friendly giant Frank Swift (who, while working as a journalist, died in the Manchester United air crash at Munich), were easily beaten 4-0 in the Charity Shield. Even when the pitches became heavy after Christmas Arsenal still looked the part of true champions. However, they were not so successful in the FA Cup, being knocked out by the eventual winners, Sheffield Wednesday, against whom, in an earlier League game, James had scored three in strange circumstances.

Billy Walker, the Wednesday manager, had told his defenders that they would be wasting their time if they marked James when he came near their goal because he had lost his goalscoring touch. James himself suggested that, in fact, he had been determined to get some goals because, in the previous week, Allison had obtained Bobby Davidson from St. Johnstone and made the comment that he saw him as the future Alex James (he was wrong about that). The comment was a red rag to a bull as far as James was concerned. Unfortunately, his hat-trick performance was the last memorable one of his career. Injuries returned. He continued to be involved but no longer as the unstoppable playmaker.

As Manchester City lost touch at the top of the table, so Sunderland, inspired by the passing skills of Raich Carter, took up the challenge. Arsenal, troubled by injuries and feeling hard done by in the Cup, were not in high spirits. Allison followed the pattern set by Chapman and decided it was time to spend some money. His purchase of Alf Kirchen, a fast and strong winger who had made his name at Norwich, where Tom Parker was manager, was wise but lucky. Spurs were keen to get Kirchen and offered £5,750. Parker, loyal to his old club, fetched Allison off the golf course to warn him. Allison offered £6,000 and clinched the deal. Curiously, Kirchen's first match for Arsenal was against Spurs and he played a big part in a 6-0 win.

The most important match of the season seemed likely to be against Sunderland at Highbury early in March. It attracted a crowd of 73,295, a record for the ground at the time and one that was never bettered. That huge number witnessed a rather poor 0-0 draw. For better drama, the fans would have had to travel to Goodison Park the following week, when goalkeeper Frank Moss fell at the feet of Everton forwards and dislocated his shoulder. He went off, had it set by Whittaker and returned to play at outside-left while Eddie Hapgood went in goal. By that time, Arsenal had a 1-0 lead but were under pressure. Then Frank Moss met a centre that had come from the right side. His timing was perfect and he blasted a shot for a terrific goal. A few minutes later, his shoulder was again dislocated and he was taken to hospital with a big, pain-defying grin on his face.

51

The loss of Moss could have been damaging because Arsenal had only one other goalkeeper available, Alex Wilson. Only a few hours before the transfer deadline, Allison persuaded Everton to release George Bradshaw, who somewhat reluctantly agreed to move south. Wilson did well, defiantly holding his place to become an important part of the team that ended the season with one hundred and fifteen goals and were four points ahead of Sunderland. They had won their third Championship title in three seasons and, remarkably, their fourth in five years. Arsenal and Highbury's lasting fame was built upon those achievements. Meanwhile Spurs were relegated.

In that same historic season, Highbury was also the scene of a match that involved a large number of Arsenal players and was to go down as being amongst the most bitter and violent of any ever played in Britain.

# CHAPTER 11
# THE 'REAL WORLD CUP FINAL'

## ENGLAND 3 ITALY 2

O F THE TWELVE FULL INTERNATIONAL MATCHES that took place at Highbury, none was more dramatic nor brutal than the one England played against Italy on 14 November, 1934. Not without good reason did it go into football's history books as the "Battle of Highbury".

The root of the aggressive nature of the match was the Football Association's determination to keep the international federation (FIFA) at arm's length and retain the presumption that no England team needed to fear the growing strength of other countries, not only in Europe but the world over. In the summer, Italy had won the World Cup. England had not taken part. Not only that, England had begun to look vulnerable. Back in 1929, they had lost to Spain, their first defeat on foreign soil. Then the Austrian "Wunderteam", managed by Hugo Meisl and coached by Jimmy Hogan, had come to Stamford Bridge and, although losing 4-3 to England, played a style of football that made their opponents look heavy-footed and predictable.

The match at Highbury was preceded by almost as much hype as some that England have played in recent years. It was portrayed as the real World Cup final. English football still regarded itself as invulnerable, at least at home, and in no need of entering the World Cup in order to prove it.

The Football Association's selection committee chose five of the Arsenal Championship-winning team: Cliff Bastin, Ray Bowden, Wilf Copping, Eddie Hapgood and Frank Moss. At the last minute, two other players dropped out and were replaced by two more from the Arsenal staff, Ted Drake and George Male. To the consternation of many, this seemed to have become Arsenal against the world champions. Not only that, the side's trainer was named as Arsenal's Tom Whittaker and the radio commentary was by the club's secretary-manager, George Allison. In the Press, the team was called "Drake's Armada". The *Daily Mirror* arrogantly previewed the match under the headline: "Ten Goal Victory Must be Our Aim".

Early in the game, Drake ruggedly tackled Italy's centre half, Luisito Monti, who suffered a broken toe and played no further part. The Italians convinced themselves that he had been the victim of a deliberate kick and set about concerted retaliation. England's response was to score three goals in fifteen minutes, two coming from Manchester City's Eric Brook, who had missed a penalty, and one by Drake. Hapgood then felt an elbow in his face. He played on but later discovered that he had a broken nose. Other members of the England side decided that two could play at that game. Copping threw himself into the physical battle with robust enthusiasm.

Gradually the Italians began to calm down. Giuseppe Meazza pulled back two goals and also hit the bar. In torrential rain England won 3-2, thanks in large measure to a fine save by Moss, but the Italians defeated themselves. The dictator Mussolini had made promises that if they achieved a victory, which would have improved the prestige of the country internationally, they would be given rich rewards including cash, new cars and exemption from military service. Nevertheless, the skill, rather than the strength and lack of discipline shown by the Italians on that day, should have been another warning that English football was falling behind.

Italy went on to retain their world title in 1938. Many in the British press refused to acknowledge that there had been anything to worry about in the Italian performance at Highbury. Indeed, the *Daily Mirror* even suggested that because of the ill-tempered nature of the game English teams should not take part in any future international matches. They listed the injuries: "Hapgood – broken nose; Brook – arm x-rayed; Bowden – injured ankle; Drake – leg cut; Barker – hand bandaged; Copping – bandaged from thigh to knee". The several injuries to Italian players were not mentioned.

# CHAPTER 12
# SEVEN-GOAL DRAKE

## 1936 FA CUP WINNERS

E VEN IF THE PLAYERS WERE STILL FEELING JADED after the exertions of retaining the title, when the new season began the Arsenal fans could not get enough of them. The average attendance for the first four matches was in excess of sixty-thousand and the total for the whole term was over a million. But there were problems. The best of the players were over thirty. Moss remained sidelined until Christmas. Hulme missed the first three months with a muscle problem. Even the rugged Drake was not immune to damaged limbs, missing several games, as did James, Bastin and Kirchen. And, even as those players regained their places, it was obvious that several other clubs were catching up in terms of skill and strength. Most of the Arsenal players looked a lot older than they were. They were tired before their years. Although the team pulled off some exciting victories, in the end they found themselves beyond hope of winning the Championship and it was not all the fault of injuries or age. Even so, they made something of a recovery once Drake was fit again.

Recalled to play against a struggling Aston Villa at Villa Park, but still having a heavily strapped knee, Drake spent the early period watching Villa attacking the Arsenal goal. It was fifteen minutes before the real trend of the game was set when he took up a through ball from Pat Beasley and scored what would be the first of his seven goals, remarkably achieved without the support of James and Hulme. His feat equalled the League record set by James Ross, of Preston, against Stoke in 1888.

Sunderland, who had not followed Arsenal in employing the third back alignment and believed that attack was the best form of defence, romped into the lead at the head of the First Division. Arsenal could not keep pace with them but, when the teams met at Roker Park, it was a dynamic match. Sunderland were playing at the top of their form, passing quickly and confusingly inter-changing positions. At half-time they held a 4-1 lead, and even Arsenal's single goal had come by way of a penalty by Bastin. Then, shortly after the re-start, Drake pulled them back with a reviving goal. Ray Bawden quickly added a third. Sunderland refused to become defensive and Connor scored with a well-aimed shot. With fifteen minutes left, Bawden got the winner for Sunderland who could not be caught in the Championship. Arsenal were left to chase the Cup.

Their passage to the Final against Second Division Sheffield United, who in the Cup seem to act like a magnet that attracts Arsenal, took them via victories over Bristol Rovers (5-1, but a more nervous performance than the score suggested – memories of Walsall would not go away and Tom Whittaker rather than Allison did the stern talking at half-time when they were a goal down); Liverpool (2-0, and James returned), Newcastle (who they had never beaten in Cup competition and here they needed a replay to get through), then tough Barnsley (4-1 at Highbury) and Grimsby in the semi-final at Huddersfield where only Bastin's goal separated the teams.

A long list of injuries now meant that the club had little choice but to remember that the Cup was the priority and that in the League they would have to field some players of little experience. In fact, they were reprimanded by the FA for sending out weak teams when holding back the best players for the competition they had a chance of winning. Drake had been badly injured while playing for England and then had a cartilage operation. He came back only a fortnight before the Final, at great cost to Arsenal's League opponents Aston Villa. His goal was enough to relegate them to the Second Division for the first time in their long history. It was decided to gamble and include him at Wembley.

Roberts and James were also still having treatment. The team had to be reshuffled. Sheffield United had a strong and determined defence while Arsenal's almost lost the game in the opening minute when their goalkeeper, Wilson, dropped the ball right on to the feet of Barclay, but he immediately pounced back and recovered from his error. United's goalkeeper, Smith, equalled that by saving a crashing shot from Crayston after a measured move that clearly reduced the confidence of the Sheffield players. Even so, Dodds hit the crossbar with an ominous header and Arsenal could count themselves lucky to start the second half on level terms.

Captained by James, they then took over the game, although not with the power and seeming invincibility of their form of previous seasons. Some well-rehearsed moves settled them down but Smith dealt with their shooting. Finally, sixteen minutes from the end, Bastin took control of a clearance, went past Hooper and played a hopeful pass through the centre. Drake chased it down, baffled Johnson with a feint and drove a left foot shot into the top of the net. Smith did not deserve that. United blazed back into the attack. Dodds again hit the crossbar but somehow Arsenal held on for their victory.

## FA CUP FINAL
(25 April 1936, Wembley)

### Arsenal 1 (Drake) Sheffield United 0

*Arsenal:* Wilson; Male, Hapgood, Crayston, Roberts, Copping, Hulme, Bowden, Drake, James, Bastin.

*Sheffield United:* Smith; Hooper, Wilkinson, Jackson, Johnson, McPherson, Barton, Barclay, Dodds, Pickering, Williams.

*Referee:* H. Nattrass.

# CHAPTER 13
# THE IRREPLACEABLE ALEX JAMES

## 1937-38 FIRST DIVISION CHAMPIONS

THE GREAT NORTH BANK, which had been uncovered terracing since Highbury had opened, was finally covered in 1935. The designer was Waterlow Ferrier, architect of the West Stand. Sadly, he died while work was continuing, victim of a motorcycle accident in London's busy Piccadilly. The famous clock was removed to the other end which, inevitably, became known as the 'Clock End'. A year later, work started on the Avenell Road side of the ground. The new East Stand would have to look almost identical to the West but needed to contain the club's offices, changing rooms, directors seating, and so on. Also, it had to boast the club's front entrance, smart and a little forbidding. Many players of those days may still have arrived at Highbury using public transport, but once they climbed the steps and went through that entrance, they were made to feel like the superstars of their day.

It had not been intended to build the East Stand for several more years but the old stand was rapidly decaying and it was decided to go ahead. Because of Ferrier's death, Major Binnie was left in charge. Although his brief was to create a mirror-image of the West Stand, he had to ensure that as well as providing four thousand seats on the top tier, there would be the same number on the lower. As a result there would be less standing room.

The first plan was to have the seating on the lower tier extend all the way down to the wall surrounding the pitch. It was soon discovered that because most of the rain drove in from a westerly direction, the fans in the front rows would get very wet. Those seats were removed and the area returned to standing room. The roof, some eighty feet above pitch level, would have only two pillars in front of the spectators. Within the stand there had to be refreshment areas.

Once the work was complete, the directors took up seats in the new stand. The area they had previously used became, perhaps, the first at any football ground to go up-market, attracting one hundred better-off spectators to the 'Enclosure Club'. Each member was entitled to two seats. Bernard Joy described it as bringing "Mayfair to Highbury". The annual subscription was ten guineas. Members had their own lift from a private entrance, a lounge, buffet and 'American Bar'.

Despite the impressive up-dating of the ground itself, there was little doubt that, on the pitch, the other First Division clubs no longer felt inhibited by a declining Arsenal. The fact that, in 1936, a Second Division side that did not even get promoted had stretched them so much at Wembley seemed to be further evidence. In the 1936-37 season, Arsenal won only three of their opening eleven matches and were struggling away from home. They pulled themselves together in mid-season, reaching the top of the table, and had a good FA Cup run, including a 7-1 win at Burnley and a 5-1 victory over Manchester United at Highbury. Meantime, Charlton Athletic, under the wise management team of Jimmy Seed and Jimmy Trotter, quietly and surprisingly climbed higher and higher. Only two years earlier the south London club had been in the Third Division South.

As the season in the League began to turn sour again, the Cup brought Arsenal a measure of compensation, but West Bromwich knocked them out 3-1 in the Sixth Round. Drake lost form and then forfeited his place because of a recurrence of a knee injury. Manchester City, who it seemed had given up all chance of the Championship in January, now found their form again thanks in large measure to the goalkeeping of Frank Swift and the wonderful skill and energy of Peter Doherty. Not that Arsenal were altogether out of the running. Indeed, immediately after their Cup defeat, and even without Drake, they took the lead and began to look like potential champions. They then endured a succession of drawn games at Highbury. Most of the leading sides were able to escape from there with at least a point in their travelling bag.

The crucial game of the season was a visit to Maine Road on 10 April when they were still leading but only by a point. Roberts had been badly injured the previous weekend and the attack against Manchester City was unfamiliar: Kirchen, Bastin, Bowden, Davidson and Nelson. Swift remained as solid as ever in the City goal and Arsenal found themselves a goal behind as a result of amazing footwork from Doherty, who beat three Arsenal defenders. City added another and went on to become champions. Arsenal ended the season behind Charlton and without a trophy for the first time since 1930, making it all the more remarkable that, in the next season, they would again be champions.

In October, 1936, the new £130,000 East Stand was opened with a match against Grimsby Town. It contained the most luxurious dressing rooms ever built. They were tiled throughout, with the floor heated so that the players could keep their feet warm when preparing for a match (there was no pre-match warming up on the pitch). The baths were more like small swimming pools and there were showers and 'cooling off' plunge baths. Uniquely, there was a zinc bath to help in the treatment of injuries. The treatment room was ahead of its time. The use of heat lamps was popular (all of the heating for the stand came from the burning of match-day rubbish in an incinerator). Because all of the training was done at the ground (or on the local footpaths when the players went for a stroll together), there was a gymnasium on the floor above the dressing rooms and a training pitch at the south end, as well as tennis courts. The dressing rooms hardly changed throughout Arsenal's time at Highbury, although modern players preferred to shower rather than use the baths.

On 1 May 1937, Alex James played his final League game for the club (against Bolton in a goalless draw at Highbury) and Bob John retired at about the same time. In spite of long-term injuries, Drake was as effective as ever but there was a depressing feeling that, particularly in the case of James, the heart had been taken from the team. James's departure left a void. Whereas in other areas, such as full back, where Eddie Hapgood's place was being challenged by Leslie Compton, the loss of a good player could be overcome, James was more than good. Allison was only too aware of the problem and, at the same time, was worried by the fact that, despite the successes, the club had fallen into substantial debt. There was a need to rely on producing their own young players, several of whom were being trained at the nursery club of Margate, on the breezy north coast of Kent.

Allison tried moving Bastin into the James role and it worked. However, the most notable move was the decision to buy a new goalkeeper, George Swindin, from Bradford City. Because his timing when coming out to meet centres was initially poor, Swindin had a troubled start at his new club. Once he had overcome that problem, he developed into one of the best goalkeepers Arsenal ever employed. Among the other newcomers were Denis Compton and Reg Lewis. Compton, of course, became an international at football and cricket and would have been even more successful if it had not been for the fact that his career was interrupted by the war and injuries. He was amazingly relaxed and an absolutely natural ball player with that mysterious ability to watch a cricket ball, or a football, and slow it down in his own perception. He required no coaching in ball control.

It was not until January of the 1937-38 season that the recomposed team got to the top of the table, taking over from Brentford who had surprised even themselves. But the most likely champions seemed to be Wolverhampton Wanderers, founded on the defensive strength of Stan Cullis and wizardry of Bryn Jones. Arsenal met them in the fourth round of the FA Cup. Shortly before that, Wolves had beaten them 3-1 in a League match, though against the run of play. Nevertheless, that caused Arsenal to drop to third place.

The Cup game at Molineux was one of the most dramatic in Arsenal's history. They scored a fortunate early goal when Drake glanced the ball in off his shin. Wolves' goalkeeper, Scott, was unsighted and it gently rolled over the line. Nonetheless, the goal had been initiated by a low centre from Bastin, who was following George Allison's orders to avoid sending over high ones that he knew Cullis would intercept without difficulty. Wolves fought back, with Jones outstanding. Slowly, though, Arsenal took control. Kirchen scored from a difficult angle. Again, Wolves recovered their composure without being able to score. The burly Bernard Joy, who had established himself as Arsenal's centre half, recalled that he could barely drag himself back to the dressing room.

In the next round, Arsenal lost to Preston by 1-0 at Highbury, leaving them to put all of their efforts into the League in which they were trailing Brentford and Wolves, although both of those sides were beginning to drop points. In spite of various injuries and the need to bring in the inexperienced Eddie Carr as centre forward (a good one, as it happened) the feeling was that winning the title was under control. Far from it. Over the Easter period, they suffered two defeats by Brentford. Drake also endured a bloody head wound in the first but came back to help out. They were then held to a draw at Highbury by lowly Birmingham. They remained top but only on goal average over Preston and Wolves. Defiantly, they went to Preston and won 3-1. On the last day of the season, they had to beat Bolton Wanderers at Highbury while Wolves could still snatch away the title.

The situation could not have been tighter. For Arsenal, there was only one way to become Champions and that was to play for victory and hope that Wolves would at least be held to a draw at Sunderland. A win for Wolves and they would finish on top.

There was nothing for it but to charge into the attack from the opening whistle. Bolton had slightly given the game away, at least metaphorically speaking, by more or less being given a week off, with only light training at Brighton as a reward for a season in which they would finish seventh, which was higher than they had expected.

When feeling the power of the opening Arsenal attacks, it was obvious that Bolton had no appetite for a battle and, after a few minutes of nominal defiance, they capitulated. Arsenal were two up after thirty minutes. At the same time, news came in from Sunderland that Wolves were losing 1-0. Yet Sunderland had no more to play for than Bolton. Indeed, they would finish the season one point behind them.

Arsenal added two more goals. Wolves had kicked off a quarter of an hour earlier and the final result was relayed to the players on the pitch at Highbury. As a celebration they scored another goal to finish 5-0 winners. So they were champions again but with a points total of only fifty-two, the lowest since 1919.

Allison continued to deliberate over whom he really wanted to replace Alex James. In the end, his choice was the Welsh inside-forward Bryn (Bynmoor) Jones, who had played so well against Arsenal. The fee paid to Wolves in August, 1938 was £14,000 (in four instalments), a record that stood for nine years and immediately put Jones under pressure. A quiet, unassuming, nervous man, he found the expectancy that came with the fee a burden. Nevertheless, he scored against Portsmouth on his debut at Highbury. Instead of being encouraged by the goal, he felt that he had been bought as a goal-maker, not a scorer. Consequently, in his opinion he was not doing the job for which the club had paid such a high fee. By the end of the season, he had lost so much confidence that he asked to be dropped into the reserves.

During the war years, Jones gained in self-esteem and played some fine games, dissecting defences with clever passes. But, by the end of it, he, like many others, lacked the pace of youth. He had not lived up to what had been expected of him. Allison kept trying to change the team's compilation. Many of the Margate 'school' were brought in, though, in the end, a lack of goals condemned the team to finish fifth in 1939 with Jones taking a disproportionate amount of criticism. Chelsea beat them in the third round of the FA Cup. The glorious years of the Chapman era were a memory. However, the club could have suffered a fate far worse than a few setbacks on the pitch.

# CHAPTER 14
## CLOSE TO DISASTER

E VERY YEAR, TRADITIONALLY, ARSENAL SENT A TEAM over to France to play Racing Club, of Paris. In November of the 1938-39 season, two aircraft were used, both taking off from Croydon, which was then London's main airport. Fog was covering northern France. Bernard Joy said: "It was not really safe to fly when the French pilots took off". But they did.

Joy recalled: "We could see the top of the Eiffel Tower as we circled Paris, but, underneath, a thick bank of cloud covered the city. The fog and cloud obscured the runway at Le Bourget". Joy reported: "My plane landed safely and then we heard the sister plane droning in with Bryn Jones and £70,000 worth of players as passengers. It seemed a long time coming down and suddenly the engines roared into full power. Our hearts were in our mouths but our feelings were nothing compared to those of the men on the other aircraft".

The French pilot had realised that he would not have enough runway to stop the plane safely and having put on the power lifted it only a few feet above the other aircraft, which had not turned off the main runway. The second plane then just missed the roof of a hanger, circled and returned with the passengers shocked and hardly in any state to play a match. Nevertheless, they rushed into Paris by taxis and drew the game 1-1.

The war years brought unreal matches. Teams were more or less made up of last minute selections of players who happened to be on leave from the forces and guest players. Out-field players played as goalkeepers (Leslie Compton among them, though he also scored ten goals against Clapton Orient), defenders played as attackers and results were meaningless. Even so, Arsenal managed to retain some of their pre-war players because they worked at the stadium as air raid wardens. The ground was closed and home matches played at White Hart Lane.

Highbury took on a new purpose. A barrage balloon was flown from the practice pitch next to the college and the rest of the ground became a first aid post and air raid patrol centre. The marble hall now contained a blast wall and the dressing rooms were turned into clearing stations for casualties. The windows were boarded over and so not badly damaged when a thousand pound bomb hit the training pitch. More bombs brought down the North Bank roof and even the goalposts were set on fire.

Tottenham's offer to open their doors to their greatest rivals greatly helped heal the wound inflicted in the Norris days. Relations between the club have often been strained by events (not least the transfer of anyone from one to the other) but there have been times when they have come close to ground-sharing on a full-time basis. Financially that might have made sense in any era, but it would have been at the expense of the fans having a base for their club loyalty, which cannot be valued in monetary terms.

Shortly before the war, the club made one of their biggest mistakes as far as talent-spotting was concerned, when they failed to retain a young inside-forward called Len Shackleton, who was to become one of the most skilful, not to mention one of the most opinionated, players of his generation. It was George Allison's mistake. He allowed Shackleton to leave for Bradford. 'Shack' then joined Newcastle and later Sunderland, where he became the great entertainer. With typical lack of faith in real skill, the FA chose him for only five international matches. He thoroughly disliked the administrators of the game at all levels and not without good reason. Famously, in his autobiography *'Clown Prince of Soccer'*, he left a page blank, explaining that it represented the average director's knowledge of the game.

Shackleton had been wildly enthusiastic about joining Arsenal as a groundstaff boy in 1938. "I packed my bags, caught the train to London, and was met at King's Cross by Jack Lambert, centre-forward hero of so many Arsenal triumphs. Having been installed in Highbury Hill lodgings, I went with Lambert for my first peep at the magnificent Arsenal stadium. It was a real eye-opener. The mighty stands, the spotlessly clean terracing, reaching, to my eyes, into the clouds, the emerald green turf: there would have been sufficient to impress the bumpkin from Bradford, but to cap the lot, I saw – and recognised immediately – several of the favoured, fabulous footballers who had helped to make Arsenal great, helped, in fact, to make Arsenal 'The' Arsenal. There they were within hailing distance, Ted Drake, Wilf Copping, Cliff Bastin and George Male, yet I did not dare hail them, even with a 'good afternoon'. Enviously, I watched the 'real players' doing their training stint while I pretended to rake the gravel or cut the turf without having the heart for either task".

Shackleton's short time at Arsenal ended when he was told by the groundsman to report to Allison's office. Shackleton recalled: "In the magnificent managerial mausoleum I stood awkwardly facing Mr Allison wishing that the pile on the ankle-deep carpet might grow and keep growing until it attained a height of 5ft 2in to hide me from the eyes of my manager. Then followed an interview I shall never forget. With each pronouncement the facts became clearer. I was washed up, was not good enough for Arsenal – or any other club for that matter. I would have to return to Bradford and become, perhaps, a miner, an engineer, perhaps a commercial traveller – but never a footballer". Allison told him: "Go back to Bradford and get a job. You will never make the grade as a professional footballer." Allison was totally wrong and though Shackleton was rarely trusted by those who selected England teams, he was to become one of the finest ball-players ever to appear in English football.

There were many occasions during the war when Arsenal still managed to pull together recognisable and formidable teams. For instance, the side that beat Charlton Athletic in 1943 was: Marks; Scott, Leslie Compton, Crayston, Joy, Male, Kirchen, Drake, Lewis, Bastin, Denis Compton. Arsenal won 7-1. Prime Minister Winston Churchill was keen to see that people continued to have some sense of normality in abnormal conditions. To an extent football provided it. Arsenal won the South A League in 1939-40, the London League in 1941-42, and the South League and South League Cup in 1942-43.

Although the club lost many promising young players in war action, they also had victims on the field of play. Kirchen, Crayston and Drake were injured while playing in those strange non-competitive but often hard-fought matches. None of them appeared for the club again. The guest players included Stanley Matthews and Stan Mortensen, who drew in the crowds, perhaps at the expense of young Arsenal players awaiting their opportunity. In spite of that, some talented, permanent new ones began to show their potential. Outstanding amongst them was Wally Barnes, who had been playing as an amateur for Portsmouth. He was a natural wing-half back; a dependable tackler with good distribution. He joined the club in 1944 and went on to win twenty-two caps and captain Wales. Laurie Scott and Reg Lewis also established themselves as first team regulars.

The war brought Arsenal to their knees financially. At the end, it was essential to bring back the glory of the 1930s. Nothing seemed to go in their favour. Denis Compton's prowess as a cricketer took him on tours, and, even when he did become available, more often than not he did further damage to his injured knee, which then became stiffened by arthritis. Barnes also had a knee problem. In addition, discipline in terms of training was not all that it should have been. Strong leadership was badly needed and it came with the return from the RAF of Tom Whittaker who, somewhat generously, Bernard Joy described as "… in many ways superior to his mentor, Herbert Chapman". Allison, who had worked beyond the call of duty to keep the team running during the war, was not altogether unhappy at an invitation to hand over the bulk of his team responsibilities.

The club had always embraced the idea of playing against foreign opposition and agreed to be one of those who would entertain Moscow Dynamo when they toured in 1945. If ever there was a warning that football in Britain needed to look over its shoulder, this was it. Dynamo drew 3-3 at Chelsea, but were clearly the better side. They then thrashed Cardiff 10-1. Because so many of the Arsenal players were still in the forces overseas, the club wanted to include guest players including Matthews and Mortensen. The Dynamo officials objected but without cause because they beat this invitation 'Arsenal' 4-3 on a foggy night at White Hart Lane (Highbury was still not ready after war damage).

Whittaker had to form a post-war team without many of the famous names of the 1930s. Also he had to replace the dependable Joe Shaw, who was welcomed by Chelsea as their assistant manager. In addition, he knew that the club faced severe financial troubles. Arsenal had not been able to play on their own ground for seven years and, when they did return, it was far from ready. As well as the north end roof being destroyed, a bomb had caused extensive damage to the south end and killed two servicemen who had been in charge of the barrage balloon. The only positive result of the war-time destruction was that later the War Damages Commission provided funds to help build the new North Bank roof. Shortly before the end of hostilities, the college behind the other end of the ground was destroyed by fire, which ended the club's links with the previous owners of the Highbury site.

For the first League game after the war (31 August, 1946), away to Wolves, the only players who had appeared in pre-war days were George Male, Cliff Bastin and Bernard Joy. The new team lost 6-1. The first post-war League game at Highbury was against Blackburn Rovers and ended in another defeat (3-1). The situation got worse. It seemed impossible to construct a solid group of players in the middle of the field. Nine of the first fourteen matches were lost. By December, relegation looked likely rather than possible. The turning point came when Barnes started to play again. On his return to first team duty, he faced Preston's Tom Finney and did so well that he retained his position at left back, although being two-footed he could play anywhere in the defence. His partnership with Laurie Scott was impressive and Les Compton brought confidence back to the whole team. Even so, there was still the need to find an influential player for the half-back line.

When it became known that the experienced thirty-one year old Joe Mercer, of Everton and captain of England, was available for transfer, Whittaker moved fast and had his offer of £7,000 accepted without further negotiation, which was not surprising because Arsenal were taking a considerable risk. Only a few months earlier, Mercer had undergone a cartilage operation and there was serious muscle wastage. Indeed, he had considered retiring early from the game to look after his grocery business. After all, he had already enjoyed a long and successful career. He was the son of a former Nottingham Forest professional player. At the age of sixteen, in 1931, he joined Everton. An England place was soon won as a wing-half from which position he enjoyed the thrill of the counter-attack. During the war, he and his Everton colleague Tommy Lawton served in the Army Physical Training Corps, which allowed them to appear as 'guest' players for Aldershot, also the powerful Army Xl.

Once Mercer arrived at Highbury, intensive massage brought strength back into the weakened leg. Meanwhile, Whittaker advised him to change his style from an attacking half-back to an anchor in the middle of the field, thus not putting him under as much physical pressure. Not that Mercer had lost his ability to tackle firmly and with good timing. Bernard Joy said: "Only one player, Alex James, has contributed more than Joe Mercer to Arsenal's greatness." Mercer had been his family's breadwinner at the age of thirteen and was a born fighter with a wonderful sense of humour and great warmth of character. Later in his career he was, all too briefly, England's enormously popular temporary manager.

Allison and Whittaker's team rebuilding continued with the unlikely signing of Fulham's Ronnie Rooke who, in his mid-thirties, had been thinking of retirement rather than a call from Arsenal. He was in the bath at Craven Cottage when he was told to report to the manager's office in the Cottage (originally the home of Edward Bulwer-Lytton, author of 'The Last Days of Pompeii'). There he found Allison and Whittaker who told him they were badly in need of a player of his ability. Rooke agreed to sign and Fulham let him go for £1,000, probably thinking that they had by far the better of the deal.

Had Arsenal been in a stronger financial position probably neither Mercer nor Rooke would have been considered worthy of any investment at all. As it was, these two were essential to a revival. Once they started playing together, the results improved. The threat of relegation became a memory. The team took Chelsea (who included Tommy Lawton) to two FA Cup replays. In the third game, played at White Hart Lane, Lewis missed a penalty and Lawton took advantage to score twice. Although Arsenal concluded their season thirteenth in the First Division – their worst finishing position since 1929-30 – considering their bleak situation earlier in the season it was quite an achievement. Rooke scored twenty-one goals in twenty-four matches, which surprised himself, not to mention Fulham.

# CHAPTER 15
# LUCKY ARSENAL?

## 1947-48 FIRST DIVISION CHAMPIONS

GEORGE ALLISON FINALLY RESIGNED and Tom Whittaker took over as manager. Chelsea realised that Joe Shaw yearned to return to Highbury to assist Whittaker and, magnanimously, agreed to release him. Jack Crayston became assistant manager. Whittaker then set about obtaining more players, including Don Roper, a winger from Southampton. Whittaker always believed that Arsenal's strength should be based on quick and clever wingers. He successfully converted Ian McPherson, previously an outside right, into an outside left and strengthened the defence by obtaining Archie Macaulay from Brentford.

The changing team embarked on the 1947-48 season much improved in strength, skill and morale. McPherson quickly proved a success on the wing, inspiring early victories over Sunderland, Charlton (twice, including a 6-0 win at Highbury) and Sheffield United. People who had not been sorry to see the mighty Arsenal fall on hard times now revived the cry "Lucky Arsenal", which in the much different period of the 1940s was far from the truth. Not even Manchester United, on their visit to Highbury, had an answer to Arsenal's superb football, losing 2-1 and seeing Rooke beat them with a shot from thirty-five yards.

Proof that the club really had turned the corner came in a match against Bolton Wanderers. Reg Lewis and Alf Fields were both injured in the first half and had to abandon the game. As captain, Mercer took it on himself to re-arrange the side. He moved to centre-half and sent Jimmy Logie to left-half. At least Arsenal had already established a two-goal lead. In the second half Mercer directed everything. The nine men hung on to retain their advantage to the end. There were no defeats in the first seventeen games.

Such a fine start to the season had a beneficial effect on the spirits of the players. Having taken top position, they retained it for the rest of the term. And that despite the fact that Fields lost most of it to that injury and the Compton brothers were pre-occupied with cricket.

Many of the matches in the second half of the season were made all the more difficult because everyone wanted to beat Arsenal. Then the forwards lost goalscoring form, leaving the defence to ensure that games were not lost. Derby interrupted the successful sequence at the Baseball Ground.

Slowly, the attack began to regain form, but the advance was almost destroyed with a surprise defeat in the third round of the Cup by Bradford City, of the Second Division. Suddenly the worries of the previous season returned. It was Manchester United's turn to go on an extended unbeaten run (thirteen games) and, in January, the teams were to meet. Confidence was further eroded when it became known that Mercer had a heavy cold and was unlikely to be available. After a series of penicillin injections, he managed to appear.

The match took place at Maine Road (Old Trafford still being closed after war damage) and attracted a League record crowd of 81,962 (there had been 84,569 there for a Cup match against Stoke in 1934). Despite still feeling far from well, Mercer did a splendid tight-marking job on the normally elusive Johnny Morris, and Archie Macaulay kept a close guard on Stan Pearson. Even so, the United defenders were equally efficient. Johnny Carey and Jack Aston were probably the best players on the field but a 1-1 draw was the fair result of an outstanding game.

Arsenal had an eight-point lead. Whittaker was becoming ever more impressive as a manager. He did his homework on opponents and restored the teamwork that had been the hallmark of the Chapman teams of the 1930s. The reliability of Swindin, in goal, was satisfying and confidence building.

The Championship title was finally won with a draw at Huddersfield. The team had left the ground before they knew the result of Manchester United's and Burnley's games. Denis Compton had no intention of waiting until the team's train had arrived in London before discovering what had happened and rushed off at Doncaster to buy a copy of the local evening paper. Only then did the players know that both of their rivals had lost. Although there were four games remaining, Arsenal could no longer be overtaken. Whittaker's first season as manager proper had seen the club win their sixth Championship and the team conceded only thirty-two goals. They scored eighty-one, of which Rooke got thirty-three. Mercer was enjoying himself and put off retirement.

# CHAPTER 16
# SWINDIN'S STRANGE PREMONITION

## 1950 FA CUP WINNERS

T HE ARRIVAL OF ALEX FORBES from Sheffield United in the second half of the 1947-48 Championship winning season had added competition for half-back places. It was also an opportunity for him to turn Joe Mercer from personal hero to team colleague. He was a Scottish international who was seen as a likely successor to Mercer but Mercer continued to be a forceful player at a time when others were disappointing. Early season matches in 1948-49 brought several poor performances and though during the autumn there was an upturn in results, the rest of the season was a mixture of encouragement followed by disappointment.

Fifth place, nine points behind champions Portsmouth, was no more or less than the team deserved. After all, their Championship winning side of the previous season had been based on players moving towards the end of their careers, several of whom suffered injuries from which they failed to recover sufficiently quickly. Laurie Scott, for instance, was the victim of a knee problem. In those days, a cartilage operation was not something from which a player could be fairly sure of making a full recovery to fitness, as Scott discovered. His place had to be taken by promoting Lionel Smith.

The season, which was also marred by the death of the Chairman, Sir Samuel Hill-Wood, did at least have one exceptional match. Oddly enough it was the Charity Shield which is not usually associated with great excitement, tension and fine football. It was played against Manchester United at Highbury. Three goals were scored by Arsenal in the first five minutes (Lewis got two). United, under the control of the peerless Johnny Carey, revived and scored two themselves before Rooke got the winner.

If in the League and the FA Cup (knocked out by Derby County in the fourth round) the team did not perform as effectively as the fans had hoped, at least the attendances remained high and the club went back into profit. Not that Whittaker was allowed to go off into the transfer market with his pockets stuffed with money.

Winning the FA Cup in 1950 came as no surprise to goalkeeper George Swindin who at Christmas time had told Joe Mercer he had a premonition that, in spite of having several players who were supposed to be past their best, Arsenal would benefit from being drawn at home four times and be the eventual winners.

There had been little to justify Swindin's prediction, which the rest of the players took with a pinch of salt. In November and December, for instance, only three wins came their way. The fans were firmly of the belief that an arduous summer tour to South America had left too little time for the players to recover. Whittaker sought to raise spirits by saying that he would put extra effort into winning the Cup (a ploy to divert attention as old as the competition itself). He also used the period in which the club lost sight of any chance of winning the Championship to make changes.

Ronnie Rooke had moved across London to join Crystal Palace and was replaced by Peter Goring who had come up from Cheltenham. It had been on the much-criticised tour of South America that Goring first showed that he had the potential to replace Rooke at centre-forward. Whittaker had also obtained Freddie Cox, a direct and fast winger who had not won over the crowds' appreciation while with Tottenham. The various changes substantially improved the team and they moved up to a respectable position in the League. Forbes and Mercer, the wing halves, were now probably the best in the League and the team gave Manchester United and Liverpool tough matches without collecting winning points. So Whittaker had to be tested on his vow to make the Cup the priority.

The path to Wembley began at home, just as Swindin had predicted. The third round tie against Sheffield Wednesday threatened danger. Wednesday had not lost for three months in the Second Division. Sure enough, although they played for over an hour with ten men (Kenny suffered a dislocated shoulder) they defied Arsenal until the final minute when Lewis shot through a gap in their defence.

Swansea City offered a gritty fight. Then, against Burnley, who had beaten Arsenal on the first day of the season, Whittaker recalled Denis Compton, who because of his knee problem had put on weight but was still an accurate distributor of the ball. It was Compton's pass that offered Lewis the chance to take the lead, which he accepted. Compton then hit in a splendid shot himself. The draw continued to favour Arsenal with home ties, the next being against Leeds United who had the youthful, mighty Welshman John Charles at centre-half. Even he failed to cope with one exceptional Arsenal move which Lewis finished after Forbes had avoided being stopped by three or four tackles.

Then there was Chelsea to face in the semi-final at White Hart Lane. They gained a two-goal lead within twenty-five minutes, both from Roy Bentley, but Cox took a corner for Arsenal and curled it intentionally or luckily direct into the net. With fifteen minutes left, Arsenal gained another corner. Denis Compton was about to take it when he signalled to his brother, Les, to move up out of defence and into the Chelsea penalty area. Captain Mercer disapproved but when the ball came over he was happy enough because Les headed in the equaliser which brought a replay which Cox secured with a rare left-foot shot in extra-time.

The Final brought a dilemma for Mercer who had been doing a lot of his training in the north with Liverpool, who had become Arsenal's opponents at Wembley after beating Everton in the semi-final. He agreed not to join them in their main training sessions. Not that Liverpool felt in any danger of his acting as a spy because they had already beaten Arsenal in two League matches that season and their confidence was high.

Because of a clash in colours, Arsenal wore resplendent gold shirts with white shorts. Liverpool changed to white shirts and black shorts. For one man, in particular, it was a golden afternoon. Reg Lewis was not a player Whittaker considered essential to his team, often leaving him out. By now, Lewis was thirty and probably thinking he would soon be locking up his career. At Wembley, he was to prove the key to victory. Because of a greasy pitch and heavy rain, Arsenal decided against playing many long, low passes and opted for a short-ball game. It worked well.

In the seventeenth minute, Jimmy Logie, the tiny, inventive inside-forward, placed a pass through the Liverpool defence. Lewis took it under his control and comfortably beat the Liverpool goalkeeper, Cyril Sidlow. Liverpool pulled themselves together. Albert Stubbins and Billy Liddell looking menacing. By coincidence, it was also in the seventeenth minute of the second half that Lewis, who had a splendid match, guaranteed Arsenal their victory after being put in possession by Cox. Following a long career in which he had won every other domestic honour, Mercer (that season's Footballer of the Year) collected the FA Cup. Not only had Swindin's premonition about a run of home matches mysteriously come true but Arsenal had actually won the competition without ever travelling outside London.

### FA CUP FINAL (29 April 1950, Wembley)
### Arsenal 2 (Lewis 2) Liverpool 0

*Arsenal: Swindin; Scott, Barnes, Forbes, Leslie Compton, Mercer, Cox, Logie, Goring, Lewis, Denis Compton.*
*Liverpool: Sidlow; Lambert, Spicer, Taylor, Hughes, Jones, Payne, Baron, Stubbins, Fagan, Liddell.*
***Referee:** H. Pearce.*

73

# CHAPTER 17
# MERCER'S FAREWELL

## 1952-53 FIRST DIVISION CHAMPIONS

INJURIES CAME IN THE WAY OF THE CLUB extending their FA Cup victory into the following season's Championship. Their results in the first half were sound enough but there were problems in the very area in which the club had become renowned – the wings. Denis Compton retired and Don Roper had lost his speed. To rub salt in the wounds, Stanley Matthews was magical at Highbury for Blackpool who would go on to win the 1953 Cup Final, known as the Matthews Final, which was accurate in the romantic sense of it at last bringing a deserved medal to the old wing-master but unfair on Stan Mortensen, the scorer of three goals.

Arsenal's troubles continued while Arthur Rowe's Spurs, with their 'push and run' style, were attracting all of the attention. Doug Lishman, who in spite of the fact that he began his playing career as a centre-half had been Arsenal's top goalscorer, broke a leg. Swindin was also injured and several players failed to live up to their reputations. As a result, fifth position for the 1950-51 season was not as bad as it might have been. It seemed worse because the champions were Spurs, and deservedly so.

In the Cup, Arsenal were held to an exacting draw at Highbury by Carlisle but went north to win the replay 4-1, which was a result that is not often remembered in the glowing reviews of the managerial career of a certain Bill Shankly! Northampton were stubborn in the next round, losing by only 3-2, and finally there was another meeting with Manchester United at Old Trafford, where a single goal from Stan Pearson brought United victory. That did considerable harm to Arsenal's self-assurance and led to several new faces being given their chances to come into the team on a permanent basis, notably Cliff Holton, Ray Daniel, Arthur Milton and Dave Bowen. Meanwhile, Les Compton played against Wales, thus, at thirty-eight years and two months, becoming the oldest player ever to make a debut for England.

The 1951-52 season was one of what might have been. Milton and Holton added a lot of credibility to the attack, which was a little surprising since Holton had joined as a defender before becoming a

74

successful goalscorer. By Christmas, the side had gone to the top of the table, where Portsmouth had been residing. In the Cup, there was a comfortable Third Round 5-0 victory over Norwich, and Barnsley were similarly well beaten. After that, injury cost the services of the reliable Forbes but the run continued. Leyton Orient, who had never before reached the Fifth Round, were overawed by their visitors, especially by the goalscoring threat of Lishman, and lost 3-0. Luton gave a better account of themselves, which was in part because Logie was injured. They even scored the first goal that Arsenal had conceded in the Cup that season, Bernard Moore beating Swindin with a diving header. Whittaker made several tactical changes at half-time. Cox equalised and then scored again before Milton added a third.

Finding themselves facing Chelsea in the semi-final at White Hart Lane was not the threat it might have been because they had twice beaten them in the League. There was now even talk of achieving the League and Cup Double. With seven League games remaining, they were on level terms with Manchester United. Then more problems. The semi-final was postponed because of snow. That also clogged up the League season. When the semi-final was played, Lewis took a heavy knock, carried on but was, as they said in those days, 'a passenger'. Even so, Logie laid on a goal for Cox after ten minutes, but when Swindin and Bobby Smith collided, the ball was not cleared properly and Billy Gray headed into an undefended goal. The replay was dominated by Cox and Arsenal won 3-0.

Much energy had been expended in those two matches and in the run-up to the Cup Final against Newcastle there was no time to rest. Some ageing limbs were crying 'enough'. Ray Daniel was then injured. The team also lost to Bolton, the first time they had been beaten in eleven League games. Injuries continued to pile up: Les Compton, Lionel Smith, Arthur Smith, Cox, Lishman and finally Logie were all victims.

Mercer, who had been inspirational, was struggling with fatigue. In his absence, and with six reserves called in, the side lost 3-1 at West Bromwich Albion. Their nearest rivals, Manchester United, took advantage. When they met at Old Trafford one week before the Cup Final and on the last day of the League season, Arsenal needed to win by seven goals to deny United the title. Not only did United win, they scored six goals to Arsenal's one (Jack Rowley, who had been in sensational scoring form, got a hat-trick). Even so, Arsenal had been two victories away from the title.

Most of the injured players made out that they had recovered in time for the Cup Final, though Whittaker himself had the suspicion that several were far from ready. Daniel, for instance, would play with a broken wrist. Lishman was in pain from a cut that had turned septic. Logie had a leg injury that was causing internal bleeding. Then, in the early stages of the game, there was another cruel blow when Wally Barnes injured a knee as he twisted on the soft turf. He went off for treatment and returned but soon had to abandon the game. The ten-man team needed to be re-arranged, with Roper moving from the wing to right back. Arsenal were defiant. Lishman hit the crossbar with a spectacular overhead kick. Thanks in no small measure to Mercer's efforts, the Newcastle attack, purposefully led by Jackie Milburn, was held. Near the end, however, Holton and Roper fell to the turf in need of attention. Although Mercer pleaded with the referee to stop the game, it continued and Mitchell crossed for George Robledo to head in the winner off the post. Later Mercer remarked that even though he had captained England, he had never felt greater honour than on that Cup Final day captaining Arsenal. Tom Whittaker said he had never been more proud of an Arsenal team.

Everything that had happened in that Cup Final concentrated minds on the challenge ahead. The 1952-53 Championship was not easily won. It came as a result of outstanding team spirit amongst a long established and mature group of players. That spirit may even have been too buoyant since matches that should have been won at a canter were turned into difficult hurdles. There were also some signs that one or two of the players were not totally sold on Whittaker's emphasis on a cautious tactical approach. Indeed, for that very reason Ray Daniel requested a transfer and later went to Sunderland.

Barnes had been struggling with his knee injury which was worse than originally diagnosed. Several changes had to be made and the season began hesitatingly. Then, after a 5-1 win over Liverpool at Anfield, where Holton scored three, thoughts turned to winning the title. Milton, particularly, was in splendid form. Blackpool, on their way to the 'Matthews Final', lost 3-1 in a match at Highbury that had few touches of magic from the ageing genius, who at that stage of his career was often more of a decoy than a positive force.

The season turned from promising to seemingly hopeless. In sixth place at Easter, hopes of winning the Championship looked hazy but the team clung on, only three points behind Preston and Charlton. Then came five successive wins in April, including a 5-3 beating of Liverpool. Preston lost at Charlton and so Arsenal were top but Preston were still the danger team. By coincidence, the last Saturday of the season brought them together at Deepdale where, having gained a crucial draw before a crowd of 60,000 at Cardiff, Arsenal knew that they could afford to lose, though not by too many goals.

Tom Finney and Charlie Wayman gave Preston victory which meant that the Championship would be decided by the season's last two matches. On the following Wednesday Preston visited Derby County and won 1-0, leaving Arsenal needing to beat Burnley at Highbury on the Friday. Burnley had been playing well and were in sixth position.

Arsenal at that time always preferred to play on a damp pitch so that the ball could be played quickly across the surface. So when there was a heavy shower shortly before kick-off, they could not have been more thankful. They were also grateful that the galvanising Mercer had been declared fit after suffering from an ankle injury.

Without a moment's hesitation Arsenal strode into the attack and forced Burnley back into their own half. Such tactics always carry the danger of being broken down by a sudden breakaway, which was exactly what happened. In a rare moment of confusion between Mercer and Swindin, Burnley snatched possession and Stephenson put them into the lead. Now Arsenal had serious work to do. They reacted with some of the most effective football of the season. In an eleven minute period, Forbes (with his first goal of the season), Lishman and Logie all scored.

This Burnley side had a lot of resilience and during the second half put Arsenal under enormous pressure. There were fifteen minutes left when Billy Elliott scored to leave the game finely balanced. Tom Whittaker had been nervous throughout and now could stand it no longer. He got up from his seat and walked to the dressing room until the players returned to tell him that they had hung on for victory and, as a result, the club had won the Championship for a record seven times, though only because of the slightest margin of goal average (less than a goal). Their goal average was 1.51 whereas Preston's was 1.41.

After the match, Mercer returned to the pitch to acknowledge the crowd's support and also to wave goodbye. It was time to retire at the top.

Coronation year also brought England's first home defeat, by the magical Hungarians. For Arsenal fans, the saddest event came on the day before the Coronation with news of the death at the age of only fifty-one of Alex James. Who can say whether he was the greatest player Britain has ever produced. There is no doubt that he ranked high among them. Certainly he was the most skilful inside-forward of the inter-war years. Arsenal's decision to pay Preston £9,000 for him in 1925 had, as we have seen, brought criticism upon Herbert Chapman because the manager had only recently paid the record £10,000 for David Jack, but the investment was not misplaced.

James, only 5ft 6in, was at the heart of the teams that won so much prestige for Arsenal. He more than anyone had routed England when playing for the wonderful 1928 Scottish team that won 5-1 at Wembley. But Chapman pictured him in a different role and the fans saw him as an amazing dribbler with the ability to pass the ball when it was right and hold it while others moved into receiving areas. After he stopped playing, he became a coach at Highbury, working mainly with young players. In a rare diversion from tradition, *The Times* carried an obituary of a sportsman. James was that special.

# CHAPTER 18
## DESPERATE TIMES

FOLLOWING THE WINNING OF THE CHAMPIONSHIP in 1953, the club went into a long period (eighteen years) of virtual hibernation. Perhaps when Whittaker could not bear to watch the last few minutes of the last game, the strain on him was taking a toll (he would have had in his mind what pressure did to Chapman). There had to be a lot of changes. Much more emphasis needed to be placed on producing young players. After all, the average age of the last Championship winning side had been about thirty.

New players brought in included Bill Dodgin (from Fulham), Derek Tapscott (Barry Town), Jimmy Bloomfield (Brentford) and Joe Haverty (St Patrick's, Dublin) while an excellent young goalkeeper had emerged from the ranks – Jack Kelsey, who was to become one of the club's most loyal and valuable servants. He had grown up in South Wales where his father, a Londoner who married a Welsh girl, was a smelter furnaceman. Jack followed him into the tinplate works in Swansea where he had to lift slabs of steel. His strength grew. He became a crane-driver, then painter before National Service. Only after that did his ability as a goalkeeper for Winch Wen get noticed and Arsenal offered him a trial. His work had given him considerable arm strength to accompany his large hands, but his first game for Arsenal, back in 1951, had seen him concede five goals to Charlton Athletic. The experience failed to intimidate him and, by 1953-54, he had replaced his mentor, Swindin.

A youth who made rapid progress through the ranks to reach the first team was Gerry Ward, who was only sixteen when he made his debut. Dave Bowen was showing signs of becoming what he turned out to be, a stalwart both for the club and Wales. But if the way forward had to be with youth, the need for experience had to be kept in mind.

It would have been difficult to get anyone more experienced than Tommy Lawton, who signed at the age of thirty-five. On his own confession, he was too slow for first division football in which he had not appeared for six years. He had been acting as manager at Brentford and though still feeling that he had some football left in him, he had not been considering a return to the top flight. He was amazed when Arsenal came calling. His wife telephoned him at Brentford and told him to get away from the ground as quickly as he could and telephone her from a call box so that nobody else could hear. When he did, his wife explained that Tom Whittaker had telephoned and said he wanted her husband to play for Arsenal. "Her message seemed like a practical joke", Lawton said later. "I told her not to be so daft, but she persuaded me to ring him, and his offer was confirmed".

Lawton was honest with Whittaker, telling him that he thought it "ludicrous" to consider returning to that class of football. Whittaker reminded Lawton that Arsenal were at the foot of the First Division and in serious need of a man of his experience to bring the best out of the younger players. He had worked with Lawton before when he was a trainer with the pre-war England team.

The announcement that Lawton was in the side to play Manchester City on the day after he signed was met with amazement everywhere. On the other hand, it also caught the imagination, which was the real point. A crowd of fifty-thousand turned up at Highbury where the club had been struggling to attract thirty-thousand, which was well below their financial break-even figure. Lawton admitted that in the match, which was drawn, he felt "more than a little out of place". He said: "I had spent too many years with lesser clubs".

Lawton acted more as a public relations man for the club than useful player. His enthusiasm was beneficial and the effect of his signing was to lift the team away from the relegation area. In that respect, he more than repaid the seven thousand five hundred pounds fee paid to Brentford and the seventeen pounds a week basic wages (the same as everyone else). Near the end of the 1956-57 season, he decided it was time to begin a new career and went off to join Kettering Town as player-manager. In all, he made thirty-five first team appearances for Arsenal and scored thirteen goals.

Jimmy Logie also departed, finishing his career at Gravesend. Meanwhile, some of the younger players blossomed, especially Tapscott. There were also some team highlights such as the period in 1955 when they went seven successive games without defeat, although they still finished only ninth. Generally, though, it became a long journey of frustration. As an example, in the 1953-54 season they lost to Third Division Norwich City in the fourth round of the FA Cup despite saving a penalty in the second minute and taking the lead.

An unlikely source of quality in the team of the mid-fifties was a former market porter, Danny Clapton. He had written in for a trial, got one and was so enthusiastic, and not a little talented, that the club seriously considered putting him directly into the first team. They waited and he got his chance in a side that contained Vic Groves, who was bought from Leyton Orient and soon made a favourable impression with his goals.

Embarrassments were only to be expected for a world famous club that was in a rut of comparative mediocrity and trying to re-build. The Cup brought one in particular (1955-56). Non-League Bedford went to Highbury and seemed to have been well beaten when, with ten minutes left, they were two goals down. Then Steel scored with a shot that probably surprised even himself, and Bedford equalised almost at the end. The replay on their own ground failed to see much improvement in the Arsenal attacking performance. The defence had looked solid enough until Cliff Holton lost the ball and Yates scored. Here was the possibility of a Cup sensation even more amazing than the defeat by Walsall. Cometh the hour cometh the man. It was Groves who dived to head in an equaliser. Confidence rose but there was still extra-time to come. Bedford did not have Arsenal's stamina and lost to another header, by Tapscott.

Although Jack Crayston was an admirable assistant manager, there was clearly a need for Whittaker to be offered more help. He had not been well but insisted on taking full responsibility, which was the very reason why Alec Stock made a brief appearance as another assistant. Almost overnight Stock irritated the players by saying that a large number of them were not good enough and would soon be released. As it happened, he was the one to go, returning to Leyton Orient after less than two months. At Orient, he had been in sole charge. At Highbury, he was firmly one of the backroom staff. Had he stayed, possibly he would soon have become manager, though at what cost to player relationships?

Whittaker, who had been manager since 1947, died in 1956, still in his job. That, together with the deaths of Alex James and George Allison, who had been known as Mr Arsenal, and the retirement of Joe Shaw, seemed to take the soul out of the club. Whittaker's former assistant, Crayston, took over just before Christmas in 1956 and the day-to-day running of the club became the responsibility of Bob Wall, a devoted Arsenal man who had been secretary-assistant to Herbert Chapman.

Crayston worked well with his inherited players and, in the 1956-57 season, they finished a creditable fifth, though fourteen points behind Manchester United's dazzling Busby Babes. However, he felt that the board was failing to release sufficient money to improve the team. Mainly for that reason, he resigned after less than two years.

It was assumed that Joe Mercer would take over but George Swindin had been working well as manager of Peterborough who had several exciting Cup runs. He was offered the position and tried without success to raise Arsenal out of their comparatively forlorn state. During his period in charge (1958-62), and despite taking on Ron Greenwood as senior coach, they simply survived, usually in mid-table positions (1958 twelfth, 1959 a more creditable third, 1960 thirteenth, 1961 eleventh and 1962 tenth). For the fans, the situation was torture because this was the era of the fine Spurs side that, in 1961, achieved the "double". Swindin suffered by comparison with Bill Nicholson.

Oddly enough, it was during this long period of largely unsatisfactory performances that there occurred the most poignant, memorable and historic match ever played at Highbury.

# CHAPTER 19
# ARSENAL 4 MANCHESTER UNITED 5

## 1 FEBRUARY 1958

### A PERSONAL MEMORY BY THE AUTHOR

*For a football-loving teenager living on the north Kent coast in the 1950s, the best on offer was less than satisfying. There was the occasional visit to Gillingham, who were then playing in the Third Division (South), or the regular Saturday afternoon entertainment watching Whitstable Town. The 'Town' consisted of a few local 'stars' who had outgrown the Canterbury and District League but were not good enough to become full-time Football League players, and a hand-me-down bunch of former pros who, after their careers had left them not much richer than when they had begun, topped up their incomes in the semi-pro Kent League.*

*My determination to see Manchester United's Busby Babes in their match against Arsenal at Highbury had probably become a nagging irritation to my parents, both of whom enjoyed watching Whitstable well enough and were prepared to leave it at that. Or at least, the expense of raising their sights as high as Highbury, even for one excursion, was not something they particularly welcomed. My pestering finally won the day. I had always favoured Arsenal but United had been champions for the previous two seasons and every single player seemed to me to be indescribably brilliant.*

*The cheapest way to get to London was by the 'Milk Train' (fare: four shillings and sixpence) which left before dawn. Unlike schooldays, on that chilly February morning there was no knock on the bedroom door and the dreaded call to get up or be late. I was dressed and ready to go. When the train arrived at Victoria, kick-off at Highbury was still many frustrating hours away.*

*I said I wanted to be at the ground early. Frustratingly, my parents resisted the idea of going straight there before the pigeons in Trafalgar Square had lifted heads from under wings. During the long wait we wandered aimlessly, killing time and eventually finding some cellar café off Oxford Street where you could get a modestly priced early lunch before midday.*

*Under duress, I was persuaded that arriving at Highbury at 12.30pm would not leave us locked out. But we were far from the first in the first queue* we found. It was, of course, the one nearest Arsenal tube station. We joined it simply because we, like thousands making their first visit to Highbury over the years, assumed that this entrance was the only way into the stadium (in a way helping to prove that the club had been right to stress the importance of having an underground station virtually adjoining the ground).

The grand main entrance and the other points of entry were unknown to us. The fact that there were eighty turnstiles waiting to click into action all round the stadium was not in our reckoning. We were used to two gates to our Kent League ground, one by the gasometers and the other near the stream into which a few referees had been thrown by some of Whitstable's more unruly fans.

We sat on a garden wall until the gates opened at 1.30pm by which time there was an atmosphere of such expectation that you could almost take it in your hands. Somehow everyone seemed to know that this was to be a special match; a special day. Did we know by some strange, fortunate tip from the gods just how special? No. It was simply our good fortune to be there. Geoffrey Green, distinguished Football Correspondent of The Times, also arrived early and in the following Monday's paper reported: "There was a whiff of the old days. There must have been some premonition about it too, since the crowds fairly poured in – a 64,000 gathering, filling the rim of the stadium far up where it cut the sky …". I would not have conceived that many years later I was to succeed the incomparable Geoffrey at The Times.

I had become slightly more confident that we would not be locked out. We rushed down the terrace beneath the West Stand, on the way almost forgetting to buy a programme (still treasured). We were among the first few hundred to arrive and went to the pitch edge fence where the view would give us only a knee-high perspective of the match, but you would be almost within touching distance of players who, to my mind, were untouchable.

The ground was almost empty; a huge, near-silent stage awaiting actors and audience. The East Stand, on the other side, was slightly obscured by the winter mist that added to the feeling that this was somewhere magical and a little mysterious. The famous clock above the open terraces ticked away the seemingly endless minutes of expectancy. In those days there was not much in the way of preamble. We were 'entertained' by the Metropolitan Police Central Band playing, amongst other things, the 'Teddy Bears Picnic' and, daringly, a selection from 'The Pajama Game'. There was not even a warm-up on the pitch by the players. How that modern, admittedly sensible, athletic necessity for those who perform at today's formidable pace nevertheless destroys the drama of the entrance of the gladiators.

To be at Highbury for the first time fulfilled a long-held ambition. And at the same time to witness one of the most extraordinary games in its history and, for the rest of your life, be able to say that you were there, was a strange and, in hindsight, haunting experience. The Busby Babes were breathtaking in their power and determination. Arsenal reeled, recovered, hit back and finally lost by a single goal. Memories become blurred by the passing seasons but one remains pinned like a picture on a teenager's wall.

Duncan Edwards sped past, a young colossus only a few yards away. He cut in and scored with a shot that I thought must have been the fiercest and most accurate anyone had ever seen. Perhaps not, but it was a moment that, nearly half a century later, stays as a highlight in a long adventure playing, watching and reporting football. I have had the opportunity to see and write about thousands of matches, some memorable, many more sent to the recycle bin of the mind. That one is the most vivid of all.

In the following week, five of the United players who had appeared at Highbury were killed. Matt Busby and Duncan Edwards hovered between life and death. Busby survived. Edwards, seemingly indestructible as a player, died in hospital. The plane carrying them back from a European Cup tie against Red Star, Belgrade had stopped to refuel in Munich and crashed in the snow and slush while attempting to take off. Eddie Colman, Geoff Bent, Roger Byrne, Mark Jones, David Pegg, Tommy Taylor and Bill Whelan failed to survive. Others suffered serious injuries. Jackie Blanchflower and Johnny Berry were never healed sufficiently to play again.

With the disbelief shared by millions, I first read about the crash in the following day's Daily Mirror, whose own Archie Ledbrooke had been among the victims. When faced with tragedy there is a macabre, involuntary inclination to cry and smile simultaneously. I long remained embarrassed by that disbelieving smile. I had been there, at Highbury, amongst the privileged, watching that still developing yet magnificent United in their last dramatic game on British soil – one to which Arsenal contributed so much.

They say that if all the people who have claimed that they were at Highbury on the day Manchester United played their last League game before the tragedy that decimated that glorious young team, the attendance would have been several hundreds of thousands. As it was, 63,578 actually witnessed an adventure of a match that in more modern, cynical times would almost certainly be impossible. There was never a hint from United that, being the away side, they would be defensive and take the odd chance if it appeared. That was not their style, and within a few minutes of the start they were storming into the attack.

85

Arsenal almost buckled. After only ten minutes United were ahead. Dennis Viollet eased the ball across to Duncan Edwards, the enormously powerful wing half who had made his debut at only fifteen and, at eighteen, was England's youngest-ever full international. Edwards was still several yards outside the penalty area when he struck his shot. Jack Kelsey, in the Arsenal goal, was never going to have the answer.

Arsenal put up some gallant resistance. It was not enough. After half-an-hour, United caught them too committed to a counter-attack. Harry Gregg, the United goalkeeper who was to become a hero at the crash scene in Munich when going back to rescue the injured, had just been forced to make an important save. He gathered up the ball and cleared it quickly and accurately to Albert Scanlon, who scampered down the left side before pulling it back across the goalmouth to Bobby Charlton, who was a comparative newcomer to the side. But here Charlton finished the attack maturely, in the way that over the next few years he would complete so many both for United and England. He hit in a wonderful shot.

Edwards and his wing-half colleague Eddie Colman then began to dominate the middle areas of the pitch, bringing the best out of the United attack, always looking to play the positive pass and intercepting Arsenal's counters with strength and positional intuition. It seemed certain that this would bring about a third United goal and probably finish off Arsenal's voice in this onrushing, vivid debate. The third came, Scanlon again instigating it by sending the ball far across to Ken Morgans, who rapped it back inside to where the formidably powerful Tommy Taylor was waiting to complete the sweeping movement. But Arsenal were not finished.

Although United spent the first quarter of an hour of the second half largely in control, the last half an hour brought a breath-clawing climax. In an extraordinary period of unpredictable defiance, Arsenal drew level, seemingly riding a tide of noise. David Herd initiated the recovery, volleying in from Dave Bowen's lob. In the next minute, Gordon Nutt sent over an inviting centre. Vic Groves headed it down and, with typical care, Jimmy Bloomfield placed the ball past Gregg. Arsenal were now full of spirit. Nutt again skipped down the wing and placed another centre. This time Bloomfield had to dive low but he headed in the equaliser. The sound of the crowd's excited appreciation was thunderous.

Bowen took control off the feet of Edwards and Colman. Bloomfield, always a stylish player, played delicate through passes. United had every right to feel that the game had turned against them. Instead they rallied and began to regain the dominant role that earlier had belonged to them.

Character as well as physical strength was called for in full measure. Charlton and Scanlon moved the ball around smoothly and Viollet completed their move with a deft header: 3-4. From the restart United simply continued in the same vein. Colman and Morgans set up Taylor in the penalty area but his angle was not hopeful. Kelsey seemed to have the danger covered but Taylor unleashed United's fifth goal.

Even then Arsenal were bold and brave. Derek Tapscott had been competitive throughout but had few chances to break through the United defence. At last he did. Bowen and Herd had provided the platform with an exchange of passes. Tapscott ran through the middle to beat Gregg. If this was to be an epitaph to this fine United side, it was also one of the most courageous performances by any Arsenal team.

United later flew to Belgrade for their European Cup tie, which they drew 3-3, sufficient to take them into the semi-finals. The crash on the way home cost twenty-three lives and there were several long-term sufferers from their injuries and shock.

# CHAPTER 20
# THE TOO GENTLE MAN

A FTER ARSENAL'S DECLINE of the mid and late 1950s and early 1960s, almost in desperation they finally decided that something out of the ordinary had to be risked. In March, 1962 they appointed a manager who had no connection with Arsenal. They were not the first, or the last, to discover that a player who had achieved almost everything was not necessarily qualified or temperamentally suited for management. Billy Wright was a quiet, modest gentle man who had won a world record number of caps (one hundred and five) while playing for England and been captain of the splendid Wolves side that had won the Championship three times in the 1950s.

It had always been assumed that if or when Wright wanted to go into management, it would be with Wolves. Instead, he had become manager of the England Under-23 and Youth teams. A call from Arsenal's Chairman, Denis Hill-Wood, surprised him but he had no hesitation in accepting a three-year contract. He had always admired the club's history and traditions.

In terms of potential, this was an interesting time to be taking over. Joe Baker had come back from Torino after Arsenal paid seventy thousand pounds and he was leading the attack with Geoff Strong. Behind them was one of football's most subtle play-makers, George Eastham, the man who challenged the traditional 'retain and transfer' system in the courts and won. They were joined by Frank McLintock and Don Howe, who were to become two of the most influential figures in the whole history of the club.

Wright, a man who had been such a stout defender himself, failed to put sufficient steel into the Arsenal defence. Nonetheless, he did a prodigious amount to promote the younger players. His team finished seventh in his first full season and there was an appearance in the Fairs' Cup which ended quickly with defeat by Liege. While the attack was flourishing, the defence was acting like an open lock gate. When, in 1964-65, Arsenal were discharged from the FA Cup in the Fourth Round by Peterborough and then finished only thirteenth in the League, the players must have been expecting a huge rollicking for their collective failure. Wright, however, seemed like a man without anger, or without the ability to let it steam out of him by throwing teacups or shouting abuse.

Frank McLintock got so frustrated that he asked for a transfer, believing that he would never win medals all the time the 'too nice' Wright was in charge. There was no bitterness in Wright, not even of losing and certainly not of the fans who lost patience, although he did once say that he gradually grew to hate the bust of Herbert Chapman in the marble entrance hall because he knew that every manager that had followed the great man had been forced to live by comparison.

Meanwhile, Highbury itself was constantly being updated and, during 1964, it became one of the first grounds to be made safe from the old problem of frozen pitches. Electric wires were laid underneath the turf, at a cost of fifteen thousand pounds, and the experiment succeeded. The wiring remained in place until 1970 when it was replaced. The demand for more seating had to be faced and eighty thousand pounds were spent on installing five and a half thousand under the West Stand that had previously been standing room only. That proposal had first been suggested several years before when the cost would probably have been less than half. At the same time, it was also suggested that a roof could be placed over the pitch, sliding back over the East and West stands, but that was considered to be too futuristic and the plan was shelved.

In the days before the Clock End and the North Bank were dramatically altered to provide modern accommodation, including hospitality boxes, to all outward appearances the ground looked little different from the way it was in the early post-war years. The imposing façade of the East Stand remained more or less unchanged since the day it was finished. The words 'Arsenal Stadium' adorned the highest point, as if always aloofly fighting a long-lost cause against the popular title of 'Highbury'. Beneath, and above the main door, was the club's motif and emblem. The metal-framed windows were typical of the 1930s era in which the stand was built.

Until recent times, when stadium tours became popular, most Arsenal fans were left to imagine what it would have been like to enter the marble entrance hall and see what mysteries were hidden beyond. For decades nothing really changed. The entrance hall was actually a little disappointing, being smaller than fans might have imagined. The Jacob Epstein sculptured bust of Herbert Chapman dominated. Offices were to the left and dressing rooms to the right. In the corridor, there was a post box. Moving up the stairway you would enter the boardroom and the guest rooms (reception rooms were also provided for the directors' wives and friends). Flowers were always placed on the tables: red and white for the Arsenal followers and the colours of the opponents on the others. The board-room contained a brace of small cannons, one of which was understood to have been fired before matches when Arsenal played at Woolwich. There was also a five-legged chair that was supposed to have been made for what must have been a particularly portly director who also suffered from gout. A carved chapel-style seat was presented to Chapman by his church in Yorkshire in 1931.

# CHAPTER 21
# A HEALING HAND

## FAIRS' CUP WINNERS 1969-70

WHILE ALF RAMSEY GATHERED together a well-motivated and efficiently organised England team that would win the 1966 World Cup at Wembley, Arsenal's spirits sank even further. So low in fact that on Thursday, 5 May 1966, while Liverpool were playing Borussia Dortmund in the European Cup Winners' Cup final which was shown live on television, they met Leeds United at Highbury before a gate of only 4,544. That represented Arsenal's lowest attendance in the First Division since matches re-started after the War. Even the lonely faithful were not well rewarded. Arsenal lost 3-0.

During the World Cup finals, the board decided that Billy Wright should be dismissed. In hindsight, it was acknowledged that his work with the development of young players was largely responsible for the upturn in results that came later. Without his dedication to that cause, Arsenal would not have achieved the Double, for which his successor, Bertie Mee, perhaps received a disproportionate amount of credit (though he was not slow to pay tribute to Wright's contribution). Sadly, Wright's dismissal hurt him badly and, for a while, it took a heavy toll on his personal life. He knew that some of the players had been giving less than every drop of sweat while he was desperate to return Arsenal to greatness.

The choice as Wright's successor was not well received by the fans who made it clear that they felt the club was acting without any sense of direction. The players were familiar with forty-six-year old Bertie Mee. He had been at the club since 1960, not as somebody who had much to do with instructing them about the way to play but in the treatment of injures. He was a well-respected physiotherapist who had worked both with Arsenal and the Football Association. Few could have predicted that he would become one of the most successful managers in the club's history. From the outset, he made it clear that he never sought to become a manager. However, he was a good organiser, could delegate and was a qualified coach. His own career as a player with Derby County had been cut short by an injury received while training in a gymnasium, although he did appear in a few war-time games for Southampton and Blackpool.

Upon his appointment, Mee tried to do what his predecessors had done and avoid living in the shadow of Herbert Chapman. In his typically considered, confident way, he said: "I am, of course, grateful for the history. But we are in the process of building our own traditions. And these will be better than the old ones. There is a new generation of fans to whom the names of Hapgood, Male, Copping and Drake have no meaning whatsoever. We have the best scout in George Clarke and the best physiotherapist in George Wright. They are identified with the present, not the past". He was also keen to re-establish the old idea that an Arsenal player should be judged almost as much for his off-the-field behaviour as his performances on it. A player who snapped his fingers at a waiter at a pre-match lunch was taken to one side. Mee said he was horrified to hear such a thing and that it would never happen again. It did not.

His first task was to improve discipline in training (probably proving that Wright had been correct in believing that there had been some laziness). In a way, he as much as anyone would have heard the players' gossip and their complaints while he was with them in the treatment room. In those days, the role of some physiotherapist was enigmatic. In fact, the medical room was seen by most of the players as a confessional, which was why, long before football clubs had media relations staff, some physios became the unofficial sources of information for the Press.

A further new appointment was also crucial to the rebuilding process. On the recommendation of Mee, Dave Sexton, of Fulham, was employed as coach. Sexton was thoughtful and undemonstrative. Indeed, some thought he would suffer from the same fault as Wright and be almost too calm and collected … quite the opposite. The players soon realised that he was one of the game's most astute tacticians and could motivate in his own quiet way. His partnership with Mee was an unusual one because those managers who tend not to be ranters and ravers usually like to employ sidekicks who do it for them.

George Eastham, a player with delicate and often mesmerising ball skills, had kept the Arsenal fans entertained even when the rest of the team regularly failed to exploit his ability. Mee was not convinced of his value and sold him to Stoke. He felt that George Graham would be a more practical contributor and bought him from Chelsea in an exchange plus cash deal, Tommy Baldwin moving to Stamford Bridge. Bob McNab came in from Huddersfield for fifty thousand pounds and proved a thoroughly sensible buy.

Alan Ball, whom Mee obtained from Everton for one hundred and ten thousand pounds, probably put his finger on Mee's qualities when he said: "He was a real gentleman. He was not a soccer tactician by any stretch of the imagination, but he was always willing to listen to his players and he surrounded himself with good coaches. He let them sort out the tactics – he got on with running the club. And he did it brilliantly".

The new manager-coach partnership began unremarkably, the team finishing a little above mid-table in their first two seasons, which was all too familiar. However, the League Cup final was reached in 1968 by beating Coventry, Reading, Blackburn and Burnley before, in a home and away semi-final, there was an historically poignant meeting with Huddersfield Town who were beaten 6-3 on aggregate. In the final, Arsenal lost 1-0 to Leeds United who, directed by Don Revie, were beginning to show the mettle and class that was to turn them into an unusual blend of the ruthlessly efficient and disarmingly entertaining. Not that Arsenal were all angels. In a four-day period, Bob McNab, Frank McLintock and Peter Storey were sent off in two matches against Burnley, one in the League and the other in the League Cup.

Gradually, the side became more settled. McLintock was a strong, commanding leader while John Radford and McNab received England caps, which had become quite a rarity at a club that in the past provided so many internationals. Becoming 'difficult to beat' is the first priority of many a new manager and, at Highbury, this more than anything turned the club's fortunes.

With Peter Storey solid and combative in midfield, Bob Wilson becoming an ever more reliable goalkeeper and Peter Simpson defending soundly, no opponent could break through with ease. "Stroller" George Graham was not really suited to an out-and-out attacking role but prospered when asked to play just behind the attack.

The 1968-69 season included a dinner at the Park Lane Hotel in London to celebrate fifty years of unbroken membership of the First Division. There was also an anniversary match at Highbury attended by members of the club's 'Hall of Fame', including Joe Mercer, Joe Hulme, Alf Kirchen, Bryn Jones and Bernard Joy. Bill McCracken, then eighty-six, was also there and talked about playing for Newcastle in Arsenal's debut match in the First Division back in 1919.

The season saw the team reach the fifth round of the FA Cup, losing at West Bromwich, and the League Cup final in which they were again beaten, this time by Swindon Town. This was a humiliating defeat that in some ways did the club a big favour.

On the way to the final, there had been two tough semi-final legs against Spurs. Radford scored in the last seconds of the first match at Highbury. The defence had held the elusive Jimmy Greaves but Spurs were convinced he would rescue them in the home leg. In fact, although Greaves did score, Radford got another goal so Arsenal won 2-1 on aggregate, a victory that was important to the raising of morale.

Although there seemed little doubt that they could overcome their surprise Wembley opponents in the final (Swindon Town were in the Third Division), for various reasons the recent composition of the team and the way they had been playing was unconvincing. Even McLintock was being criticised for going forward without enough consideration for what would happen if an attack broke down. With the headstrong Bobby Gould at centre forward, Ian Ure, big and strong but not the most reliable centre half, and insufficient guile in the middle of the field, there seemed to be a lot of work to be done before thoughts could be turned to winning major trophies. As for the League Cup against a team of much lower status, surely there was ample talent?

Swindon did warrant some respect. They were leaders of their division and had beaten two First Division teams, Coventry City and Burnley, as well as the eventual Second Division champions, Derby County, on their way to Wembley. They also had a player of the calibre that Arsenal lacked – a goalscoring winger, Don Rogers. That was ironic since it was players with that ability who in the past had brought so much glory to the club. Also, Swindon had the support of every neutral in the country.

Arsenal had received little in the way of praise for reaching the final with their 'purposeful' football. They arrived at Wembley with confidence again deflated. Many of the players had been suffering from 'flu. When they looked at the pitch they were even more subdued. It was far from the pristine surface of fame. Absurdly, the Wembley authorities had allowed the Horse of the Year Show to be held there. After that gallons of rainwater had been pumped away, leaving a soggy mess of sand and mud.

In spite of their reputation for defensiveness and directness, Arsenal tried hard to play good football. In the conditions, it was not easy. One player who seemed able to rise above the mire was Rogers who scored two memorable goals. Surprisingly, Swindon had taking the lead after 34 minutes through a defensive muddle in which Ure attempted a back pass to Wilson who had no chance of reaching it. Roger Smart nipped in to score.

There were only four minutes of normal time remaining when

Swindon's previously unbeatable goalkeeper, Peter Downsbrough, who had faced nine corners in not much more than ten minutes, came out of the penalty area in an attempt to clear but kicked the ball directly to Gould who headed in.

The Arsenal players who had been ill and missed training could have done without extra-time. In it, Rogers brought himself lasting fame first by deflecting in a corner then running some fifty yards with the ball and beating Wilson. Afterwards, he said that at the end of ninety minutes he had looked at the Arsenal players with their socks rolled down and they all looked exhausted. He thought to himself 'That'll do me'.

Don Howe said Arsenal should have wrapped up the game by half-time, which was true. Then he added that Arsenal would "not take too much notice" of the result, which proved patently inaccurate. The result hurt and he knew that the team of that day had too many weaknesses. As a result, he worked even harder on making better players of those already on the staff. Thus the elevation of such influential ones as Ray Kennedy, Eddie Kelly, Charlie George, plus the crucial decision to move McLintock to centre half. McLintock, more than anyone, had been exasperated by the Wembley defeat because it was his fourth appearance there and he had never been a winner.

Several of the team admitted that their humiliation at Wembley was actually the foundation of a new sense of pride and dedication. They were determined not to suffer a similar fate in the rest of their careers. They were also mindful that as Arsenal players they had the best of everything and needed to give of their best in return. A small insight into what it meant to be an Arsenal player in the late 1960s was given by Alan Ball shortly after he arrived from Everton. "They really make their players feel important. When they travel to away matches they do it in style. It's the best of everything. The coach they travelled in had just about everything. There was waiter service and three-course meals. Anything you wanted was available: smoked salmon, beef salads, every drink you could think of and cigars – even After-Eight mints. It was luxury all the way down the line and on foreign trips it was Champagne service on the flight and only the best hotels". Booze and cigars courtesy of the club, let alone After Eights! Arsene Wenger would be appalled.

The other good thing that came out of the League Cup final debacle was that because Swindon were not eligible for the Inter-Cities Fairs' Cup, Arsenal, who finished fourth in the First Division, gained a place in the following season's competition. It would be the first opportunity in a

European tournament to discover whether a new spirit had really arrived.

They stormed through the early rounds: beating Glentoran (3-1 on aggregate), Sporting Lisbon (3-0), Rouen (1-0) and, in the quarter-final, Dinamo Bacau by an extraordinary 9-1 thanks mainly to a 7-1 win at Highbury in the second leg. The semi-final brought them up against Ajax who were developing the wonderful side that went on to win the European Cup three times and had lost in the final to AC Milan the previous season. A 3-0 home win with a couple of goals from Charlie George, including a penalty and one from Jon Sammels, allowed Arsenal to go to Holland and suffer a 1-0 defeat without it costing them their place. Bearing in mind that Ajax included such brilliant players as Krol, Muhren (their goalscorer) and Cruyff, that victory was a considerable boost, especially for George, the local boy, who was becoming such a favourite with the Highbury crowds. It took them into a home and away final with Anderlecht.

## FIRST LEG
Brussels, 22 April (attendance 37,000)

### Anderlecht 3, Arsenal 1

*Anderlecht:* Trappeniers; Heylens, Velkeneers, Nordahl, Kialunda, Cornelis, Dessenghere, Devrindt, Mulder, van Himst, Puis.
*Arsenal:* Wilson; Storey, McNab, Kelly, McLintock, Simpson, Armstrong, Sammels, Radford, George (Kennedy), Graham.

*Scorers: Anderlecht: Devrindt, Mulder 2. Arsenal: Kennedy.*

The opening game seemed, at the time, to be such a devastating defeat for Arsenal that their chances of ultimate success appeared remote. Jan Mulder scored twice and Devrindt got a third. Arsenal reeled before, towards the end, the inexperienced teenager Ray Kennedy managed to score with a header. He had made only two starts in the first team and been a substitute twice. Even allowing for his goal, a recovery at home looked unlikely. McLintock, a man of moods, was fed up, believing he would be playing in another final on the losing side.

## SECOND LEG
Highbury, 28 April (51,612)

Bertie Mee's appointment as manager may not have conformed to the usual pattern of choosing high-level former players, but his ability to bring together good individuals and turn them into an excellent team was beginning to show. The core of the side was now Wilson, McLintock, Simpson and McNab, all solid in defence, Sammels and Graham in midfield and Radford, George Armstrong and the confident young Charlie George up front.

Anderlecht had much more European experience, having competed in various competitions for more than a decade. They had several of the Belgian national side including Paul van Himst, probably the finest player in that country's history. Not only that, their comforting lead from the first leg put them in what seemed to be an unassailable position.

Although himself far from convinced that his team had much hope, McLintock tried to express all the right, captain-like things in the dressing room before the game. He said there was no reason why they should not win, especially as Kennedy had scored an away goal. He reckoned they could build on that because he had seen weaknesses in the Anderlecht defence.

Less than half-an-hour into the match, another of Arsenal's emerging youngsters, nineteen-year-old Eddie Kelly, controlled the ball with cool assurance and pulled back a goal with a powerful shot to give his team hope of a recovery. The crowd created a massively encouraging atmosphere that clearly put doubts into the minds of the Anderlecht players. While the whole Arsenal side played with tireless energy, one of their number was inspired. Young Kelly defended and attacked with equal spirit. The rest picked up his dedication, especially after his goal. "I could have jumped out of the stadium when I saw it go into the top of the net" he said.

The job was still far from done. McLintock was convinced that Anderlecht could not defend all that well in the air but he was afraid of their counter-attacking qualities. He wanted more balls played to the head of Radford but most headers were comfortably received by goalkeeper Trappeniers. However, McLintock's theory proved right, though before that Mulder had a shot that crashed against a post, as did Nordahl.

When Radford added a second goal with a header from McNab's cross victory was in sight (Arsenal were ahead on the basis of the goal scored away from home) and in the seventy-first minute George slipped a clever pass through to Sammels who scored the third to bring about a clear aggregate victory. Sammels was rarely praised by the Arsenal fans but was now. For the team's captain, McLintock, the victory marked the end of a personal feeling that he would never win a major trophy. He had played in four FA Cup Finals (with Leicester and Arsenal) and never been on the winning side. At the conclusion, fans ran on to the pitch. George lost his shirt to one of them and after McLintock collected the cup from Sir Stanley Rous he was carried shoulder high round the pitch.

Sammels later remarked: "For us, that great victory was both a beginning and an end. An end to the strange conviction that, somehow, destiny was against us and that fate had decreed that Arsenal would never win anything again." Unhappily, even his performance in that final failed to win over much long-term support for Sammels himself and he left the club still underestimated. Bob Wilson echoed Sammels sentiments by saying: "There were rumblings in 1969 when we finished fourth in the League but, if I had to put my finger on one turning point which made a good, hard-working side into a progressively better one, it was the Fairs' Cup win".

*Arsenal: Wilson; Storey, McNab, Kelly, McLintock, Simpson, Armstrong, Sammels, Radford, George, Graham.*

*Anderlecht: Trappeniers; Heylens, Velkeneers, Kialunda, Martens, Nordahl, Deseanghere, Puis, Devrindt, Mulder, Van Himst.*

The treatment of Sammels by the Arsenal fans was in part understandable since he was one of those players who more often than not performed only moderately well by comparison with the finest of his era. In a team context, that in itself should have been enough to satisfy the crowds but Arsenal fans have always set their sights higher than, on occasions, they could reasonably expect. Even in Herbert Chapman's era, expectancy levels were too demanding. In 1931 he said: "The football spectator can be, and often is, cruel". He looked back to a day when he called a young player into his office to sign on. "To my amazement he covered his face with his hands and burst into tears. 'It's no use' he said, 'I'm no use to anyone in football and I had better get out. I can't stand it any longer. The crowd is always getting at me. I'm going home and I hope I shall never kick a ball again'".

Chapman said that he had been appalled at the the barracking that Alex James and David Jack had received in their early days at Highbury. When looking back over the years, it is possible to believe that Arsenal crowds have been less forgiving than the fans of many other clubs. Sammels suffered more than most. On one occasion, in 1969, he was only warming up for a match against Wolves when he heard some of the crowd booing him. During the game, he was jeered whenever he got the ball.

# CHAPTER 22
# THE DOUBLE

## 1970-71

VICTORY IN A EUROPEAN COMPETITION may have been a
significant moment in the club's long journey but the Fairs' Cup
was not considered to be of such moment that Arsenal could begin
the following season full of hope that the domestic Championship was a
comparatively simple objective. After all, it never is. Realistically, ending
the previous season in only twelfth place suggested that they were still
inferior to a substantial number of League clubs, most notably Leeds and
particularly the stylish Everton, who had won the Championship twenty-
four points ahead of them and won twenty-nine matches to their twelve.

There were several problems in the weeks of the close season before the
one that brought the club their first Double. The powerhouse of midfield,
Peter Simpson, had a cartilage injury. The fixture list offered little in the
way of comfort because the opening game was against champions
Everton. Bertie Mee needed to do a lot of homework. The Everton midfield
of Alan Ball, Colin Harvey and Howard Kendall was the best in the
country. A lot of responsibility fell on Storey, who had to mark the non-
stop Ball, while his own position at right back was given to Pat Rice. The
game ended in a 2-2 draw, Graham and George cancelling out goals from
Ball and Royle. But George was also a casualty, breaking his ankle and not
playing again until the new year, leaving Kennedy to take his striker's
place with good support from Radford.

This was the era of Don Revie's utilitarian but sometimes brilliant Leeds
United who, early in 1971, held a seven point lead which, bearing in mind
the practical way they played, seemed to put them beyond anybody's reach.
When they had come to Highbury in September, Arsenal were reduced to
ten men (Kelly rashly, and a mite bravely, kicked the fiery Billy Bremner
and was sent off). A draw was much more significant than the result suggested.
It told of a strength of character in the Arsenal team that would grow.

Once Simpson returned from injury and Graham fully settled into a
midfield position, Mee felt that his players were ready for anything.
Anything perhaps excluding the defence of the Fairs' Cup, in which they

went to Rome and drew 2-2 with the notoriously short-tempered Lazio who equalised late in the game with a penalty awarded against McLintock for handling the ball, which he disputed. In the street after a reception for both clubs, several of the Lazio players attacked Kennedy, leading to a punch up between many of the players of both sides.

The cause of the trouble may have been a fault in the translation of a speech by Denis Hill-Wood in which he referred, with tongue in cheek (he thought), to the referee's decision over the penalty. This deeply offended the Italian players. Arsenal got their own back less violently by winning the second leg 2-0 at Highbury but after beating Sturm Graz and Beveren Waas, they eventually succumbed to FC Köln on away goals

The Championship was secured, thanks mainly to a run between early October and mid-January of fourteen matches without defeat. At other times, there were strangely careless performances, including a 5-0 away defeat by Stoke. Leeds looked the more likely winners. At the same time, however, Arsenal had been progressing through the early rounds of the FA Cup. Yeovil, who on their famous sloping pitch had rarely made a Cup match easy for anyone, were dismissed unusually painlessly by 3-0, followed by Portsmouth (3-2 after a draw at Fratton Park). Meeting Manchester City at Maine Road was a predictable test but one that would not be shirked by Charlie George, who had become Arsenal's most prized player. Tall and strong, he also had a touch that was not greatly inferior to that of George Graham. His two goals against City took his team into the sixth round. And, all the time, Bob Wilson was having an outstanding season.

Mee now had a problem. His players faced two games a week for the rest of the season. The Cup demanded as much attention as the League. After beating Manchester City 2-1, they had a tough replay against Leicester City at Highbury, where George won the day with a header from Armstrong's centre. They were happy to avoid Liverpool and Everton, who were drawn against each other, and faced outsiders Stoke City in the semi-final at Hillsborough where they were 2-0 down at half-time and it could have been worse (the earlier drubbing in the League was nagging away). But Storey drove a blistering shot past Gordon Banks. Even so, going into injury time the probability was that Arsenal would not be moving on to achieve their Double. Then Banks was bundled down and had to give away a corner, which Armstrong took. When the ball came over, McLintock met it and sent a header towards the inside of the far past. John Mahoney risked everything by pushing it away with his hands. The referee had no choice but to give Arsenal a penalty. Storey still had to beat

England's Banks but did so to force a replay at Villa Park that Arsenal won with goals from Graham and Kennedy. The Double was now on

The League season was still far from over. Ten more Championship games had to be faced. Leeds now had fifty-four points from thirty-five matches while Arsenal had forty-eight from thirty-two. In other words, Arsenal needed to win all three in order to stand equal with Leeds who they still had to confront at Elland Road. On 17 April, West Bromwich Albion pulled off an unlikely and controversial win at Leeds (the winning goal involved two players who were clearly offside) while Arsenal were beating Newcastle at Highbury, thanks to a typically inventive goal by George which offered them top place.

They were fortunate to benefit from the debatable win by West Bromwich and the fact that their own next game was at home to Burnley, who were struggling at the foot of the First Division and, as expected, lost, if only by 1-0. George was again match-winner, albeit from the penalty spot. Single goal victories had become Arsenal's trademark – one that was enough to keep Leeds under pressure. Even so, there was more drama to come.

West Bromwich were again central characters in the adventure. They ended Arsenal's sequence of nine wins by drawing 2-2 with them at The Hawthorns, meaning that Arsenal still had a game in hand over Leeds and were a point ahead. They met at Elland Road with Leeds knowing they had to win and could call on the confidence that had come by reaching the final of the Fairs' Cup (they beat Juventus on away goals). Arsenal would happily have settled for a draw and clearly had that in mind throughout a first half in which they defended unhesitatingly, forcing Leeds to put even greater effort into the second half.

Considering Leeds' reputation for almost ruthless determination as well as subtle touches, the game got to near the end without many problems for referee Norman Burtenshaw. Ambling Jack Charlton went forward and had the ball at his feet in the Arsenal penalty area. He blazed his shot while the Arsenal defenders implored Burtenshaw to give offside. The ball hit a post and rebounded to Charlton who returned it into the net. George retrieved it and angrily belted it into the crowd. McLintock went after Burtenshaw and argued with him, seemingly endlessly. The controversial goal stood and Leeds held out despite seeing a header from Graham fly frighteningly close to their crossbar. Television replays showed that Burtenshaw and a linesman who did not flag were right, which was as well since it quelled the controversy in time for the Cup Final which, coincidentally, Burtenshaw was to referee.

On 1 May, Leeds beat Nottingham Forest at Elland Road to make sure that Arsenal had to beat Stoke at Highbury. They made hard work of it and saw Radford miss a clear opportunity shortly before half-time while not long afterwards they lost Storey with a leg injury. Kelly went into midfield and quickly made quite a difference by moving up into the penalty area to accept a clever pass from Radford. Kelly stayed calm and drove home an accurate shot. It was the winner and Arsenal were left knowing that Leeds had finished their season on sixty-four points while they had sixty-three with one more match to play.

They required only a scoreless draw to take the Championship by the extraordinary mathematical margin of 0.013 of a goal. Defeat or a score draw would give Leeds the title. Only a scriptwriter could have written that the last game was to be against Spurs at White Hart Lane.

The crucial match was arranged for the Monday night (3 May) before the Cup Final. Even without anything more at stake than local pride, Spurs would always give of their all against Arsenal. As it was, they needed more points for European qualification. Yet in a way both sides could have afforded a goalless draw. Spurs required three points but still had to play Stoke. Meanwhile, Spurs' manager, Bill Nicholson, viewed the situation in his typically philosophical way. After all, he had experienced the sort of challenge Arsenal were facing. A decade earlier, he had organised his superb Spurs side to win the country's first Double of the twentieth century. He also took into account the fact that Arsenal's six defeats in the season had all been away from Highbury (they only lost one home game which was against Crystal Palace in the League Cup in November when they had more auspicious things on their mind).

Pride was a prominent factor. Nicholson remarked: "We are tremendously proud of our Double achievement. I suppose some other club has got to do it again sometime, but we will be doing our best to make sure it isn't Arsenal". There was also a not insignificant matter of Tottenham's players being on a four hundred pounds per-man winning bonus. As for the Leeds players, they all went off to play in a testimonial game in Hull, but their minds were on London. In the meantime Bill Shankly, the matter-of-fact Liverpool manager, was hoping that Spurs would give Arsenal an energy-sapping game ahead of the Cup Final.

One change had to be made from the Arsenal starting line-up that had played against Stoke. Storey had not recovered from his injury, so, deservedly, Kelly would play from the start. Huge crowds built up around the stadium. Probably something in the region of one hundred and fifty thousand set out with the intention of watching the game. It was obvious that a full house of just over fifty thousand would still leave at least twice as many locked out. The roads were so solidly blocked that even the Arsenal coach moved at less than a walking pace. McLintock said he was amazed that nobody was killed in the crush.

The noise inside was tumultuous and prolonged. The match began in cat and mouse fashion, though far less quietly. McLintock said he tried to shout orders: "But I might just as well have been talking to myself. You just couldn't hear a thing out there". Bob Wilson and Pat Jennings, the two goalkeepers, were soon in action. George forced Jennings into a spectacular deflection over the bar and Wilson dived importantly and painfully at Joe Kinnear's feet. Martin Peters, in the Spurs midfield, was always going to be the player most likely to do the cool thing in the heat of any moment. He clipped the Arsenal crossbar with a swerving shot that, unusually, had Wilson grounded.

Arsenal, without the hard-tackling Storey, looked uncertain. McLintock admitted: "I was a bag of nerves". Yet it was the captain who pulled the team together. The ever robust Kelly responded well and, from the wing, George Armstrong began to stretch the Spurs defence. Arsenal dominated the last few minutes of the first half but, early in the second, Spurs put together a number of well-constructed moves. Wilson again had to risk diving at the feet of Kinnear. Bob McNab quickly came to Wilson's aid, sparking nervous rather than bad-tempered pushing and shoving. There was too much work to be done to let the game become lost in ill-discipline. Arsenal fans were horrified to see Alan Gilzean move in for a free header. The elegant Scottish international, who in those circumstances never seemed to fail, confessed later that he took his eye off the ball at the last moment and missed it "by an inch".

Bertie Mee was sitting next to his Chairman, Denis Hill-Wood, allowing Howe to make the decisions from the bench. Howe said: "There had been a few scares but I never felt that we were in real trouble. We had worked on containing Martin Chivers and our back four looked solid. It looked all over like a no-goals draw".

As the game approached its final few minutes, Arsenal were beginning to feel relieved that the result was exactly the one they wanted. Yet the dilemma was still there – try to score for the outright win or cling on to the equally productive goalless draw. Charlie George gave them the answer. There were three minutes left when this gangling, lank-haired, wonderfully talented and so popular ball player and goalscorer came moving in from a wide position. Jennings raised his big hands to create a barrier by the near post. No shot came. George chose to swing the ball across the goalmouth towards Radford who headed strongly forwards. Jennings turned and somehow slung himself along the goalline to push the ball away. The Spurs defenders were so amazed that they seemed to stand and watch in admiration while the quicker-thinking Armstrong took up the attack, clipped the ball back across the goalmouth and Kennedy headed in off the bar.

Although the Arsenal fans leapt and shouted as if the title had been won, it had not. Not at least for a further dramatic three minutes in which, if Spurs had equalised, Leeds would have been champions. Kennedy recalled thinking that when Spurs came back at them he began to wonder whether it would have been better had he not scored at all. Even in the last minute, when the whole of the Arsenal team had lodged themselves in their own penalty area, Wilson had to dive into a melee and grab the ball before hearing the final whistle from referee Kevin Howley who was officiating in the last and most dramatic League game of his career.

The Arsenal fans invaded their neighbour's pitch. McLintock was lifted high. George virtually collapsed into the arms of Howe who said: "This is only the start. Next season we're going to win the European Cup". In the event, by the following season he had left the club. Bob Wilson remarked that although Spurs would be credited with winning their Double with a more attractive style of play, "they did not win it under such tremendous pressure". Bill Nicholson went into the Arsenal dressing room with Champagne and, up in Hull, Leeds' centre-half Jack Charlton was told the result. He was asked what he was going to do. To which he responded: "Get drunk out of my mind".

It was nearly half-an-hour before all of the players managed to get back to the dressing room. Howe was concerned that they might have been injured in the celebrations. "I was worried. The fans were ripping at the players' shirts. Some wanted their boots which, of course, they had to wear on Saturday. I was frightened that they would tread on someone's foot and keep them out of the Final. We pleaded with the police to go out to rescue the players but they said that if the lads couldn't get off, how could they get on. But, thank goodness, no one was injured and all that went missing was a few shirts".

Bertie Mee said that the attitude of the Tottenham club was magnificent. "There had been an awful lot of bad feeling between the two clubs in the past but I like to think I helped break that down. I am sure they were disappointed that they hadn't beaten us but they entertained us marvellously after the match".

The players were less cautious about their celebrations than perhaps Howe

104

had originally intended. They went to the White Hart pub in Southgate and enjoyed a private party until the early hours. But even Howe made no attempt to stop them. "We believed it was better for the players to fully unwind", he said.

There were many thick heads the next morning and disciplinarian Mee, slightly reluctantly but sensibly, gave the players a day off. The one who most needed time was Storey who was only on the margins of fitness after his injury. Although Kelly was an able deputy, Mee decided he wanted Storey in his Cup Final team.

Arsenal's ground staff had been working hard to ensure that the players were ready for the special demands of Wembley. They had even allowed the grass to grow a little longer at the training ground and a pitch was marked out with exactly the same dimensions as that of the national stadium.

The Press had never been so keen to get interviews but, after giving them access on the Wednesday, Mee stopped all of it for the rest of the week. He even told the players not to answer their own telephones. He also tried to ensure that they were not troubled by any superstitions. They stayed at the Grosvenor House Hotel in central London rather than in the one they had used before losing in the League Cup finals of 1968 and 1969. On the day of the Final, they spent the morning at the South Herts Golf Club which had been a good omen before previous Wembley matches.

The preamble to the Final was very different for Liverpool who had more time to be put under media pressure because they were not involved in the Championship title race. Arsenal were too busy to have time to think much about the biggest challenge the club had faced. Would they now suffer the effects of too many high-pressure games?

Howe recalled that in the days before the pinnacle of the historic season: "We kept telling the players that we could win the Double, but we really didn't think so. So that when we had beaten Stoke in the League, it was the first time that we really came face to face with the prospect. There had been no time to get all tensed up. In fact, the players came off the field looking drawn and tired at the end of a long season, but rarely has a team had such ambition for success. If there was any suspicion of tension, the old heads like McLintock and Graham kept it under check".

On a sunny afternoon, conditions at Wembley were perfect but in a tight first half few opportunities came to either side. Early in the second, Radford began to look dangerous, though more as a provider than finisher. 'Stroller' Graham did indeed start to stroll through the Liverpool midfield and had a header defended on the line by Alec Lindsay. Not that the escape seriously worried Liverpool or added much to Arsenal's confidence. After all they had one of the most reliable defences in the League and the game was steeped in a careful attitude which brought about extra-time. Two minutes into that and the high-stepping Steve Heighway swept inside from the left wing. Wilson anticipated a centre but Heighway drove the ball in off the near post.

A tactical decision probably won the game. Graham was told to move up into the front line of the attack. Charlie George, who was struggling on this oppressively hot afternoon, was switched into midfield. Shortly before the end of the first period of extra-time, Radford lifted the ball into the Liverpool penalty area. Kelly was the first to reach it and simply knocked it forwards. Half the Liverpool team seemed to be between him and the goal but somehow the ball eluded them all. Graham came on the scene and swung a leg at the ball. He claimed that he got a touch but the goal belonged to Kelly.

There was a temptation on the Arsenal bench to be satisfied with a draw and regroup in time for a replay. Graham was ordered back into midfield in a holding role and Charlie George, who only a year before was virtually unknown, went forward again. It was a decisive move. Nine minutes from the end, George, socks down, found himself with the ball some twenty yards out. He was too tired to bother running it into the Liverpool penalty area and decided to have a shot at goal. It is of no consequence that the ball took a slight deflection. It sped into the net. At first George raised his arms but then, with his legs already buckling with exhaustion, he fell on to his back, arms still raised as if posing for what would become a famous picture.

So, at last, McLintock was soon able to raise his own arms, to grasp the Cup. It was not a universally praised victory. Arsenal's football was seen by many critics as always being too circumspect. Maurice Smith, writing in *The People*, went as far as to say: "Arsenal and Liverpool … Cup Final of the decade, the clash of the giants? The match worth £90 a blackmarket seat? Not on your flippin' nelly."

Even if the Final was criticised, the Double team could not be seen as anything less than the best Arsenal unit that had been put together since the days of Herbert Chapman. Bertie Mee and Don Howe deserved as many medals as the players. Mee summed up the achievement by saying: "We were well organised but we had a lot more skill than people gave us credit for. The players would appreciate each other's weaknesses and compensate for them. And they were able to play to each other's strengths. Our experiences in Rome against Lazio and places like Romania forged a bond".

One of the secrets of the success was the close relationship between Howe and McLintock, who were near neighbours. They would often travel to training together and it was in the car that, as Howe explained: "The most brutally honest discussions took place". The end product of those discussions was the Double, which had not even been achieved by Chapman ... not bad for a manager (Mee) who did not particularly want to be one.

## FA CUP FINAL
(8 May 1971, Wembley)

**Arsenal 2** (Kelly, George) **Liverpool 1** (Heighway)

*Arsenal: Wilson; Rice, McNab, Storey (Kelly), McLintock, Simpson, Armstrong, Graham, Radford, Kennedy, George.*

*Liverpool: Clemence; Lawler, Lindsay, Smith, Lloyd, Hughes, Callaghan, Evans (Thompson), Heighway, Toshack, Hall.*

*Referee: N. Burtenshaw.*

# CHAPTER 23
# HOWE TO DO IT!

## 1978-79 FA CUP WINNERS

THE DOUBLE CAME AT A PRICE. The club's thoughtful coach, Don Howe, decided it was time to spread his wings and go into management, leaving to take charge of West Bromwich Albion. He said later that had Arsenal given him an assurance that when Mee left he would have been given a chance to manage at Highbury he might have stayed. His departure had a dispiriting effect. Disappointments quickly followed. The challenge of the European Cup was, not for the last time, too demanding. Ajax were far too experienced and skilful for them in the quarter-finals of the 1971-72 season. The Championship title was also given up all too easily to Brian Clough's exciting Derby County.

By comparison with the excitement of the previous season, even reaching the Cup Final for the second successive year was not considered anything more than a shadow of the near past. Leeds United's "Sniffer" Allan Clarke beat them in a dour game when he dived to head the winning goal, although along the road to Wembley at least they had beaten Derby, not to mention Swindon!

As the Double winning side began to be eroded by time and injuries, so Bertie Mee seemed to lose sight of the need to rebuild. Alan Ball, who had come from Everton for a British record fee of £220,000, commented: "I could see that things needed to be done to improve the team but nothing was happening", which was why he later asked for a transfer. He had great respect for Mee and thought his personal protest might spur him into action, or at very least raise questions at board level. He later admitted that the attempt was a mistake and he asked to come off the transfer list.

The early 1970s was a period in which George Best was in decline but still the most famous player in the land. Every club wanted to find a new Best and Arsenal were no exception. In Scotland, a slight, long-haired young winger had been publicised as the most likely successor in the new world of footballing pop-stars. Peter Marinello made his debut for Hibernian when he was only seventeen and had shown rare skill and individuality within the limited demands of the Scottish League. Arsenal decided to invest one hundred thousand pounds (a huge amount in those days) to bring him to London, which was a mistake in more ways than one. Marinello was headline news and he soon fell in line with what the popular newspapers had anticipated. Off the field he played the part of the new generation of Beatle-style 'celebrities' while on it, and despite scoring on his debut against Manchester United at Old Trafford, he failed to live up to expectations.

Perhaps the highlight of Marinello's brief career at Highbury was the European home leg against Ajax against whom he had an impressive match, yet it was a performance remembered more for missing a goal. "They never mention the own goal by George Graham which cost us the tie," he said. He was reported to have been offered a further three-year contract but decided to join Portsmouth. Looking back, he thought it was a bad move because Arsenal were moving into a new era of bright young players including Graham Rix and Frank Stapleton. He felt that, had he stayed, he might have matured with them.

There was a brief time in the second half of the 1972-73 season when the team held the lead by beating the eventual champions, Liverpool, at Anfield. They finished as runners-up, only three points behind and lost only one more game than the champions but, by and large, the standard of performances did not raise hope of a return to the glamorous days of the Double. There was also the sadness of hearing that Eddie Hapgood had died at the age of only sixty-four. A true sportsman, he remained a loyal Arsenal man to the end.

The years became leaner. In 1973-74 they finished only tenth, and 1974-75 sixteenth, just four points outside the relegation zone. So, in 1976, after the club had finished even lower (seventeenth) and twenty-four points behind the champions Liverpool, Mee decided it was time to go. The decision to appoint Terry Neill as his replacement was a throwback to the days when it was always assumed that the new man would be a former Arsenal stalwart, although this was somebody who only a fortnight before had been managing Spurs.

Arsenal fans were surprised at the decision and the players were less than happy with the fact that their popular coach, Bobby Campbell, was not offered the job. Indeed, at a meeting they voted unanimously to tell the board of their feelings. Nevertheless, Neill came in and there is little doubt that the players' loyalty to Campbell caused friction. Some performances under Neill were alarming. Seven consecutive League games were lost – the worst run in the club's history.

The new manager had made one particularly sound move in the transfer market by buying Malcolm Macdonald from Newcastle for £333,333. "Super Mac" scored twenty-five League goals in his first season. He and Birmingham City's Trevor Francis went into the records of unique performances by both scoring hat-tricks in the same game, which ended in a 3-3 draw. The clever ball-player, Alan Hudson, was also bought from Stoke, but the crucial arrival was that of Don Howe, who had realised that he was not a born manager and would be happier back at his old club doing the job he most enjoyed – coaching.

Howe worked hard on rebuilding a team with a stout defence (in 1977 Pat Jennings signed after thirteen years and four hundred and seventy two appearances for Spurs) and positive spirit. Success was not immediate but the side he taught reached the 1978 FA Cup Final, only to be defeated by a single goal from Ipswich Town. This was a season in which the smaller clubs had done well but it was generally believed that Ipswich would not be good enough to hinder Arsenal at Wembley. In the event, they may have scored only one goal but their performance was so superior that they could have won by three or four.

Early in the game, the willowy Paul Mariner struck the Arsenal crossbar. The hard-working John Wark twice hit the post and a header from George Burley would surely have gone in had it not been for one of Pat Jennings's familiar on-the-line saves. Bobby Robson, later to be the much under-valued manager of England, had told his Ipswich team to make sure that the Arsenal left-back, Sammy Nelson, was stopped from going forward or being given enough time to initiate attacks. Nelson had been doing that all through the season. David Geddis was giving the job of man-marking a defender.

Despite their opportunities, it took Ipswich seventy-six minutes to make their breakthrough. Curiously, it was Geddis who sparked the decisive move by beating Nelson and sending the ball across the penalty area. The big Arsenal centre-half Willie Young tried to clear but screwed the ball to Roger Osborne and he cracked it in before exhaustion got the better of him and he asked to come off.

Arsenal came alive again in terms of trophy-winning in 1979, although their appearance in another Cup Final against Manchester United hardly roused the nation. On the way there had been several struggles. They needed five matches to beat Third Division Sheffield Wednesday (three were played at Leicester in the space of one week). Notts County were overcome with less difficulty. Nottingham Forest, then League champions

110

and soon to be European champions under the eccentric but wily guidance of Brian Clough, were overcome on their own ground where they thought they were invincible. After beating Southampton and Wolves, the Final brought them up against old, recurring rivals United.

Possibly it was the fact that the sun was beating down on Wembley, but despite the fact that there were fifteen internationals on the field, the bulk of the Final was a torrid game in which only Arsenal's newcomer, Brian Talbot, bought from the previous season's winners Ipswich Town, seemed to have the energy to keep running. Yet it contained one of the most dramatic finishes in what was dubbed the 'Five Minute Final'.

Don Howe was convinced that United's liking for pushing forward as quickly and as often as possible from midfield was also their Achilles heel. He wanted the ingenious Liam Brady to become the target for counter-attacks and told the players to remember that the United defence tended to bunch in the middle and did not defend the far post at crosses. His assessment, based on the homework done by Wilf Dixon and George Male, was spot on.

Brady, cool in the sun, played with imagination as well as to order. He provided the basis of Arsenal's first real attack, sending a good pass to Frank Stapleton who cracked a quick cross to David Price who in turn managed to avoid a tackle and drag the ball back towards Alan Sunderland. He and Talbot more or less headed the ball at the same time. Talbot was credited with the final touch to take his new club into the lead.

United were not all that troubled. There was plenty of time left and they began to build up a string of corners, forcing Jennings into several good saves. Even so, there was something indecisive about their play. Suddenly, Howe's instructions led to another Arsenal goal. United had been attacking. When one move broke down, they found themselves facing a five-man Arsenal breakaway led by Brady, who had the ball at his feet. He got to the edge of the penalty area and looked across to see whether United had left anyone unmarked at the far post. They had, and there was Stapleton to head in the cross.

United, the more attacking side in the first half, were two down. In the second they had several more opportunities. Arsenal held them in a dour, competent way that had the fans yearning for more excitement. Five minutes were left when Terry Neill asked Steve Walford to replace Price. His motives were not altogether clear. Perhaps he wanted to give Walford a taste of the big occasion when Arsenal seemed more than likely to coast through the final minutes, or maybe it was simply a rash, spontaneous decision. Howe said it was made because Price was exhausted after a marking and counter-attacking game. Be that as it may, the effect was to disrupt the defence.

United suddenly raised some defiance. A free-kick from Steve Coppell found Joe Jordan who returned the ball across the penalty area. Gordon McQueen lumbered up from defence and hacked at the ball. Whether by luck or judgement, he made contact and it flew past Jennings. That left only four minutes. Two of those Arsenal survived, but not without some panic. Hundreds of Arsenal fans had already left the stadium, hoping to avoid the crush and confident that their team had won. Sammy McIllroy ran the ball down the right side, swept past David O'Leary, cut inside Walford and crashed the ball in for the equaliser.

Extra-time seemed inevitable. The momentum had swung towards United. Arsenal re-started the game and went into a concerted attack. Brady was again the key. He seemed to magnetise defenders into approaching him then swing away. Graham Rix had gone down the line. Brady flicked a pass out to him. Gary Bailey, in the United goal, anticipated Rix's cross but somehow misjudged the fact that it was swinging away from him. Sunderland, who had damaged a knee, still managed to charge into the space that was again available at the far post and pressed the ball over the line.

### FA CUP FINAL
(12 May 1979, Wembley)

**Arsenal 3** (Talbot, Stapleton, Sunderland)
**Manchester United 2** (McQueen, McIlroy)

*Arsenal:* Jennings; Rice, Nelson, Talbot, O'Leary, Young, Brady, Sunderland, Stapleton, Price (Walford), Rix.

*Manchester United:* Bailey; Nicholl, Albiston, McIlroy, McQueen, Buchan, Coppell, J. Greenhoff, Jordan, Macari, Thomas.

*Referee: R. Challis*

# CHAPTER 24
# ONE NIL DOWN, TWO ONE UP

## 1986-87 LEAGUE (LITTLEWOODS) CUP WINNERS

IN THE LONG PERIOD BETWEEN WINNING THE FA CUP and obtaining their next trophy eight years later, the club had several near misses. They reached their third successive Cup Final in 1980 (no other club had done that in the twentieth century) but Second Division West Ham's Trevor Brooking scored the winner with only the third headed goal in his long career. Arsenal felt aggrieved because they had worked so hard to get to the Final. Their semi-final against Liverpool had become the longest in the history of the competition. There was a 0-0 draw at Hillsborough, then two 1-1 draws at Villa Park. Eventually the tie was settled at Highfield Road, Coventry, where Brian Talbot scored. In all, the two teams had played for four hundred and twenty minutes. Not only that, Arsenal had to endure two League games in between the semi-final and the Final nine days later.

The Hammers had not been given more than an outside chance to win at Wembley. After all, although they had the still stylish Brooking, who at thirty-four was nearing the end of his career, the rest were largely inexperienced, not least Paul Allen who was seventeen-years and two hundred and fifty six days old, making him the youngest player ever to appear in the Final. Against them was an Arsenal defence containing Pat Jennings, Pat Rice (who would become the first player to appear in five Finals for one club), David O'Leary, Willie Young and John Devine (in all they had sixty-six caps).

O'Leary was the cool, guiding hand in the centre of the back line. He ranked amongst the best players Arsenal ever employed. He had taken a regular place in the Republic of Ireland team at the age of only eighteen, having won the first of his sixty-eight caps in the 1976-77 season. Born in Dublin, he came over from Ireland to join Arsenal as an apprentice and was taken on as a professional when seventeen. His fine judgement in anticipating the intentions of the opposition meant that, rather like Bobby Moore, he always seemed to have time to intercept, particularly in the air, and come away with the ball. His distribution was also outstanding and he enjoyed taking the ball downfield to join the attack. That Arsenal played in three successive Cup Finals had a lot to do with his reliability.

At Wembley against West Ham, the team played as if tired, which they must have been. West Ham looked spry. After Brooking's goal, the Hammers comfortably contained their experienced opponents. In fact, they would have added to their own tally had not Allen been hacked down by Young just outside the penalty area. Under modern laws that would have been interpreted as blocking a goalscoring opportunity; a clear sending off offence.

In the following week, Arsenal went to the Heysel Stadium in Brussels and played Valencia in the European Cup Winners' Cup final, losing in a penalty shoot-out that came when most of the Arsenal players were worn out after playing an impossibly demanding sixteen matches in forty-six days. Their best performance of that competition had come earlier when they were still fresh and went to Turin to become the first British club ever to win on the home ground of Juventus. By the time they got to the final, many of the players were more than ready for their summer break. Valencia, managed by Alfredo Di Stefano, of Real Madrid fame, had gathered together a formidable side containing Mario Kempes and Rainer Bonhof.

For the first ninety minutes, the teams cancelled each other out, as they also did in extra-time. So, for the first time in the history of European competition, the result depended on penalties. The controversially introduced novelty brought the final to life. Kempes, the power and inspiration of Argentina in their home World Cup victory in 1978, dramatically missed with the first. Brady went forward but he too seemed nervous about this new pressure and also failed. Eight penalties then went in and, in sudden death, Arias scored to give Valencia a 5-4 advantage. Rix, as accurate a ball player as anyone in Britain, had to score. The Valencia goalkeeper, Pereira, gambled and was diving across the goal even as Rix struck the ball. He was right and blocked the shot.

This was surely the season in which the "Lucky Arsenal" tag could finally be laid to rest. With two League games still to play, there was a chance to qualify for the following season's UEFA Cup. Both had to be won. Only two days after the final against Valencia they managed to beat Wolves 2-1 away but in the last game against Middlesbrough, also away, they simply ran out of energy and went down 5-0. Looking at the statistics of the season that was not surprising. They had become the first

114

English side to play seventy competitive matches in a season. However, the most unwanted record was to be the first team ever to go through a European competition unbeaten and then lose in the final.

The defeat in Brussels marked the beginning of negativity. Although Terry Neill had experience of managing Hull City and Spurs, he had not seemed ready for the special demands of Highbury. After finishing third in 1980-81 and fifth in 1981-82, his team were patently struggling in the League and suffered a 3-1 home defeat by Walsall in the League (Milk) Cup in November, 1983. That was probably the last straw.

The obvious replacement was a man who had given most of his working life to the club as player and coach, Don Howe. Although he was popular and had the reliable assistance of Terry Burton, he should have known that coaching was his forte while managing was a complex mix of problems not all to do with producing a successful football team. In less than three years, and after hearing a lot of wild rumours about who was likely to take his place, he resigned. The team, left under the temporary stewardship of Steve Burtenshaw, had become comparatively dull, a fact reflected in poor attendances.

The early 1980s had seen the arrival on the Board of David Dein, whose title of "Vice Chairman" has always been a modest description of his actual standing within the club. From the beginning, Dein was a man with Chapman-like progressive ideas. Without his drive and large shareholding, the club would almost certainly have trundled along with a world famous name but virtually no 'brand'. His initiatives turned Highbury into the vibrant new-old stadium it became in its last days. He was the one who was determined that Arsene Wenger would become manager. He continually looked ahead to the days of a proper European League, which, in the era of jet travel is geographically not a problem but could further alienate week-in-week-out fans. And the new stadium would not have come about without his enthusiasm.

Dein is not Arsenal but without him they would almost certainly have remained in the comparative mediocrity of the early to mid-1980s. For all that, Arsenal's achievements of the 1990s and early 2000s did not have the fans singing 'There's Only One David Dein'. His profile is high in the game itself, especially at the FA, but remains almost shadowy as far as Arsenal's supporters are concerned. The same could be said of the dedicated former Managing Director Ken Friar, who has spent all of his working life at the club and is, without doubt, one of British football's most respected and valued administrators.

To put the club's situation in the mid-1980s into perspective, when they beat Liverpool in September, 1984 it was the first time since 1972 that they had been top of the table. It was not surprising that they were looking around for a new manager. Alex Ferguson, then successfully in charge of Aberdeen, was one of those believed to have turned them down. So, in May, 1986, once again the club decided to give the responsibility to a former player, George Graham, "Stroller" of the Double team, who had never seemed to raise sweat but was a master at setting up moves. His appointment was surprising but, in the light of what he achieved, a wise move by the club's board. His managerial credentials were limited, having done a good job at Millwall, which was very different from being asked to revive one of the most famous clubs in the world. However, Graham had a deep love of Arsenal and their traditions and instilled that sense of pride in all of the teams he produced.

If any of the players thought he would be telling them to play as he had done, they were badly mistaken. For a start, not many of them had the languid skills that in his day made it unnecessary to charge round the field. A few of the seniors had known him from playing golf and enjoying some of the social life that went with it. Now, though, they discovered that he could detach himself from that and work them harder than they had ever been worked. He was also aware that the club's shareholders had been appalled when learning that four players had been convicted of drink-driving offences. They were looking to him to stop the rot.

Tony Adams probably put his finger on Graham's managerial style when he said: "He liked to foster an atmosphere of creative tension". Possibly Graham's most valuable long-term decision was to encourage and promote the youthful Adams who, in spite of his later personal problems rooted in alcoholism, was to become the foundation stone of the new Arsenal, linking up with the more mellow but equally commanding David O'Leary. Howe had been bringing Adams along slowly, too slowly for the ambitious young man's liking. It was only when Steve Burtenshaw had taken over as caretaker manager that he got an extended run. After that he became properly established as the rock in the centre of the famous Arsenal back four or five which, in later seasons, Wenger was well advised not to retire off too soon.

Graham made it clear that fitness was paramount. Pre-season training under his rule was always torturous and there was not much let-up when competition began. He said that all of the Arsenal teams, from the youths to the seniors, would play in the same style (shades of Chapman), which was to be dependent on having a sound defence and a midfield that could stop the other side from having freedom. There were a few players, notably Charlie Nicholas, who suddenly realised that this manager was not going to give bonuses for pretty football. As Adams said: "It was a bit like being back at school".

Graham knew what he wanted and which individuals he did not think were part of his plans. Paul Mariner and Tony Woodcock were not amongst them. He searched for ball winners, workers, players upon whom he could rely, which was why he took Perry Groves from Colchester. On the other hand, he later sold Martin Keown to Aston Villa, which was not such a clever idea.

Graham's attention to the detail of not allowing opponents to enjoy themselves really came to light early in the 1986-87 season. His dependable but not over-exciting team had a run of seventeen First Division matches without defeat, which took them to the top of the table. The era of Graham's theory that stopping the other side scoring was the route to success may not have been popular with the fans of opponents but it certainly opened the door to the club's revival.

Christmas Day, 1986, marked Arsenal's official centenary. Two days later the real celebration was held. By then the fans had a new belief and were in high spirits for a home match against Southampton, which was attended by an impressive array of players of the past, including George Male and Ted Drake, survivors of the Chapman days.

That celebration year ended in appropriate excitement but also disappointment. Both Arsenal and Spurs had reached the quarter-finals of the FA Cup and the League Cup.

They met in the semi-final of the Littlewoods (League) Cup. Arsenal won in a thrilling second leg replay against a Spurs side that David Pleat had organised with a totally different outlook to that of Graham.

Pleat had Glenn Hoddle and Chris Waddle playing as providers for Clive Allen, who was scoring goals almost at will. Spurs won 1-0 at Highbury in the first game and, early in the second, at White Hart Lane they went two goals up, predictably scored by Allen. Arsenal, thanks to one from Viv Anderson and a spectacular second by the ever-determined Niall Quinn, managed to pull the score back to 2-2 to force a replay at White Hart Lane. In that, Allen continued his scoring run to put Arsenal behind. Substitute Ian Allinson equalised and David Rocastle scored the winning goal. That result inspired the title of the club's fanzine 'One-Nil Down, Two-One Up' and set up a final against Liverpool.

When fielding an injury hit team, Arsenal had already lost to Liverpool in a League match at Highbury in March and, in the final, they were not considered mature enough to face what may not have been one of the better Liverpool sides but one with greater experience. They were mindful that Ian Rush would be a big threat, which put a lot of pressure on the young Tony Adams, yet with O'Leary at his side and Viv Anderson and Kenny Sansom as full backs, he had plenty of support. In any case, he was never short of confidence. The group worked well in unison, especially when drawing the attention of linesmen to opponents they caught offside – or claimed they had. Their arms-raised appeal was to become a trademark gesture. Even so, they were right to identify Rush, rather than Kenny Dalglish, as the biggest threat. Sure enough, after twenty-three minutes, with a quick turn and shot he scored.

In the Press Box, most journalists had made Liverpool, with their provenance, clear favourites. Now they were emphasising that Liverpool had never lost a cup match in which Rush scored. To their surprise Arsenal began to take charge. Charlie Nicholas, whose performances for the club usually contained some breathtaking moments but not enough of them, managed to push the ball over the Liverpool line in a goalmouth muddle. Perry Groves, who had been sitting on the bench, came on near the end and almost immediately went on a long run down the left side. He turned the ball across to Nicholas who scored with another stab rather than real shot. Nevertheless it was good enough to secure the trophy.

Curiously, in the first match of the season after beating Liverpool in the League Cup final, Arsenal found themselves facing the same opponents at Highbury. Liverpool got their revenge, winning 2-1, but the term improved with a run of ten successive League wins. Nicholas, popular with the fans, was considered wasteful and perhaps even a luxury by George Graham. He was transferred to Aberdeen in mid-season. That allowed Paul Merson to get more opportunities to join Alan Smith in attack. Merson, like Adams, over-indulged in the good life and suffered its consequences. Nevertheless, there is no doubting the prodigious contribution he made to Arsenal. With his fine ball control, purposeful, strong running and ability to burn the candle at both ends yet play with amazing energy and enthusiasm, he contributed much more than anyone who knew about his problems would ever have believed possible.

The formation of the famous Arsenal back line took shape when the club let Viv Anderson go to Manchester United and bought Nigel

Winterburn from Wimbledon. Steve Williams, who was too opinionated for Graham's liking, was sold to Luton, giving more chances to Michael Thomas. Another significant change came about after Kenny Sansom was injured. Adams, only twenty-one-years-old, was made temporary captain; the youngest in the club's history.

The season was one of promise and sertbacks, which arrived in equal measure. A long period in which goals were hard to find took away any chance of winning the Championship and things were not made better by some remarks by Sansom which brought about a row with Graham. There was only ever going to be one winner in that situation. Sansom lost the permanent captaincy to Adams, who was to lead the team by example and not a little verbal 'encouragement'.

No further trophies came their way that season but, after a string of Littlewoods Cup victories over Doncaster Rovers, Bournemouth, Stoke City, Sheffield Wednesday and Everton, in which only one goal was conceded, there was an appearance in the final against Luton Town, who would not have been favourites even if they had fielded their regular team instead of one beset by injuries and in low spirits. That was not immediately obvious at Wembley because Brian Stein completely baffled the Arsenal defence to give Luton an early lead.

Stein was a continuing danger, forcing John Lukic into a brilliant save. Eventually Groves was substituted by Martin Hayes who scrambled in a goal which was quickly followed by another finely struck by Alan Smith. By then Luton were in retreat. Even so, they survived a controversial penalty (David Rocastle stumbled in the penalty area) when Winterburn's effort was deflected round the post by Andy Dibble. With five minutes left, Luton's Danny Wilson equalised and, almost on the final whistle, Ashley Grimes drove the ball into the middle of the Arsenal penalty area, where Stein turned it in for a most surprising 3-2 victory.

That disappointment could be balanced against the work Graham was doing in assembling one of the best and most determinedly competitive of all Arsenal teams. Apart from having the home-produced Adams, he had obtained Lee Dixon and Steve Bould to bolster the defence. The style of play was practical, disciplined and difficult to disturb. It won few praises from neutrals, who complained that it did nothing to raise the standards of British domestic football and was unattractive. On the other hand, it was what was needed to take the club back into Championship contention. Unfavourable comparisons were made with the earlier Double-winning side. None of that mattered much to Graham who knew

119

that the key to success was pulling off victories when it really mattered.

The great surprise in 1988 was Wimbledon's beating of Liverpool in the FA Cup Final. Perhaps it should not have been all that unexpected. After all, they were coached by Don Howe!

## LEAGUE (LITTLEWOODS) CUP FINAL
(Wembley, 1987)

**Arsenal 2** (Nicholas 2) **Liverpool 1** (Rush)

*Arsenal:* Lukic; Anderson, Sansom, Williams, O'Leary, Adams, Rocastle, Davis, Quinn (Groves), Nicholas, Hayes (Thomas).

*Liverpool:* Grobbelaar; Gillespie, Venison, Spackman, Whelan, Hansen, Walsh (Dalglish), Johnston, Rush, Molby, McMahon (Wark).

# CHAPTER 25
# THOMAS SOMERSAULTS INTO HISTORY

## 1988-89 FIRST DIVISION CHAMPIONS

C RUCIAL TO THE STYLE OF PLAY THAT GRAHAM designed was the tall, slim Alan Smith. His ability to control a ball sent downfield high or low and lay it off or make for goal himself (he scored a total of thirty-six in the 1988-89 season) represented the work of a complete professional. At first, results were not particularly promising and later Liverpool, who had been the outstanding team through most of the 1980s, led them in the run-in, but it was a curious season in which most of the leading teams failed to benefit as much as usual from home advantage.

In the middle of January, Arsenal enjoyed a clear lead at the top, but the season was soured when Paul Davis was suspended for nine matches after breaking the jaw of Southampton's Glenn Cockerill. They played outstandingly to beat Everton 3-1 at Goodison Park (a result that turned them into Championship favourites). Slowly, though, Liverpool edged back. Arsenal suffered what many observers thought was a damning 3-1 defeat by Nottingham Forest at Highbury in March. Then struggling Charlton also went to Highbury and questioned Arsenal's credentials by drawing 2-2.

Graham was getting increasingly concerned that, of all things, it was the defence that seemed to be letting them down. His answer was to look abroad to the tactic of having three central defenders, with one (O'Leary) operating behind the other two. He also hoped that this would offer Winterburn and Dixon more opportunities to press forward on the counter-attack. Both full backs were fairly quick. Graham was assuming that this tactic would also allow David Rocastle to move up and become a useful potential goalscorer. The tried, tested but predictable four across the back defensive tactic was put aside and safe victories followed. Yet Liverpool, who had been unbeaten since the turn of the year, persisted and the race was neck and neck, with Nottingham Forest in close pursuit.

When Forest and Liverpool met in an FA Cup semi-final at Hillsborough, a day that should have been full of drama and excitement turned to tragedy. Ninety-five fans were killed in a crush that had only one beneficial outcome: the speeding up of safer, all-seater stadia, not least at Highbury.

The Championship turned on a re-arranged match against Norwich at Highbury. Norwich had been having an outstanding season, even leading the Championship until Christmas time, but they had declined and the game against Arsenal was a last opportunity to renew their challenge. This was a match in which Graham's tactical philosophy was obvious and justified. The full backs pushed forward with such relentless effort that 5-0 was a modest outcome. Yet the promising situation changed when, thanks largely to brilliant goalkeeping by Peter Shilton, Derby achieved a 2-1 win on their own patch, allowing Liverpool to look ahead to another trophy-winning season.

When unpredictable, battling Wimbledon came in search of revenge for their 5-1 thrashing on their own ground back in August, they drew 2-2 at Highbury and Arsenal's chances seemed to have disappeared. By the time it came to the last game of the season, a re-arranged fixture at Anfield, Liverpool had to avoid being beaten by two clear goals to take the title. Only twice before in the whole history of the Football League had the top two teams played each other for the Championship on the last day of the season. For the first time, the title would be decided on a day when there were no other matches.

Liverpool had already won the FA Cup, as if in tribute to the fans who died at Hillsborough, and had just beaten West Ham 5-1 to take the Championship lead. They were aiming for their second Double in four seasons. They also had a slightly better goal difference than Arsenal, who had not achieved a victory at Anfield on their previous seven League visits over fourteen years.

In so many respects, this was a match of inconceivable drama. To begin with, there was the near memory of Hillsborough but, for Liverpool, the conclusion could have been the claiming of the two titles. On that Friday, the players emerged from the dressing rooms looking sombre rather than excited. They took flowers to the fans. And the fans were subdued; at least comparatively speaking.

In those days, Liverpool were not just a good footballing side. They were hard, really hard in a way that in contemporary football, with its cheating, quick-to-fall guys, seems to have gone out of the game. Arsenal had to match them, tackle for shuddering tackle. Of course, the fans were unaware that several of the team had spent the early part of the week at various levels of intoxication. Fortunately, those players were still young and fit enough to get away with it.

Liverpool were used to pressing forward with a power too great for virtually any midfield in Europe, let alone in the League. Here they were frustrated. On the other hand they could afford to be. After all, they only needed to stop Arsenal scoring to become the Champions. Only? Graham had told his team that they had to keep the game tight but at the same time keep Liverpool under pressure ("If you let them play they'll hurt you"). He added that he would be quite happy to see a goalless first half.

Even then the atmosphere was not like the Anfield of fame. It was mellow; quiet with the memories; quiet with nervous anticipation. Perhaps that had something to do with the fact that in the first half there were few opportunities to cheer near misses or thrilling attacks. Graham walked to the dressing room fulfilled in his wish to keep the first half rigid and on no account concede a goal. All was going according to his plan.

In the early part of the second half Arsenal attacked much as they had in the first, with caution so that Liverpool had few chances to break them down and counter. Suddenly the deadlock was broken. In the fifty-second minute, Winterburn lifted a free-kick across the goalmouth and Smith headed in. Or at least, that was what Arsenal believed. Liverpool suggested several alternatives. Smith was offside; he never touched the ball before it went into the net from an indirect free-kick; the linesman had flagged for something. The Arsenal players were quick to tell the referee what he should be doing – allowing the goal to stand. In spite of that, he took the second opinion of the linesman, before accepting Arsenal's demands that the goal was indeed a goal. The teams were equal on points. Liverpool still had a one goal advantage on goal difference and achieving the Double was tantalisingly within their reach. But now, without Rush, who had been injured in the first half, they were struggling. Even so, Arsenal still had to score another goal.

With ten minutes left, Thomas sprinted through, only to miss with his shot – just a rehearsal someone said later. Five minutes to go. Less than two minutes to go. Injury time. John Lukic, in the Arsenal goal, chose what seemed like a ridiculous moment to throw the ball out. Yes that had so often been the start of successful attacks in the past. Surely, though, this was not the moment to do anything so time-consuming? In his pre-match talk, Graham had emphasised the importance of patience, but even he was probably thinking that there was a time and a place for relying on well tried tactics – this was neither.

So the ball went out to the dependable, much criticised, much underestimated Lee ("If you're good enough for England so am I") Dixon. He was not going to hesitate or even think of playing the so familiar, safe square ball to or Bould. He drove one of his equally accurate forward passes to who laid the ball off to Michael Thomas, who would probably not even have been playing if Paul Davis had been fit. Everyone could sense that the referee had already decided it was pretty nearly time to close up the game. On went Thomas. Steve Nicol tried to cut off his path into the penalty area. All he did was to deflect the ball back to the Arsenal player. Thomas saw Bruce Grobbelaar moving out to meet him so chose not to wait, lobbing the ball over the eccentric but often spectacularly effective goalkeeper for a memorable, breathtaking, unique goal.

Liverpool had one final chance. From the kick off they had only one choice, to tear downfield, but Thomas had gone back with them, gained possession and, placid as you like, played the ball back to Lukic. Hard man Dixon later confessed that he had tears in his eyes and was almost praying that the final Liverpool attack would not come down his side of the field because he could not see properly. The referee, let alone the Arsenal fans, could stand no more drama and called time. Liverpool had been deprived of the Double. Arsenal, with a largely home-grown team, had won the Championship title in the closest, most dramatic finish there had ever been. Thomas turned a somersault to celebrate the victory. Liverpool were on their knees in defeat.

# CHAPTER 26
# A QUESTION OF DISCIPLINE

## 1990-91 FIRST DIVISION CHAMPIONS

IN SPITE OF THEIR DRAMATIC WINNING of the previous season's Championship, Arsenal were still not the dream team to which George Graham aspired. They finished only fourth in 1989-90 and were quickly removed from both cup competitions. Not one of the club's staff appeared in the World Cup finals in Italy. Although Graham was full of what seemed to be extravagant claims about what his side would do in the 1990s, for the players it must have been difficult to set fresh targets. Even the younger ones were drained by the exertions of winning the title. That was obvious in the season's opening game, the Charity Shield in which Liverpool got a modicum of compensation by winning 1-0. In the first League match, Manchester United won 4-1 on their own ground. The chances of this becoming the start of a decade of success seemed remote.

It was only when Graham reinforced the squad that hope emerged. He bought Anders Limpar from Cremonese to add width. David Seaman was brought in from Queen's Park Rangers for £1.3m (a record for a goalkeeper) to replace Lukic, who despite hard-won popularity with the fans was sold to Leeds. And Niall Quinn was allowed to leave for Manchester City. The sometimes under-valued but single-minded Brian Marwood also left. Typical of Graham, he added yet another big, strong defender to the squad in Andy Linighan, who cost £1.25m when bought from Norwich. Linighan had to accept that he would be spending most of his time on the bench.

Discipline on the field, which fans had expected from a team organised by Graham, was not always maintained. In fact, a match against Norwich involved one of the worst brawls ever seen in League football and was witnessed by television viewers. Norwich had taken a two-goal lead. Arsenal then retrieved the situation and, almost at the close of the game, were awarded a penalty. Dixon put the kick away for victory. Then several players started pushing each other and quickly almost all of the others joined in. The police came on to break it up. Later the Football Association fined Norwich fifty thousand pounds and Arsenal twenty thousand.

Off the field there were also problems. Paul Merson was fined for drink-driving and failing to stop after an accident. He and Steve Bould were accused of drunken behaviour during a dinner in London organised by various club sponsors. On another occasion, several players were sent home after heavy drinking during a tour of the Far East. Later came the court case involving Tony Adams that had been hanging over him and the club for several months.

In spite of behind-the-scenes problems (several players quickly realised that it was not wise to disagree with Graham, or even voice an opinion) the arrival of Limpar made the team of 1990-91 really come alive and show signs that they could take the place of Liverpool as the dominating force in English football. One of the high points was the December beating of the previous season's champions 3-0 at Highbury, although, at about the same time, came another sign that self control amongst several of the players was not all that it should have been. Indeed, to a greater or lesser degree, that fault has remained with the club over the past two decades and conflicts with the era in which they used to judge a potential new player as much by his manners as his ability on the pitch.

Another serious indication that Graham was building a team that could overwhelm some of the best in the land came in a visit from Chelsea. Limpar scored his first League goal and gave the Chelsea defence a torrid time, while Merson stormed through midfield with pace and style. Arsenal won 4-1. Paul Davis was also in great form. On the debit side, Alan Smith was not achieving much at this time and was under pressure from the more muscular reserve centre-forward, Kevin Campbell. Playing them together did not seem to enter Graham's thinking, at least until midway through the season.

Then the disciplinary problem re-emerged. A shameful-looking mass brawl in a top-of-the-table match against Manchester United at Old Trafford was, as is so often the case, a confusion of intentions. Nonetheless, it was one of those discreditable scenes that did nothing to improve football's already declining standards of behaviour. Arsenal had been controlling the game. They had a huge band of travelling supporters that out-voiced those of United (which is not all that unusual at Old Trafford). When a short corner from Davis arrived at the feet of Limpar, he tried an instant shot that fooled Les Sealey, in the United goal, so much that he failed to get his hands on it until it had crossed the line. The referee thought so too. The United crowd and their players wanted to believe that it had not and that they had been cheated. Just after Seaman had pulled off a couple of superb saves, the game turned nasty (it had always been on the verge). A 'determined' tackle by Nigel Winterburn on Denis Irwin sparked what looked like a roughhouse.

Certainly some players senselessly and enthusiastically joined in. Winterburn and Brian McClair could hardly wait to get at each other. Others genuinely attempted to break it up. From the Arsenal point of view, there was probably an element of not wanting that old northern taunt about being 'Soft Southerners' to be seen to have any basis in truth. They pushed and shoved with no consideration for the way their actions would discredit their club and football in general. Inevitably, United's fiery Paul Ince quickly acquired a taste for some 'afters' and, equally predictably, Alex Ferguson got involved. Others on both sides made real efforts to drag team-mates from the scene. The headlines the next day failed to give a balanced response.

The incident lasted for not much more than a minute and it is doubtful if any player landed a serious blow. Nonetheless, the FA punished Arsenal by deducting two points and United one. Both clubs were fined fifty thousand pounds. In effect the FA had offered Liverpool a clear road to the Championship. The Arsenal board reacted angrily at seeing their club being criticised for irresponsible behaviour and fined Graham and five players two weeks' wages. In reality, the incident had an uplifting effect on the spirit within the squad – a bonding that had come out of something that could not be condoned.

The points punishment was seen by Graham and most of the team as another challenge. However, they were falling behind Liverpool and, lurking in the background, was the knowledge that the inspirational Adams was awaiting his court appearance for drink driving. When the case came up he was given a prison sentence of nine months, with five suspended. Arsenal had temporarily lost a colossal influence. In a way, though, Graham, had been justified in what had earlier seemed the unnecessary luxury of buying in more defenders than he needed when the season had begun. Bould and Linighan became the defensive anchors.

Arsenal were to be without Adams for thirteen matches. However, before that and despite a 6-2 defeat by Manchester United at Highbury in the League Cup, a 3-0 win over Liverpool, also at Highbury (where Graham played O'Leary as a sweeper to confront Ian Rush), confirmed that this was a serious attempt at the title. Limpar was in devastating form, though not making himself popular with Graham by insisting on turning out for Sweden whenever asked. In the FA Cup, Sunderland were overcome, then came a four-game FA Cup tie with Leeds. In the third replay, Dixon and Merson finally broke Leeds at Elland Road. Shrewsbury gave them a tough game but went down 1-0 and Cambridge United were no walk-overs, losing by only 2-1 at Highbury.

So the semi-finals were reached and another meeting with Spurs, this time at Wembley. Consequently, Arsenal were still on course for the Double. Adams returned, remarkably fit, and played his first match of freedom at Anfield. Liverpool were leading Arsenal by three points at the top. Merson's winning goal gave Arsenal the psychological edge. Confidence was high. Campbell was establishing himself in the attack and David Hillier proving a strong-tackling worker.

The decision to hold the FA Cup semi-final at the national stadium was controversial, although after the disaster at Hillsborough and bearing in mind the massive demand for tickets for the north-London derby, there was justification. Spurs were also pleased to have the chance to play to a larger crowd (more than seventy seven thousand) than they could have accommodated at White Hart Lane because it had become clear that their financial situation was serious.

The match itself will long be remembered for one special contribution. After four minutes, Paul Gascoigne, standing thirty-yards from goal, took a free-kick for Spurs. He hit a huge drive that rose above the outstretched hands of David Seaman to put Spurs ahead. Gascoigne, such a talent that went to waste, was outstanding. Later, in a link with Paul Allen, he baffled the Arsenal defence and his clever pass allowed Gary Lineker to put them two up. Although Smith retrieved a goal, typically heading in from the far post, Lineker added another in the second half by avoiding Adams and Seaman.

The question after that defeat was whether the disappointment would have a detrimental effect on morale before the run-in to the League season. In midweek, the team came out seemingly in serious, determined mood against Manchester City at Highbury but the Wembley defeat had obviously lodged in the back of their minds. City pulled off a 2-2 draw. Arsenal were still ahead of Liverpool but the fight was on because Liverpool were failing to do what had previously been their forte: closing down games when ahead. They even lost 3-0 at Luton. Kenny Dalglish had resigned, leaving the club in the hands of Graeme Souness.

With three matches of the season remaining, Arsenal had a three-point lead over Liverpool. On the next to last Saturday, they began their match at Sunderland early in the evening after Liverpool had finished their game with Chelsea, who had won 4-2. Arsenal were satisfied to tease out a goalless draw. So there were two games left for each of the contenders, but Arsenal had what on the face of it seemed a comfortable four-point lead. The trouble was that their next opponents were Manchester United, at Highbury, on Bank Holiday Monday. Again, because of the demands of television, that game and Liverpool's at Nottingham Forest had staggered kick-off times. Arsenal had the advantage of starting second.

By the time they kicked off they were elated. Liverpool went down to a winning goal from Ian Woan and Arsenal were able to go on to the Highbury pitch already victorious and with their fans singing and chanting in triumph. To their great credit, the players tackled the match professionally and with a will to win, even though the need had gone. The marauding Dixon had performed exceptionally well throughout the season as an adventure-seeking full back, safe in his tackling and distribution but also the provider of numerous accurate crosses for Smith in particular. Here he provided the same service and Smith scored after twenty minutes then calmly added another, this time with a fine shot from the edge of the penalty area. Later, he gratefully accepted when Dixon offered him the chance to complete a hat-trick from the penalty spot, which he did.

United, who earlier in the season had beaten Arsenal in the League Cup, managed to get a late goal. By then, the trophy was already being taken to the pitch edge for Adams to collect and parade round the ground. Graham stood back, almost out of sight, and let his players enjoy the moment. The final game against Coventry was merely a continuation of the celebrations – a 6-1 win, also at Highbury. Arsenal's lead at the top was seven points over Liverpool - remarkable in view of the deduction.

Joy was blunted by sadness. Two of the finest players ever to appear for Arsenal, Joe Hulme and Cliff Bastin, both died aged eighty-seven and seventy-nine respectively.

# CHAPTER 27
# THE WRIGHT CHOICE

## 1992-93 FA CUP & LEAGUE
## (COCA-COLA) CUP WINNERS

BECAUSE THE BAN ON BRITISH CLUBS, imposed after the tragedy at the Heysel Stadium in 1985, had been lifted, Arsenal were allowed to enter the 1991-92 season's European Cup, which has always been the most reliable test of true quality. The target was to prove enduringly elusive. In the club's return to facing the best Continental opposition, it was natural that they would be out of touch with the demands. Who knows whether they would have done better if Graham's latest signing had been available.

Ian Wright had cost £2.5 million when he came from Crystal Palace and, in the long term, would more than repay the club for their confidence. However, he had been signed too late to play in Europe. He introduced himself to the Arsenal fans by scoring against Leicester in a League Cup tie, then got three against Southampton on his League debut.

The European campaign began well enough with an overwhelming 6-1 home win over FK Austria, of Vienna. It included four goals by Alan Smith. A 1-0 defeat in Austria was not something over which it was necessary to fret, except, perhaps, that the style in which Arsenal played was very English; tough, uncompromising and not with many hints that against more subtle opponents they would have the necessary variation of tactics or the required imagination.

The next European test was a big one – Benfica. A confident, defensively impressive performance at the Stadium of Light meant that they could face the champions of Portugal at Highbury well satisfied with their 1-1 draw. Colin Pates then added to confidence with an early goal in the return but the Brazilian Isaias suddenly took control in midfield. He was well known for his ability to score from long range and, sure enough, blasted in a shot from thirty yards. Arsenal began to feel threatened, and rightly so. In extra-time, Kulkov and Isaias added two more goals. Arsenal's performance was a clear sign that they were well below the standards of the top European teams. George Graham went on the defensive, complaining that clubs in the English League were involved in far too many matches. He said they were playing into the hands of the "foreigners who think we are crazy playing the number of games we do". Old excuse, and not entirely accurate.

The European frustration was compounded by unpredictable League results and early eviction from the League (Rumbelows) Cup by Coventry. Things got worse when they were then knocked out of the FA Cup in the third round by Wrexham, for whom the veteran Mickey Thomas scored eight minutes from time to cancel out an earlier goal by Smith, who had been badly out of scoring form. Seaman was then beaten again, by Steve Watkin. Significantly, Wright had missed the game because of a suspension, but the fans were not in a mood for more excuses. Pressure built on Graham.

Apart from buying the successful Wright, who scored twenty-four League goals in his first season, Graham had not reinforced the squad in the way the fans would have liked. A lot of money had gone into ground improvements. As far as Arsenal's league performances in the opening season of the new Premiership were concerned, there was little to remember. Indeed, only twice did one of their players score more than one goal and their total of goals (40) was even worse than Nottingham Forest, who were relegated. Obviously the atmosphere at Highbury had been eroded by the rebuilding work going on but the customers were more concerned about a lack of rebuilding on the pitch.

Predictably, the main financial backers and company with the most to gain, BSkyB, publicised the 'Premiership' with absurd hype, such as "A Whole New Ball Game". And this after England had again been found wanting internationally by getting knocked out of the European Championship in the opening round of the finals. The fear amongst football's more serious thinkers and writers was that the Premiership would, in time, cut itself off from any responsibility towards the smaller clubs and, supported by large amounts of television money, encourage the bigger ones to import players rather than cultivate their own. There was also the feeling that by having numerous matches available live on television, people would become blasé about the game as a whole. To some extent that has happened.

Smaller clubs have been hard hit and the "not more football" attitude of the television viewing public has grown. By 2005, the appetite for attending Premiership matches had reduced (there was no longer a 'full house' notice outside every ground) but not withered sufficiently to cause panic. What may well have changed is the background of the spectators themselves.

Clearly it requires a good income to buy Premiership tickets. Many less well off fans have been priced out of the market. On the other hand, it is understandable that when a club of Arsenal's status reduces ground capacity, they welcome the "salmon sandwich" spectators and corporate entertainers who help cover the cost of the lost gate money.

The 1992-93 Premiership season had begun poorly for Arsenal with a 4-2 home defeat by Norwich and, after that, there was no continuity. Although the bookmakers had made them clear favourites, the flowing football and free-scoring of 1990-91 had all but disappeared. A final mid-table position, twenty-eight points behind Manchester United, looked like a bad memory from earlier times. The inter-play between Alan Smith and Ian Wright, which was to become so important, had not yet been refined. Off the pitch there were also problems.

Many fans were unhappy about the decision to turn the famous and enormously popular North Bank, where some sixteen thousand of their dedicated number had always stood, into a twelve thousand capacity, all-seated area. It was accepted that this would satisfy the tightened safety regulations, but a substantial number of fans believed it was also another move away from financially accessible entertainment for the majority towards luxury for the well-off minority. Arsenal were by no means the only club to come in for this sort of criticism, although in their case the gradual but dramatic reduction of the ground's capacity from the days when attendances of over fifty five thousand were commonplace, had played into the hands of those who believed that profitable exclusivity was the club's aim.

The Arsenal Bond, which was intended to help finance the 'improvements', was introduced. This also came in for a great deal of criticism. The publicity got worse when one of the tabloid papers pointed out that a mural that had been set up behind the goal in front of building work going on at the North Bank end did not contain a black face or that of a woman amongst the thousands. It was changed to become 'more representative', or politically correct.

Behind the scenes Graham had been trying to increase the strength of the squad. He had obtained John Jensen, of Brondby, and, in mid-season, he managed to get Martin Keown back from Everton for £2 million, which proved to be money well spent. But the squad had been depleted by the selling of Michael Thomas to Liverpool and David Rocastle to Leeds. Sadly, Rocastle later died from cancer, aged 33. He was a super player and a super guy.

With Premiership results unpredictable, it came as a big relief to have success in the two domestic cup competitions. David Seaman came to the rescue in the first League (Coca-Cola) Cup match against Millwall. After a 1-1 draw at Highbury, the second leg ended 1-1 after full-time. Seaman defied Millwall in the penalty shoot-out. Derby were equally stubborn opponents, losing a replay in which Seaman was again outstanding. Wright showed no mercy to his old club, Crystal Palace, in the semi-final which Arsenal won 3-1 at Selhurst.

There was a curious coincidence when the draw for the third round of the FA Cup was made and Yeovil Town came out as opponents. They had also opposed Arsenal in 1971, the year of the Double. Wright made sure that there were no slips against a club that had a big reputation for giantkilling and had actually scored three in that original match. He got three on his own. The tie against the champions, Leeds, at Highbury in the next round proved much more strenuous. Leeds took a two goal lead through Chapman and Speed but eventually they were hauled back by the in-form Parlour and Merson. The replay was equally testing though far more open. Wright got two more goals and Arsenal won a terrific tie by 3-2 after extra-time.

Nottingham Forest were much less obstinate, crushed by Wright's goal-run (two more). And so the quarter-final was reached and a tie against Ipswich Town. Tony Adams, with a large plaster on his head following what a club spokesman called an "accident at home", still managed to head Arsenal into the lead, which built up to a 4-2 win and a semi-final against old neighbours Spurs at Wembley. Again Adams pulled the rabbit out of the hat. Merson sent over a free-kick to where Adams had run. The Spurs defenders seemed static. Adams, as so often in his career, simply nodded the ball into the net. By coincidence, the Final would be against Sheffield Wednesday, the team they were also to face in the League Cup final.

Full of confidence, Arsenal faced Wednesday in the League Cup final with little doubt that they would win. Merson was in particularly good form, full of running and with the talent to pick out players with an instinctive grasp of the best one to find in any situation. The midfield, however, was unfamiliar, with Paul Davis hurried back after a hamstring injury and Steve Morrow, who had been loaned out to several clubs, called up for a rare full match. Although John Harkes gave Wednesday the lead, the game went on to be dominated by a player who, like Adams, was persecuted by flaws in his own character. In Merson's case it was, primarily, gambling, with several other problems thrown in. Yet he was amongst the most exciting and inventive players ever to wear an Arsenal shirt. Meanwhile, Morrow did excellent work in controlling Chris Waddle.

In the twentieth minute, Merson equalised with a wonderful swerving volley. Arsenal built on that, dominated and, in the sixty-eighth minute, Merson created the securing goal. His cross was well met by Morrow who turned the ball into the net with a deftness that defied his long wait for first team opportunities. Unhappily, in the ensuing excitement Adams lifted Morrow almost on to his shoulders, then dropped him. Morrow suffered a broken arm and was not able to play for the rest of the season. Adams was mortified. This was one of the very rare occasions on which he was not in the forefront of a prolonged celebration.

Sheffield Wednesday were soon to have a chance of revenge. There have been many disappointing FA Cup Finals at Wembley and this was certainly one of them. Partly that was the result of Wright, the great entertainer, having to play with a broken toe and Wednesday's unpredictable Waddle having one of those all too frequent days when he promised much and achieved little. Wright did manage to head Arsenal into the lead. Wednesday were persistent without being exciting and got a sixty-eighth minute equaliser through David Hirst to force a replay on the following Thursday at Wembley. In between, Arsenal also had to play against Manchester United in a testimonial for David O'Leary.

The weather on the day of the replay was dreadful. Rain beat down and traffic jams caused a delayed kick-off. Perhaps it was the frustration of waiting to start that had something to do with the fact that the match began with some reckless tackling. Mark Bright was cautioned for a challenge on Linighan, who had to carry on with a broken nose. Somewhat surprisingly, Wright, who rarely waited for a second invitation to get involved in controversial situations, steered clear of the troublespots and took Arsenal into the lead, neatly lobbing the ball over Chris Woods. Waddle needed to restore some credibility and volleyed in the equaliser, albeit after a deflection.

Chances came and went. Extra-time was almost over when Merson took a corner with as much energy as he could still muster. The ball curled across goal and Linighan managed to lift his tired body over the defence and head firmly downwards. For Linighan it was a poignant and rewarding contribution. He had long been one of Arsenal's back-up squad. Now he was the star of the moment. However, the player who had made all the difference, all season long, was the ebullient Wright, who had become every bit as popular as Charlie George had been in a previous era.

No other club had ever won the FA Cup and the League Cup in the same season. In addition, George Graham became the first person to win the Championship and the two domestic cup competitions both as a player and manager.

# FA CUP FINAL
## (15 May 1993, Wembley)

**Arsenal 1** (Wright) **Sheffield Wednesday 1** (Hirst) **aet**

*Arsenal:* Seaman; Dixon, Winterburn, Davis, Linighan, Adams, Jensen, Wright
(O'Leary), Campbell, Merson, Parlour (Smith)

*Sheffield Wednesday:* Woods; Nilsson, Worthington, Palmer, Anderson
(Hyde), Warhurst, Harkes, Waddle (Bart-Williams), Hirst, Bright, Sheridan.

*Referee:* K. Barratt.

# REPLAY
## Wembley (20 May)

**Arsenal 2** (Wright, Linighan) **Sheffield Wednesday 1** (Waddle) **aet**

*Arsenal:* Seaman; Dixon, Winterburn, Davis, Linighan, Adams, Jensen, Wright
(O'Leary), Smith, Merson, Campbell.

*Sheffield Wednesday:* Woods; Nilsson (Bart-Williams), Worthington, Harkes,
Palmer, Warhurst, Wilson (Hyde), Waddle, Hirst, Bright, Sheridan.

*Referee:* K. Barratt.

# COCA-COLA CUP FINAL

**Arsenal 2** (Merson, Morrow) **Sheffield Wednesday 1** (Harkes)

*Arsenal:* Seaman; O'Leary, Winterburn, Parlour, Adams, Linighan,
Morrow, Merson, Wright, Campbell, Davis.

*Sheffield Wednesday:* Woods: Nilsson, King (Hyde), Palmer, Anderson,
Harkes, Wilson (Hirst), Waddle, Warhurst, Bright, Sheridan.

*Referee:* A. Gunn.

# CHAPTER 28
# TOO MUCH BOTTLE

## 1993-94 EUROPEAN CUP WINNERS' CUP WINNERS

QUALIFYING FOR THE EUROPEAN CUP WINNERS' Cup of 1993-94 offered another chance to test the ability of the squad against teams from different backgrounds and ones likely to be more artistic than the Arsenal of reputation (the 'boring' tag did have quite a deep foundation of truth). But this was to be an outstanding season that began unconvincingly with a 5-4 defeat on penalties by Manchester United in the Charity Shield and another (3-0) by Coventry City on the opening day of the League season.

Graham risked further accusations of producing grey teams by guiding the side through the early matches with regimented and not very exciting football. His later decision to release Limpar to Everton seemed a further reduction of any possible flair, while Merson was continually played in a wide role whereas it seemed obvious that he was creative enough to play more centrally behind the attack. David O'Leary had also left to finish his illustrious playing career at Leeds. All in all, there was a clear impression that the pressure of playing on several fronts in this season was going to be too much.

It was the Premiership performances that suffered, albeit nobody told Ian Wright, who scored twenty-three goals. At least, the fans could experience a period after Christmas when their team were unbeaten for more than three months, though some of the football was tough on the eye. In the domestic cup competitions, there was not much to cheer. Both FA Cup and League Cup campaigns lasted only as far as the fourth rounds.

The Cup Winners' Cup challenge kicked off against Odense, who provided a surprisingly difficult examination. Although Arsenal won 3-2 on aggregate, there was not enough in the overall performance to justify the view that this was a season in which everything had to be concentrated on the European adventure. Because the main man, Adams, had been missing from the first leg, perhaps there was a lack of drive behind the scenes. He was available for the next round against the experienced Standard Liege but Wright was serving a suspension. Unlikely though it seemed after Wright's goalscoring feats, the team got along pretty well without him – an aggregate win of 10-0 including a seven-goal win away. Merson was in his element.

The quarter-final first leg against Torino in Italy brought a typically solid and goalless performance that at least set up a more interesting return at Highbury. Torino were not easily broken down and it required one of Adams' headers to overcome them from a free-kick by Davis. Excellent marking of the more talented of the Torino players paid off. The semi-final promised an interesting clash with Paris Saint-Germain, who were heading the French league and led in their attack by George Weah. They were orchestrated by David Ginola. The quality of that side had been emphasised by their beating of Real Madrid in the previous round.

To the relief of the Arsenal fans, Graham decided that it was an occasion on which to depend on Wright rather than the heavier and less enterprising Kevin Campbell, who had enjoyed an extended run in the League. Within thirty-five minutes, Wright headed in a free-kick from Davis. Ginola nullified that advantage. No matter. There was confidence that at Highbury the tie could be finished off. Campbell was restored to the attack and, ironically in view of the fans' attachment to Wright, scored the decisive goal. Paris Saint-Germain had not been allowed to settle. If they had, they would almost certainly have won because there was no doubt that they were the more talented side.

In the days before the final against the holders Parma, in Copenhagen, Graham made several heart-felt responses to the familiar accusation that the teams he had produced were dull and lacked the ability to entertain in midfield. His attitude had always been that Alan Smith was such a dependable target man that it would have been wrong not to reach him with long balls as and when necessary. In any case, he always seemed sceptical about Merson's capacity for hard work. He was also concerned that in Copenhagen his team would not be able to make up for the absences of such influential players as Keown and Wright, who was suspended. He knew that Parma, coached by the future England boss Sven-Goran Eriksson, had some exceptionally gifted ball players, including Gianfranco Zola (later of Chelsea) and Tomas Brolin. He decided to play Smith and Campbell together, rather than isolate one of them.

Yet again it was the diligent and often unsung Dixon who started the crucial move. Goodness knows how many goals he initiated over his long career with the club. This time it was a long throw that the Italians failed to clear. Smith took it under control and immediately hit a ferocious shot that clipped the post and went in. In truth, though, Parma were playing a standard of football that was well in advance of anything Arsenal could produce. What Arsenal had, however, was the ability to defend a marginal lead, which, under the guidance of Adams, they did with familiar rigidity.

Although Brolin did hit the post, Parma were thoroughly frustrated, especially by Seaman who, in spite of the fact that he was playing with some cracked ribs, made several terrific saves. The often underestimated Bould was immensely reliable but it was a combined defensive performance of the highest order ... if you appreciate that sort of thing!

Disciplined, self-preserving football was at the hard heart of the Arsenal game, which made it all the more odd that several of the players still seemed unable to discipline themselves off the field. As an example, Tony Adams and Ray Parlour faced accusations that while visiting a pizza restaurant in Essex they set off a fire extinguisher. Meanwhile, the whole gory details of Merson's involvement with drugs, drink and gambling came out in the *Mirror*. And so it went on. When he took over, Arsene Wenger could only have been amazed that so many of the players who had achieved so much could also have been so wildly adolescent.

(Copenhagen, 4 May 1994)

### Arsenal 1 (Smith) Parma 0

*Arsenal:* Seaman; Dixon, Winterburn, Bould, Adams, Davis, Morrow, Merson (McGoldrick, 86), Selley, Campbell, Smith.

*Parma:* Bucci; Benarrivo, Di Chiara, Minotti, Appollini, Sensini, Brolin, Pin (Melli, 70), Crippa, Zola, Asprilla.

*Referee:* Krondl (Czech Republic)

Creative Continental-style football may have been overcome in order to win the Cup Winners' Cup but defending that title in 1994-95 with too little real skill of their own was obviously going to be a test and one carried out largely without George Graham, who epitomised the club's pragmatic attitude to the game. Graham had been frustrated by what he claimed was a lack of financial support from the board. He said he wanted to buy certain players but that the fees and conditions were too much for the club to accept. Stefan Schwarz did agree to join from Benfica but the existing players were beginning to get unsettled by difficulties over new contracts. Some probably thought that winning a European competition would open a pot of gold. According to them, the lid stayed firmly closed.

Several of those who had worked so tirelessly for so long were clearly getting to the point at which their stamina would be questioned by less hard-worked opponents. Not that some of them helped themselves by their lifestyles. The signing of John Hartson and Chris Kiwomya hardly raised the roof amongst the fans. The team's performances staggered from modest to poor. Liverpool knocked them out of the Coca-Cola Cup in the fifth round and they were dismissed from the FA Cup by Millwall in a third round replay at Highbury. Then the club was hit by alleged scandal.

It was reported that Graham had received a large amount of money (reported at £285,000) from the agent Rune Hauge for his involvement in the buying of Jensen and Pal Lydersen. The board heard Graham's version of events and he offered to hand back the money. On 20 February, the news was released that he had been dismissed for "failing to act in the best interests of the club". He vowed to contest the decision. A few hours later, under caretaker manager Stewart Houston, the team played Nottingham Forest at Highbury and won 1-0. It was their first home win for four months.

Any attempt to put Graham's eight years at Highbury into perspective depends on who gives an opinion. If there was a consensus amongst the players it was of begrudging praise. They knew how he had driven them, scolded them unmercifully, bullied and challenged them to create a team that was short on individual skill and long, very long, on dogged determination not to lose. Alternatively, he, too, had given his all and been a powerful leader. As for the fans, like most followers of any club, they would probably forego pretty football for success, and Graham had given them a reasonable share, though, with the benefit of hindsight, they questioned whether he had done enough in the development of young players.

Finding a replacement for Graham would be an enormously difficult task. The Board needed time to consider, which was why they put the solid, cajoling Stewart Houston in charge on a temporary basis. Houston's main task was to keep the club competing in the lucrative European competition. There had been an easy 6-1 aggregate win over Omonia Nicosia and a more difficult 4-3 aggregate victory over the Danish side Brondby before one of Europe's most accomplished clubs, Auxerre of France, came into view for the quarter-final.

Proof that Auxerre were indeed an imposing team came at Highbury where they drew 1-1. For the away leg, Houston simply recommended to the players that they tried to stifle the imagination out of the improvising French. Once Ian Wright had scored against them, Auxerre found themselves tightly controlled all over the field.

Sampdoria, in the semi-finals, were an even greater challenge. Coached by Sven-Goran Eriksson, who had a good knowledge of the British game and Arsenal in particular, they were a team with plenty of clever individuals. Admittedly, Arsenal had won a lot of praise from foreign managers for the way they could close down a game, blocking the routes of some of Europe's most inventive players. The question was whether that would be sufficient to repeat the previous season's achievement.

Eriksson was among the managers who had been impressed. At Highbury, he organised his team to play some delightful football. The absence of Ruud Gullit was hardly noticed. It was anticipated that it would be a rugged match. When Wright charged into the Sampdoria goalkeeper, Walter Zenga, Adams toed the ball across the goalline, but the referee had to disallow the goal.

After his success in the previous season's final, Bould was up for further glory. A shot from Hillier was well defended by Zenga but the ball was only deflected out to Bould, who cracked it back to give Arsenal the lead. A couple of minutes later and he was up in the attack again, heading from a corner. The ball rose over the defence and even over the head of Adams and the upraised arm of Zenga, then under the crossbar. Sampdoria replied, Jjugovic scoring. Merson then spotted that Wright had got a rare area of open space up ahead and played a typically accurate forward pass. Wright controlled the ball well, avoided a couple of defenders and lifted it over Zenga. Yet again, Sampdoria came back. Jjugovic was offered too much room and turned in a fine shot. The doubts about Arsenal's lack of originality and the feeling that Sampdoria would have enough of it to win on aggregate came flooding in.

Results had not been going well in the League and there was even the possibility of a late-season relegation struggle. A couple of wins before the return against Sampdoria in Genoa raised spirits a little but the match soon turned any renewed confidence into more doubt. Mancini noticed that Seaman had moved several yards out of goal and decided to attempt a lob over his head, which succeeded. Seaman was undoubtedly one of the finest goalkeepers England had ever produced, but his susceptibility to being caught in just this way was a lasting blot on his otherwise distinguished reputation.

Just after the hour, Merson sent over a corner. Hartson flicked the ball on with his head and Wright was near the goalline to deflect in, more by luck than his usual precision. The rugged nature of the game meant that Wright was given a tough time and, with ten minutes left, he was saved further punishment by being replaced. Sampdoria were relieved to see the main danger man head for the bench. They struck a free-kick against Arsenal's defence but Bellucci knocked in the rebound. He was also waiting when Lombardo moved quickly downfield and hit in a third goal, which put them 5-4 ahead on aggregate.

In a fraught final three minutes, Schwarz managed to penetrate the Sampdoria wall with a long free-kick that found its way home. Amazingly, full-time arrived with the scores level at 5-5 on aggregate. Surprisingly, extra-time brought no further goals, leaving the match to be decided on penalties. Merson was left with his to give Arsenal victory but Zenga saved. Then Seaman saved (his third from five shots) from Lombardo, so Arsenal went through to the final in Paris where they would meet Real Zaragoza, conquerors of Chelsea in their semi-final.

The climax was memorable for something Seaman would have wanted erased from his memory. In extra-time Zaragoza's Esnaider, who had scored in every round, added another to his tally but Hartson equalised. There was less than a minute remaining when Nayim (formerly of Spurs) found himself in an unusual amount of open space near the halfway line. His options were limited. None of the Zaragoza strikers had much energy left. He noticed (not altogether surprisingly) that Seaman was some ten yards off his line. Nayim speculated on a dipping, high shot that soared over the stranded goalkeeper's head. Seaman ran back as if in a nightmare, feet seemingly dragging him in quicksand. There was no chance of a recovery and, as the ball dropped under the crossbar, he could only reach out a despairing hand and assist it over the line. How unfair that in future any video of his career would have to highlight this almost comical mistake. He deserved better.

The board had always made it clear that Houston was appointed as interim boss, though he must have felt that if the team had won against Zaragoza they would have had no choice but to give him more consideration for the full-time post. And consideration would have been all that he received because the man the club had in mind was Bobby Robson, whose experience at home and abroad made him the obvious choice. At the time Robson was managing Porto, who he had just guided to the Portuguese title. He had also recently signed a new contract. In spite of that, he came to London and met the Arsenal board. He thought that he had a verbal agreement with Porto's president that if a major British club asked him to become manager, he would be released. That proved a false hope. The president insisted that Robson worked out his contract.

So the Arsenal board had to look elsewhere and chose Bruce Rioch, who had been managing Bolton Wanderers for the previous three years. The evidence of his period in charge at Highbury made it inevitable that in hindsight the decision would be interpreted as a mistake, but almost instantly he made possibly the most important signing the club was to pull off in twenty years.

Dennis Bergkamp came from Internazionale for £7.5 million. Arsenal had never previously paid so much for anyone, yet after an unimpressive beginning to his new career at Highbury, the Dutch international was seen to be a bargain. While in later years much well-deserved praise would be heaped upon Thierry Henry, and though Ian Wright almost alone lifted spirits during years of otherwise flat football, Bergkamp was to become the most important all-round influence.

A man of quiet, introspective intelligence (though not without a sharp edge to his game that belied his apparent cool nature), Bergkamp would prove to be the mastermind behind innumerable Arsenal victories. Not only that, he represented a new approach to the way football was to be played at the club ... stylishly, which annoyed Spurs fans who had, rightly, considered that it was their club that championed the more attractive football in north London. Tottenham's chairman, Alan Sugar, went as far as to say that Bergkamp had been bought by Arsenal only because "they need a bit of cosmetic marketing". The remark would come back to haunt him when Arsenal took over as the team to watch rather than endure.

Rioch also spread his net to Italy to obtain Sampdoria's England international David Platt, who was an enigma. He could be powerful, accurate and a good finisher. He could also be anonymous. There has always been a school of thought that he was never as good as his reputation. Perhaps so, but he, like Bergkamp, was astute and reflective. Clearly the club's Vice-Chairman, David Dein, was leading the club into the modern world of big transfer fees, which had previously been avoided. The excitement caused by the new arrivals was balanced by the fact that Alan Smith had to announce the end of his distinguished career, victim of persistent knee trouble. Schwarz moved to Italy, which was also a considerable loss.

Adams wrote in his revealing and soul-searching autobiography *'Addicted'* that he was appalled when Rioch watched Bergkamp have some fairly quiet League games and then suggested that playing twice a week was too much and that he should only appear in one. Adams could not believe that a player costing so many millions could be excused matches. Amazingly, in spite of his drinking, Adams was still turning out as often as asked and not slowing down. Heavy drinking amongst many of the game's leading players was nothing unusual. In fact, most top clubs had groups of them. Adams and Merson, however, were in a league of their own.

Rioch came to the sensible conclusion that the way forward was to blend the team's traditional defensive nature with a more positive approach. In some ways he was unlucky. The semi-finals of the Coca-Cola Cup were reached in 1995-96 and defeat at the hands of the eventual winners, Aston Villa, came only through away goals after a 2-2 draw at Highbury. Although League results went reasonably well, a serious knee injury to Adams was a blow to the whole team. Nevertheless, they finished fifth. Again it was Manchester United who showed them the way.

The season ended with the outward impression of a group of players happier because of the release from Graham's intimidating approach. Surprisingly, in all the years of Graham's career at Highbury there was never a serious examination of why a manager with such a reputation for discipline could appear to allow several of his players to be drunks, drugs users, gamblers and playboys. Put another way, though, those were the days in which Arsenal's problems were probably not much worse than those of other clubs. There was a drinking culture that was accepted and some managers even ignored it on the grounds that it fostered close friendships that could be turned into better team spirit. In fact, quite a few managers happily joined in. To suggest that the problem has gone away would be to ignore the headlines that have continued to drag football into disrepute. For alcoholism, now read binge-drinking.

Bergkamp was never one of the hard-drinking school. On the pitch, he also became an example to the young players who were coming through. At the other extreme of personalities, and in spite of his problems, Merson seemed to be given a new lease of life. Not that the impression of team-spirit being improved stood up to close scrutiny. Wright was not endearing himself to Rioch. His reckless ability to draw the attention of referees was irritating. In addition, Parlour and Platt, as well as Adams, were all missing for lengthy spells with injuries.

Only fourteen months after his appointment, Rioch left the club. In his favour, at least he got the side into the UEFA Cup with a victory over Bolton on the last day of the 1995-96 season. Clearly the board felt that while he had done some good things in giving the fans a more enjoyable team to watch, future success was not by any means an assured conclusion. Speaking at the annual general meeting, Chairman Peter Hill-Wood said Rioch did not share "our" vision for the future, but he was thanked for taking Arsenal into Europe. Hill-Wood's vision for the future was founded on a belief that the standards of League football were nowhere near as good as hype would have the public believe. Arsenal had to be a cross-European borders force.

At that time there were no public hints that the club might decide to move out of Highbury. Indeed, at the annual general meeting, Hill-Wood said: "We got into Europe, but I don't think anybody in this room would think that the squad we have is actually going to challenge Manchester United just at the moment. It needs to be strengthened and we hope it will be. This club needs success. We all want it, none more so than the board of directors. If you look around the stadium, it's a magnificent stadium. We've spent £40 million over the past ten years on it".

That annual meeting also emphasised that the fans were fed up with hearing "nothing but bad things about the club" as one shareholder put it. Frustration at failure to sign any of the few top class players that might have been available was obvious, but most people at that meeting seemed prepared to accept that Rioch's indecision about which ones he wanted to join Arsenal had been the biggest problem.

Back to the forefront came Houston. George Armstrong, the reserve team coach, and Pat Rice, in charge of youth development, were happy to stay in the background. Rice's enduring contribution behind the scenes cannot be over-stated. His work with the younger players was later well maintained by Liam Brady, one of the most skilful players ever to wear the Arsenal shirt.

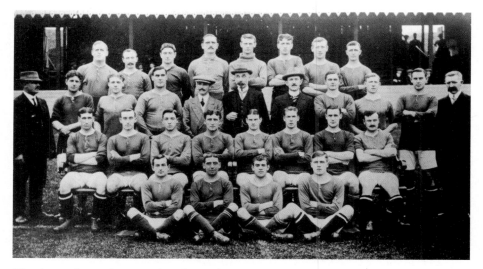

The Arsenal squad pictured at the Manor Ground in 1912 when the club was still called 'Woolwich Arsenal'. The move to Highbury came in the following year.

Herbert Chapman: the man who more than any other established Arsenal's fame through his team-building, trophy-winning and numerous innovations both on and off the field.

The famous early1930s team built by Herbert Chapman. Back row (left to right):
Parker, Jones, Moss, Roberts, John, Black.  Front row (left to right): Herbert Chapman,
Hulme, Jack, Lambert, James, Bastin, Tom Whittaker (trainer).

Alex James: midfield conductor
of the highly successful team of
the 1930s. Arguably the finest
inside forward in the years
between the wars.

Ted Drake: phenomenal goalscorer in the 1930s. He got 42 in his first full season at Highbury, including seven hat-tricks.

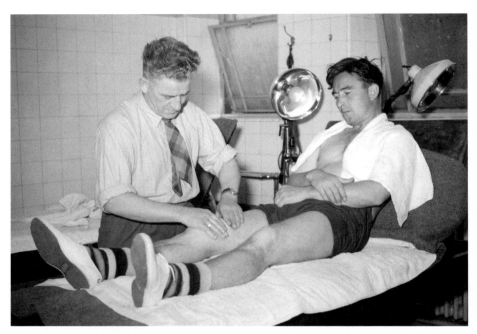

The finest of all the footballer-cricketers, Denis Compton, being treated for a persistent knee injury by physio Jack Milne in 1947.

Outstanding captain Joe Mercer holding the 1950 FA Cup (others, left to right: Wally Barnes, George Swindin, Laurie Scott, Alex Forbes, Leslie Compton, Jimmy Logie.

Tom Whittaker: relentlessly hard-working and successful manager between 1947 and 1956, in which period Arsenal were twice champions.

Manchester United's Mark Jones (foreground) and, on the right, the immensely powerful and gifted Duncan Edwards playing at Highbury on the Saturday before the 1958 Munich air disaster. Both players perished.

George Eastham stands in the famous marble hall. Eastham's passing and ball-mastery during the 1960s shone through one of the bleaker periods in Arsenal's history.

Physiotherapist turned manager, Bertie Mee shrewdly guided the team to the club's first Double in 1970-71.

Charlie George: the fans' favourite. Goalscorer, creator, character and for years the spirit of Arsenal. Here, in 1973, he challenges Manchester United's Martin Buchan.

A goal for history. In the last match of the 1988-89 season Michael Thomas scores Arsenal's second at Anfield to stop Liverpool taking the Championship and win it themselves. Liverpool only needed to avoid defeat by two goals to secure the title.

Liam Brady: one of the best in a long line of Arsenal's creative inside forwards.
He went on to prove his ability and surprising resilience by establishing himself
with Juventus.

George Graham with the European Cup Winners' Cup in 1994. The Arsenal player with a touch of gold became the club's manager of steel resolve. Under him, the teams of the late 1980s and 1990s were taught that medals were not won by being generous to opponents.

Quite how Paul Merson managed to burn the candle at both ends but remain a flaming nuisance to almost every defender who ever tried to snuff out his glorious skills remains a mystery. Here, in 1996, Coventry's former Arsenal man Kevin Richardson tries his luck.

Probably the most popular striker in Arsenal's history, Ian Wright strips off his shirt to reveal another celebrating scoring 179 goals to beat the club record set by Cliff Bastin. Lee Dixon joins the celebration.

Captain Courageous: Tony Adams was the power and guiding influence behind Arsenal's most defiant defence. Here former colleague Emmanuel Petit, playing for Chelsea, gets the ball but Adams gets his man!

David Seaman: a goalkeeper of rare ability and enviable longevity. Remembering his few howlers only serves to emphasise his extraordinary reliability.

Arsene Wenger...the best of
Arsenal's managers?
Whether or not that claim
can be justified, the fact is
he hauled the club into the
modern cosmopolitan era.

A young master of ball
control against a master of
midfield. Here Wayne
Rooney seeks to avoid the
tenacious attention of
Patrick Vieira.

Of all the fine foreign players brought to Arsenal in recent years, Dennis Bergkamp has been the most consistently important in terms of changing the course of matches.

The Arsenal player most feared by opponents everywhere. Thierry Henry's pace, perception and crafted skills on the ball place him amongst the best strikers of any era.

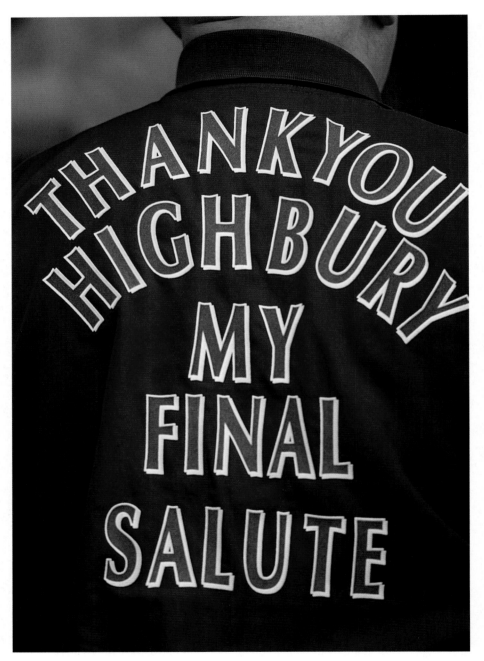

Enough said!

# CHAPTER 29
## ARRIVAL OF THE 'HEADMASTER'

HOUSTON WAS IN CHARGE FOR ONLY A FEW WEEKS because, on leaving Highbury, Bruce Rioch accepted the manager's job at Queen's Park Rangers. Houston joined him. Rice stepped into the breach, aware that the board members were really only biding their time before they could officially appoint Arsene Wenger, who was managing Nagoya Grampus Eight of the developing Japanese League.

Dedicated students of world football knew that this was a coach of consequential talent; a Frenchman who had seen and experienced his home country go to the leading edge of player development. He was an observant talent-spotter. It had been Wenger who had first seen the exciting potential of, for example, George Weah and taken him to Monaco who later decided they could do without the services of the manager who was to take Arsenal into a new era of achievement. For that reason Wenger had gone to Japan, which could well have been a huge mistake but he felt that he needed to extend his experience before being ready to take on one of Europe's leading clubs. The gamble was that going to Japan could have been interpreted by those very clubs as a sign that he lacked ambition.

Among the few British players who knew about Wenger's talents as a coach was Glenn Hoddle, who played for him in Monte Carlo. Hoddle, and others who knew him well, were convinced that Wenger's future was not in Japan.

While with Monaco, Wenger had nourished the growth of splendid young players, including Emmanuel Petit. During his seven years as chief coach there, the club not only won the French title and cup but they never failed to be in the top three, as well as reaching the final of the European Cup Winners' Cup. His short time in Japan was also remarkable because he took Grampus Eight from third bottom to second, and they won the national cup.

Arsenal (or more specifically David Dein) had done their homework and realised that if they appointed Wenger it would not be as if they were gambling on a foreign coach whose knowledge of the game in Britain was inadequate. Wenger had been following English football for years, often attending games at Highbury as well as White Hart Lane. On the other hand, he had never played the game at its highest international level, which, in the eyes of British players, was likely to bring about the usual undermining 'show us your medals' attitude. He had appeared for Strasbourg, Mulhouse, Mutzig and Vauban, clubs that Arsenal's internationals might consider to be on a par with teams from the Conference.

Soon after he arrived at Highbury, he was asked at one of the Friday media conferences whether he had been any good as a player. "I was the best," he said, adding, with his convincing appreciation of English wry humour, "the best in my village." What so many British players always choose to ignore is the fact that some of the best managers of all time have not been highly successful players, and some of the most successful players have failed to become good managers.

The village in which Wenger grew up was Duttlenheim, which had a population of two thousand five hundred. He must have known that he was never going to make the grade at the very top of the international stage but he can claim that as an amateur he appeared in the French Championship for Strasbourg and in a UEFA Cup tie. At the same time, he graduated from Strasbourg University, where he studied English, German, sociology and economics. One summer, he came over to England and, in Cambridge, took a month-long English course. Little did he know that, in the future, he would often be mentioned as an example of a foreign manager whose command of the English language put English managers to shame.

The key to his joining Arsenal (there were other offers) was that when he first met their Vice-Chairman, David Dein, the two got along famously. The club still needed to overcome the shadow of scandal that had led to the dismissal of George Graham, which was a strange affair in view of the fact that Graham was devoted to the club and deeply interested in its history and traditions. In Wenger, Dein must have been confident that Arsenal would be employing a man of reliable integrity and with a reputation for maintaining discipline.

Dein's faith in Wenger was not dislodged by shameless, media-engineered rumours about the club's future manager's private life. Nor was Wenger put off. A lesser man would have abandoned any thoughts of coming to a country where the popular Press could not only end a manager's career but almost destroy him mentally. Bobby Robson and Graham Taylor were but two who suffered abhorrent headline treatment. Wenger and Arsenal's board braved it out. Indeed, at one point, Wenger stood on the steps outside the main entrance at Highbury, faced the media and told them to put up or shut up, only more elegantly. Nobody said a word. He had confirmed what he told them: "I am a strong person and this is a strong club".

Officially his contract with Nagoya Grampus Eight should not have expired until the beginning of 1997, but Arsenal were lurching from problem to problem. At least Ian Wright was in jubilant, scoring form and would later beat Cliff Bastin's club record of one hundred and seventy eight goals, though that achievement should be put in perspective. Bastin's goals had been scored in only two competitions, the League and the FA Cup, while Wright had benefited from many more appearances, including those in the European competitions and the League Cup.

The first public statement about Wenger had come at the club's annual general meeting. It slipped out by accident when Chairman Hill-Wood said he had an understanding with a future manager but that he would not reveal the name. When a member of the audience asked with whom this understanding had been made, the chairman replied "Mr Wenger". Later in the month, Wenger flew over from Japan and was introduced to the media. He made quite an impression. No question was side-stepped. He spoke confidently. He knew about the expectations and potential. He did not need to be reminded that he was inheriting a team growing old. It was clear that he would be arriving with every problem already under consideration. And, refreshingly, he did not resort to cliché-riddled manager-speak.

As far as the players were concerned, the first time they came across him as a group was on the day after he gave his impressive press conference. He was looking ahead to the UEFA Cup game against Borussia Monchengladbach. The first leg at Highbury had resulted in a close 3-2 defeat. For the return in Germany, Wenger said Rice would remain in charge but if he asked for advice it would be offered. With Tony Adams returning after eight months following knee operations, there was a lift in confidence, but the side that went into the game lacked midfield depth and had a strange looking defence that included four natural central defenders: Keown, Linighan, Adams and Bould. At least Wright was still in scoring form and put Arsenal ahead before Juskowiak scored. Merson then hit a terrific twenty-yard shot to bring the aggregate scores level at 4-4. After that Arsenal wilted, as Effenberg and Juskowiak added further goals. At half-time, Wenger had suggested several tactical changes. The team reacted with suspicion. They must have felt that this was an intrusion (Rice was an Arsenal man through and through and this was a 'foreigner' about whom many of the players still knew little more than did the fans). Wenger had spoken about winning over supporters – but first he had to win over the dressing room.

So he took over without much initial respect from players who would get to within close sight of the Championship title. Meanwhile, probably the majority of fans were still wondering who on earth was the man taking over 'their' club's team. Some may have recalled that in Glenn Hoddle's time as England manager Wenger's name had been mentioned when the FA had been searching for a technical director. That job would not have suited him because there would have been too little player contact. Privately, Wenger had said that his time in Japan had made him ready, mentally, to take over as manager of a large club.

He was introduced to the Arsenal fans before a match against Sheffield Wednesday on 16 September, the day Rice had begun his short time directing the team. Wenger was actually still in Japan but appeared in a video recording on Highbury's 'Jumbotron' screens. A large proportion of the fans could hardly hear what he was saying and must have thought: 'This guy looks like my old headmaster'. Some may well have been wondering why, if he was supposed to be so good, he had been managing in Japan. By the time he took over at Highbury on a permanent basis later in September, Arsenal had lost their place in Europe but were doing quite well in the League.

Wenger was convinced that there was a lot wrong with the way most British clubs prepared themselves. In spite of the demanding nature of League football, he was not at all sure that most players were as fit as they ought to be. He was not impressed by the individual technique (ball control) of the average British-born players who, with some exceptions, had long been overtaken by their Continental and South American colleagues. In spite of the European Cup successes of Celtic, Manchester United, Liverpool, Aston Villa and Nottingham Forest, when it came to the World Cup, British-born players were routinely seen to be lacking in technical refinement and individuality. As a result, the moment he arrived to take charge at Arsenal's then modest London Colney training ground, which they rented from University College, London, he insisted that the players would appear in the morning and the afternoon. He felt that would not only improve them on the field but, perhaps, help to keep them away from the perils of booze and gambling.

His decision to retain Pat Rice as coach was crucial. Had he not done so he would have alienated himself from the players almost before he had begun. He quickly worked on their diet, which one recalled as being named 'Rice With Everything'. Some of the older players were more reluctant than the younger ones to accept the new regime without question. After all, they were pretty sure that within a few months they would be on their way, to be replaced by Wenger's own choices. By and large, they were wrong. Wenger greatly appreciated not only their achievements but their experience and team spirit. He actually lengthened their careers at top level. Whether that was his intention before he arrived is another matter.

As for the training ground, he was determined that it would be replaced by something more modern. In the meantime, he decided that while the training itself could continue at the University College grounds, the players would use the much more comfortable (and expensive) facilities of the Sopwell House Hotel, near St Albans, where there was a gymnasium, pool and restaurant. Friday at Sopwell was media day. The regular guests, and local ladies who lunched, looked on bemused as one of the lounges or, in good weather, the patio area, was taken over by journalists and broadcasters for interviews with Wenger and the players.

Early League results that season had been patchy. Wenger took complete charge in October for a match against Blackburn Rovers at Ewood Park. He surprised the players by telling them to go through a routine of pre-match stretching exercises, which in athletics would be normal but for them seemed all too much like being treated as if they were a bunch of ballet dancers. They won 2-0 and, in time, the stretching became an accepted preparation that all of them realised was beneficial. As for new diets, the players only rebelled, light-heartedly, after Wenger suggested that they were eating too much chocolate. On the way back on the coach from that win over Blackburn, a group at the back began to sing "We want our chocolate back"!

League results picked up. Wenger's first significant test was against Manchester United, who over the next few years were to become Arsenal's and his personal relentless rivals. Not that United were in spirited form ahead of the game at Old Trafford in November. Roy Keane was suspended, replaced by a novice David Beckham, and the defence had been looking fragile. There were incidents in this match that, looking back, brought early hints that the relationship between the clubs, and between Wenger and Alex Ferguson in particular, was about to become even more icy than in the past. Ian Wright and the tetchy Peter Schmeichel were involved in a dispute. Wright was booked.

Seaman came under some heavy challenges that ended with rib injuries and the game was decided when he made a poor clearance directly to Nicky Butt who turned the ball across the penalty area. Nigel Winterburn tried to intercept but the ball hit him and deflected into the goal. Wenger brushed the defeat aside with talk of being impressed with the team's positive attitude, and a 3-1 win over Spurs in the following match certainly confirmed his confidence. It also emphasised the influence that Dennis Bergkamp would hold over the coming years. Everything he did in that game exuded the highest class.

Problems then began to multiply. Seaman missed nine League games with his damaged rib and Bergkamp was also injured. Losing in the fourth rounds of both domestic competitions to Liverpool (Coca-Cola Cup) and George Graham's Leeds (FA Cup) did not help. The fans could be excused for wondering whether the schoolmasterly Wenger would be wise enough to turn the season round and bring some consistency behind the scenes. He responded by signing the teenage Nicolas Anelka from Paris Saint-Germain. It was a raid on French talent that soon became familiar. PSG were angry that Arsenal were able to snatch away such a promising young player because he had not yet signed a contract. That Arsenal gave them £500,000 in return, which they were not obliged to do, did little to dispel their fury.

Anelka was only seventeen. Wenger had seen in him what he described as "a rare combination of strength and flexibility allied to tremendous speed off the mark". Even so, Anelka was far from the finished product. He had not even established himself as a regular in the PSG side, although he had appeared alongside Thierry Henry in the French national team that won the European Junior Championship.

The era of large numbers of foreign imports arriving throughout the Premiership was already established. Arsenal had done their research when, on the advice of Wenger even before he became manager, they had approached AC Milan and signed Patrick Vieira, who was to become the main driving force in the successful seasons to come. Wenger had, from the beginning, insisted that although he wanted to see better ball control, he demanded that the team's traditionally hard tacklers be quicker into the challenge. In Vieira, he had a fine example for the rest to follow.

Vieira's first match was on the same day that Wenger was introduced to the home crowd. In that game against Sheffield Wednesday, Arsenal were a goal down at half-time. Vieira then came on for Platt and the game ended with a 4-1 win. He had won over the crowd in only 45 minutes, and those minutes certainly paved the way for Wenger's arrival. Vieira was to be his commander-in-chief on the field.

Emmanuel Petit, predictably captured by Wenger from his old club Monaco, was another success. Gradually the 'Headmaster' was importing the nucleus of the French World Cup squad, while insisting that he wanted to keep the hardened backbone of home-born players. Gilles Grimandi and the experienced Dutch international Marc Overmars (who was a gamble because he had been badly injured) also boosted the group. And later they kept coming: Luis Boa Morte, Alberto Mendez, Alex Manninger, Christopher Wreh and even an English-born player, Matthew Upson! If the fans began to think that they would soon be watching an all-new Continental team, that impression was furthered when Wenger allowed the immensely popular Paul Merson to go to Middlesbrough.

Wenger's first season showed him that Highbury was no fortress that would afford automatic advantage. All of the leading contenders for the Premiership title won there, including the eventual champions, Manchester United. But there were some satisfying moments, including a late season 3-0 win over Chelsea at Stamford Bridge, but much of the term brought dull performances that did not greatly enhance the reputations of the newcomers from abroad. However, the season ended with the club better placed than had been anticipated after the poor start. In fact, they narrowly missed finishing second to Manchester United, which would have provided a European Champions' League place, if it had not been for a draw with Blackburn Rovers, who were accused of unsporting behaviour.

When, towards the end of the game, an Arsenal player was injured Rovers kicked the ball into touch. When play was resumed Blackburn threw the ball towards an Arsenal player, Nigel Winterburn, as is the convention, but Chris Sutton intercepted and won a corner from which Blackburn equalised. Wenger was livid. In a future Cup game, the situation was reversed, although Arsenal did the gentlemanly thing and offered a replay.

Even in Wenger's initial season, there was some evidence that he was not going to sit back and allow Alex Ferguson to take any advantages in the psychological war of words that was to continue for years. Ferguson was concerned that in attempting to win both the Championship and European Cup, the demands of the League fixtures would threaten his team's chances. He asked that the season be extended. Wenger reacted by saying: "It's wrong for the programme to be extended so that Manchester United can rest and win everything". Ferguson fired back with a reply that probably instigated their long-running antagonism: "He's a novice and should keep his opinions to Japanese football". From then on battle lines were drawn. At the same time, Wenger was already being accused of overlooking poor discipline on the field. At one point in the season, his players were shown four red cards in only eight games.

Training at London Colney was more demanding than ever before and Wenger was not going to tolerate excuses. The players were not at all happy about being asked to return for afternoon sessions and probably thought they had won that battle when he decided to abandon the idea. Then it dawned on them that all he had done was extend the length of the morning ones. His ideas about training took some of the players by surprise. They had been brought up in the belief that competitive four or five-a-sides formed the basis. Seaman recalled that not long after Wenger arrived, the manager was supervising one such match and blew his whistle with the score 2-2. His view was that the players had done enough of that and should move on to some other more specialised work. Several told him they couldn't stop without a winning goal. Wenger told them that these competitions had to be timed as part of the overall structure of training. Liverpool's Bill Shankly would have been horrified. In his day, five-a-side matches never ended until the team for which he was playing had won.

When Wenger arrived, he viewed the University College training ground as somewhere he would not tolerate for long. Later (1999) the new, ultra-modern centre was opened and was state of the art. Apart from treatment rooms, gymnasium etc it also contained a high quality restaurant where Wenger could keep an eye on the players' diet. On the other hand, the traditional Friday media meeting soon began to eat more deeply into the journalists' own lunchtime. Unlike other managers, Wenger would always appear, though not necessarily at the arranged time. His priority was with the players. After that, he would be tireless in his determination to satisfy everyone, with separate conferences for daily papers, Sunday papers, national radio, national television and local media. In addition,c there was also the Club Call to be recorded.

*In my experience* (the author recalls), *he never complained about committing himself to those duties which he carried out with good humour and always a shrewd sense of publicity. He knew exactly what headlines he wanted and what we wanted as well. In later years, his on-going spat with Alex Ferguson did give his talks a more bitter edge, but on all other occasions he remained remarkably level-headed. Not only that, his English was faultless. Quotes from most English managers usually required translating! In spite of his amiable attitude towards journalists, it has always been on his terms and he never crosses the dividing line between a professional relationship and becoming chummy.*

As for the players, they were to discover that he was also pretty good as a psychologist. Whereas those who had worked with George Graham would regularly have been blasted with criticism, Wenger was much more sparing, believing that over-use falls on deaf ears.

Everybody soon realised that Wenger was going to be absolutely dedicated to his work and prepared to put in as many hours as it took. However, his privacy remained absolute. He moved into a pleasant but hardly 'Footballers' Wives' house to the north of London where he lives with his partner of many years, Annie, and daughter, Lea. Clearly, he would rather spend what little spare time he has with his family and watching football videos than going out on the town.

# CHAPTER 30
# THE DOUBLE AGAIN

## 1997-98 BERGKAMP – THE MASTER

APPROACHING THE 1997-98 SEASON, Wenger's squad looked much more cosmopolitan. Change had been essential. The old squad had begun to creak. Wenger was particularly pleased to get Overmars from Ajax and looked to him to give more power and positive finishing, especially in matches at Highbury where the team had not performed as well as they had away. At his pre-season media conference, he managed to make a virtue out of failure in the 1996-97 cup competitions by saying that the squad had not been big enough to send out strong teams every three days. This season, he would have no such excuses, especially as he now had some first hand experience of managing in England.

All seemed well, except for the fact that Adams was injured and missed several of the early games and there were slight doubts about whether a strike-force of Bergkamp and Wright would be sufficient – Overmars was not a renowned goalscorer. However, in an early-season match against Southampton, who did good work in frustrating the two most reliable goalscorers, Overmars did get a goal and Bergkamp seemed to take that as some sort of challenge, adding two more. Bergkamp continued to mesmerise opposing defences and his hat-trick against Leicester City, who nevertheless drew 3-3, was described by Martin O'Neill as the best he had ever seen. Berkgamp's left-foot drive for one of the goals was the highlight of his personal season and, in October, another of his goals took Arsenal to the top of the table (a position they could not retain). In the meantime, Wright was still searching for the club record for a goalscorer and it was clearly beginning to annoy him that it was slow in coming.

The subject of the future of Highbury continued to be raised. The Chairman now made no secret of the fact that the club was looking for possible sites in order that they could consider a move in about five years. For the time being, he said, they were very happy with their existing home, which had cost a considerable fortune in up-grading.

The UEFA Cup place was soon lost to PAOK Salonika, who did not have to face Bergkamp on their own ground. At the same time, Wenger did not seem to know his own mind about his preferred formation, often changing from three central defenders to two and back again while, somewhat confusingly, saying that 4-4-2 was the accepted style of world football.

For the game against PAOK in Athens, Wenger had decided to play the youthful Anelka with Wright up front. Wright found it difficult to strike up an understanding and, in any case, without Bergkamp's shrewd passing he was left with little in the way of provisions that he could turn to goals. PAOK won 1-0 and a large part of the criticism for Arsenal's performance fell on the shoulders of Wright, who had been such a favourite but was now tending to have too many days on which he forfeited possession. In reality, what Arsenal needed when Bergkamp was absent was a player of Paul Merson's ability, but Wenger had let him go too soon.

Despite problems over finding the right strike partnership, the pursuit of Manchester United was maintained. Bergkamp's brilliance was the prime reason. His competitive attitude was higher than ever, which accounted for a spate of cautions. For one day, however, he was completely upstaged by the declining but still ebullient Ian Wright, who at last was able to lift his shirt and reveal a T-shirt emblazoned with '179 Just done it'. Not only did he break Bastin's record but he did it in style with a hat-trick against Bolton Wanderers, at Highbury of course. The record-breaking goal itself was a mere tap in from a couple of yards but the crowd treated it as if he had scored the most exquisite goal in all of Arsenal's history. A few years later, Thierry Henry remarked: "For me, Ian Wright was a legend and still is a legend, and for me to beat his record would be amazing". Bergkamp added: "Ian was an out and out goalscorer who could score goals out of situations that even I thought were impossible.".

Probably the day on which Bergkamp was proclaimed the new king of Highbury was also the very one on which Wright was honoured for his goalscoring record. Wright was presented with a silver cannon. The Highbury crowd roared his name but, when the match against West Ham was over, they realised that while Wright at his peak was an instinctive and remarkable goalscorer, Bergkamp was now a master of many more things. Arsenal won 4-0 and Bergkamp was magnificent as the mastermind.

For the return against PAOK at Highbury, there was doubt about the fitness of Overmars. However, Bergkamp gracefully ran through the PAOK defence and scored but PAOK responded strongly and a poor clearance by Seaman led to Vrizas nipping past Adams and knocking Arsenal out of the competition. The challenge of Europe had again been too much, and it was not as if they had been up against one of the more illustrious sides.

There was now a nagging worry that Arsenal were over-reliant on Bergkamp and, to a lesser extent, Overmars, who missed three successive League games in which the team failed to score. When Bergkamp was then suspended for three matches there was even talk of a 'crisis'. Some of the new players were clearly not ready to take regular places. Christopher Wreh did not look capable of developing into a high class player and Anelka was still a boy in a man's shirt, which was not surprising since he had been plucked out of a totally different environment. On the other hand, his potential was enormous. He scored his debut first-team goal against Manchester United in a psychologically important 3-2 win over the champions at Highbury. It came from a shot sent in at speed from just outside the penalty area. Peter Schmeichel, in the United goal, was astounded. It also upstaged an excellent headed goal by David Platt whose time at Arsenal only occasionally raised the old rafters.

The ever-expanding authority of Vieira was a substantial plus. When he was left on the bench for a home game against Blackburn Rovers, the team had little real power in midfield and, to make matters worse, Adams was never a match for Chris Sutton. Blackburn won 3-1. Rovers had decided in advance that they would counter power and speed with power and speed. It worked and other clubs took notice. Four defeats were suffered in six mid-season matches. The defence had become brittle. The whole situation displeased the older established players who discussed it with Wenger, making it perfectly clear that they were fed up with 'carrying' several of the foreign imports who, they said, were not closing down attacking players in midfield. Even Bergkamp was criticised.

The foreign players could have pointed out that Adams, upon whom so much had depended in the past, had on-going injuries and was not quite the battling, English-style captain of the past. Sadly, Wright was past his sell-by date, and the departure of Platt was widely rumoured. Wenger took notice and stiffened the midfield area by having Vieira and Petit take more defensive responsibility while insisting that if Vieira did go forward, Petit had to cover the vacant space.

In the second half of the season, the team's spirit improved, but performances often lagged behind. In fact, they were lucky not to get knocked out of the FA Cup in the third round by Port Vale who took them to a replay, extra-time and penalties. There was a far better show in the fourth round against Middlesbrough, for whom Merson transparently wanted to show how wrong Wenger had been to release him. He scored after an hour but, by then, Arsenal had already taken a two-goal lead and won fairly comfortably, even without the services of Wright and Seaman.

By this time, George Graham was established at Leeds. When he brought them to Highbury early in 1998 he saw Overmars snatch two match-winning goals. Afterwards, Graham made several pointed and semi-serious comments about Arsenal not playing to their full potential, not just in this game but in the League as a whole. Wenger took it in good part and mentioned that he would like to do as well in his career at Highbury as Graham had in his.

The semi-final of the Coca-Cola Cup was reached. In the first leg against Chelsea at Highbury Overmars and Stephen Hughes scored and Adams looked revived physically and mentally. The second leg was much different. The midfield players lost concentration and Chelsea won 3-1. So there would not be a Treble this season, but at least the League title was still in sight, partly because Manchester United suffered an unlikely home defeat by Leicester City that seemed to put doubts in their minds about holding on to the lead and the title.

The journey through to the Cup Final was tiring. In the fifth round Crystal Palace took Arsenal to a replay in which Bergkamp and Anelka scored. If United were under pressure, it was also growing on Arsenal who then had to take on West Ham in another replay. As predicted, the Hammers, who had held them to a 0-0 draw in the League in March, were in a good vein of form and Arsenal seemed to have lost their opportunity when Bergkamp was sent off after he elbowed Steve Lomas. Indisputably, Bergkamp was one of the most accomplished of post-war players (too often at the expense of England in international matches) yet his studious nature has never precluded him from engaging in the more abrasive aspects of the game. Anelka grabbed a goal. John Hartson equalised and the game moved on to penalties. After five kicks, the teams were still deadlocked.

Captain Adams, who had never liked taking spot kicks, had no choice but to put himself forward for the next one. Naturally, the home crowd, who can be uncomfortably personal at Upton Park, made the expected 'donkey' noises. Adams held his nerve and almost tapped the ball in. Abou went forward for West Ham and within seconds was in misery having not found the goal but the post. At this time, the gap between Arsenal and Manchester United in the League had been reduced to nine points and Arsenal had three games in hand.

Of greater significance than the Cup victories was a successful March visit to Old Trafford in the League. United were having a strenuous season trying to maintain their Championship position at home and, at the same time, playing in the Champions' League, in which they had reached the quarter-final round. On top of that, on the day of the game against Arsenal they were unable to include the in-form but now injured Ryan Giggs. In spite of the pressure upon them, United put up a defiant display but Overmars played superbly (he had slowly but surely won over the doubters). He linked with Anelka who provided him with the pass that led to the only goal. Arsenal were 'go'for the Double. A key factor was that Alex Manninger had proved such an able deputy for the absent Seaman.

Two typically mean 1-0 League wins over Sheffield Wednesday and Bolton maintained the League momentum and improved confidence in the run up to the FA Cup semi-final, which was against Wolverhampton Wanderers at Villa Park. They made easy work of what is always a psychologically demanding game. Chris Wreh put them ahead after only twelve minutes and they remained in command for the rest of the match. The ability to take a goal lead and retain it for as long as necessary had become a trademark, although in this game Wolves were markedly inferior.

The next Cup opponents would be Newcastle United at Wembley but, before, that there was a dress rehearsal when Newcastle went to Highbury and lost 3-1. The main cause of their defeat had been an inability to control Anelka who was beginning to look a special player. Arsenal's self-esteem was increased when Bergkamp was released from suspension. Blackburn Rovers may well have thought that having done well at Highbury earlier in the season they would be able to control Arsenal at home. They were wrong. Arsenal wanted revenge. In less than two minutes, Bergkamp blasted in a devastating shot. Before the game had reached fifteen minutes, Parlour had scored two more.

By half-time, Parlour had made the score 4-0 and it finished 4-1. This was one of those matches in which Parlour showed his worth. His tireless running, sound tackling and reliable passing had always impressed Wenger and ensured that the Englishman retained his place even under competition from the foreign legion. Indeed, it could be argued that when, eventually, Wenger let him go, the team never quite got over the loss of his industry.

Now Arsenal were on a run. Wimbledon were thrashed 5-0 (Petit got his first goal). The timing of the big wins was perfect because Manchester United were dropping points. Arsenal had their heads in front. Of the five remaining games, they had to win three. Barnsley, dangerous because they were battling against relegation, were defeated on their own ground after Bergkamp bent a wonderful shot inches inside the post. Overmars finished the job following an inviting pass from Platt. The satisfied squad travelled home knowing that they only needed two more wins to secure the title and perhaps go on to win the Double.

Derby were next up at Highbury and they were in a foul mood, having just lost to Leicester City by 4-0. Memorably, their manager, Jim Smith, walked into their dressing room after that embarrassment and said he was seriously thinking about putting them all on the transfer list. The 'Bald Eagle' may have been flying a kite but he was extremely angry. Arsenal found them hard to break down but Petit got another goal. Suddenly the whole team believed that the Championship was there for the taking, even Bergkamp (the PFA Player of the Year) who knew he would miss the crucial games because he had pulled a hamstring. Only Everton to beat in the last home game of the season! It was a match that turned into a huge celebration.

Adams said that it was a game they just could not lose. There was no way that they would be left still needing a win away from home at Liverpool or Villa in the last two matches. Cheekily he told the still concerned Wenger that if he didn't understand why he (Adams) was so confident he had not yet understood that "we don't get into these positions to let it slip". Adams was right. Arsenal were greatly favoured when, early on, Everton's Slaven Bilic conceded an own goal. That put their minds at ease. Overmars scored two more. Now full of confidence, Adams saw that substitute Steve Bould had moved forward into midfield, found him with an accurate pass and kept on running. Bould then returned the ball to Adams who took the weight off the pass before hitting in a splendid and well deserved goal. He said that, after the final whistle, he walked round the pitch savouring the moment and drinking in the atmosphere rather than the alcohol he had consumed after winning the Championships of 1989 and 1991.

Even Sir Alex Ferguson gave Arsenal credit, saying that only a special team could have strung together ten successive victories in the run-in to the title. Seemingly, he had come full circle from the time when he said Wenger was a novice who knew nothing about English football. "He deserves immense credit for integrating his English and foreign players into such a cohesive, powerful and highly motivated unit". High praise indeed from a manager who usually begrudges every moment that an opposing side is in possession, let alone taking the Championship trophy out of his hands. Wenger had become the first foreign manager to grasp that prize.

The second Double in the club's history was within their reach. Forgivably, the two remaining League games were not taken too seriously and both were lost. For the Cup Final against Newcastle, the only part of the team about which, at first, there seemed some debate was up front. Wright had recovered from injury and was available. Then, on the Friday, Bergkamp, whom everyone had thought would be available after his hamstring injury, tweaked it again in training and was ruled out.

Wenger, who seemed less confident about the Final outcome than most of the players (his talk on the morning of the game was little more than a team announcement, totally ignoring any mention of Newcastle) chose Anelka and Wreh as the strikers. Overmars and Parlour, the wide players in midfield, were always quick to go forward to provide the attackers with service, but Overmars was also willing and able to cut inside and show everyone just how good he could be as another goalscorer.

That Saturday afternoon at Wembley was blazing hot and some players were probably thinking about conserving energy. Arsenal began poorly, lacking the organisation that had become the main feature of the second part of their season. Then they got into their formidably rapid stride. Petit slid through a good forward pass and the speeding Overmars took the ball under his control. He comfortably beat Shay Given. Alan Shearer looked appalled. Early in the second half, however, he was given his first serious chance and hit the post. He was soon to regret that. Parlour, as ever, was full of energy and sent an easily controlled pass to Anelka who ran on and blasted a shot past Given. Parlour kept running to congratulate Anelka but few others had the energy left to do the same. Or was it, perhaps, a lack of inclination to give the controversial goalscorer his deserved praise?

### FA CUP FINAL
(16 May 1998, Wembley)

**Arsenal 2** (Overmars, Anelka) **Newcastle United 0**

*Arsenal:* Seaman; Dixon, Adams, Keown, Winterburn, Parlour, Viera, Petit, Overmars, Anelka, Wreh (Platt, 62).

*Newcastle United:* Given; Pistone, Dabizas, Howey, Pearce (Andersson, 73), Barton (Watson, 76), Lee, Batty, Speed, Shearer, Ketsbaia (Barnes, 86).

*Referee: P. Durkin.*

The enigma of Anelka would follow him throughout his career in English football until he left Manchester City in 2005 to join Fenerbahce, of Turkey, for £7m. From Arsenal's point of view, he may not have fully entered into the spirit of the team, which was all important, but he did score some important goals and his departure to Real Madrid in the 1999-00 season for £23m was good business since he had been bought from Paris Saint-Germain for a fraction of that.

His move to Spain highlighted the problems a club can face when a player under contract is determined to get away and is assisted by a stubborn agent (in Anelka's case, his brother Claude). Arsenal had complained to UEFA that they believed Real had made an illegal approach while they were in legitimate consultation with Lazio. Claude was determined that his brother would go to Real. The situation remained unresolved until Lazio finally withdrew their offer. Madrid made a formal approach and signed Anelka on a seven-year contract. David Dein was furious that players and their agents could choose to ignore contracts. That has become a fact of football life and the spectre would re-appear.

On the weekend of the Cup Final victory, north London (south of White Hart Lane) became a huge party. Wenger had now been fully accepted by the fans as being the remarkable coach that he was even before arriving at Highbury. At the same time, the players had grown to respect as well as like him. In a way, though, the success was also down to the fact that he was prepared to listen to what they had to say. After all, having never been a player of their standard, he had to work especially hard to win their admiration. Crucially, he had taken into his thinking the views of the experienced defenders Adams, Bould and Keown when, in the middle of the winter of that Double season, they told him that the team badly needed to tighten up.

Considering the exacting excitement of the Double season and other factors, it was probably inevitable that the 1998-99 season should be an anti-climax in terms of silverware. The only trophy that came Arsenal's way was the Charity Shield, which was taken with a 3-0 win over Manchester United. Several of the squad (particularly the victorious French) had been fully involved in the summer's World Cup finals. Ian Wright had transferred to West Ham and David Platt retired. The close season had not seen Wenger make many moves in the transfer market (Nelson Vivas came from Lugano and David Grondin from St. Etienne) and it was obvious that the loss of such a goalscoring master as Wright needed to be considered. Wreh had been doing moderately well but there were still some doubts about his consistency. A goalscoring midfield player would fit the bill. Later in the season he arrived in the pugnacious shape of Freddie Ljungberg, a Swedish international from Halmstad.

The League season was not by any means unexciting because the team challenged Manchester United throughout. Simply, it was all comparative after the Double. Even on the last day of the season, there was a chance that the title could be retained. Arsenal needed a win over Aston Villa at Highbury while, at the same time, hoping that Spurs would do the unthinkable and give them assistance by at least drawing with United at Old Trafford. When news came though to Highbury that Les Ferdinand had taken Spurs into the lead, the Arsenal fans were faced with a dilemma: cheer a Tottenham player or just be thankful, in silence. The cheers won but United fought back with goals from David Beckham and the former Arsenal player Andy Cole.

Throughout Wenger's time at Highbury, one frustration continually challenged all of the outstanding achievements. Arsenal could not reproduce the quality of their domestic football in major European competition. Partly with that in mind, Wenger was keen to obtain the young (22) but experienced former Ajax player Nwankwo Kanu, who had been playing with Internazionale without really being appreciated. Kanu had endured a heart valve operation, which had cost him many matches, yet Inter were reluctant to permit his release.

Eventually Kanu arrived at Highbury in the middle of the season and, though often being used as a substitute (Wenger was keen not to rush him), soon started scoring brilliant goals, which helped make up for the fact that the team's disciplinary record became poor and costly. Injuries are not usually avoidable; suspensions ought to be. Wenger was criticised for failing to do more in the way of curbing some ugly, rash and self-defeating tackling.

The European Cup offered a chance to prove that Arsenal were a match for anyone. They made a controversial decision to play their home matches at Wembley. It was clear that many more fans than could be accommodated at Highbury would want to see the games. There was also the feeling that the club needed that fact to be made absolutely obvious so that when the final decision was made to leave Highbury, there would be plenty of evidence to support what would be an historic and not unanimously popular move. Proving that Arsenal had outgrown their old home was essential.

The club emphasised the limitations that Highbury imposed on them, including the loss of seating in the front rows because European regulations dictated the size of advertising boards. That did not seem to be such a formidable obstacle to dozens of other clubs in European competition with comparatively small grounds. By returning to Highbury for European matches in 2000, the club seemed to see the logic of the argument that home advantage is only as good as the home in which you play and the atmosphere it creates.

What the club did not seem to realise, or simply did not want to accept when they made the decision to play at Wembley, was that this world-famous stadium had not been a comfortable or continuously advantageous home for England (their 1966 victory was an exception). More often than not, the atmosphere was subdued by the fact that the pitch was too far from the spectators. Rarely was there a feeling that the 'visitors' were setting foot on the celebrated turf full of trepidation. Ferenc Puskas and his wonderful Hungarians had changed all that back in 1953. Every visiting player not only wanted to go home and boast that he had played at Wembley but needed to be seen to have a good game.

It would be absurd to suggest that the difficulty of creating a club-like atmosphere at Wembley led to Arsenal's failure to overcome the European challenge, but it did not help. Not only that, away from Britain they began their adventure with a sometimes fluent but too often careless 1-1 performance against Lens, wasting a large number of goalscoring opportunities. The experienced Panathinaikos were beaten by goals from defenders Adams and Keown at Wembley but, on the same pitch, Dynamo Kiev were – predictably in view of their pedigree – altogether more skilful and got a draw. Bergkamp had managed to glance in a cross from Dixon. In the last minute, Rebrov equalised from what looked like an offside position. Considering that Vieira and Petit were both suspended, it could be claimed that Arsenal had done reasonably well to draw but, in reality, they were outplayed all over the pitch. Andrei Shevchenko was particularly impressive, leading from the front but combining strength with subtle touches.

The team Arsenal sent to Kiev was far from their strongest. Bergkamp, as almost always in subsequent years, was left at home because of his hatred of flying (what this has cost Arsenal over his time with them is incalculable). Adams, Anelka and Overmars were out injured. The attack was demonstrably weak. Worse was to come when Bould suffered a hamstring injury. Arsenal lost 3-1 and knew they had to beat Lens at Wembley.

Bergkamp and Vieira were out and Petit serving a suspension. Adams could manage only half the game. The squad did not have the depth of quality to survive. Mickael Debeve scored the only goal (from an offside position, but the linesman failed to notice). In their frustration Parlour and Dixon were sent off for kicking an opponent and feigning injury respectively and Arsenal played the formality of their last game against Panathinaikos without several of their regular first team players but won 3-1. Wenger said that going out of the competition at the early stage really hurt.

The domestic season was a combination of some fine performances, usually masterminded by Bergkamp, and disappointing ones. In fact, the term was memorable because another team in red won the Championship, the FA Cup and the European Cup ... Manchester United, of course. Much is made of the distant relationship between Wenger and Sir Alex Ferguson. On this occasion, Wenger had to concede that United, who had to go through a qualifying round of the European Cup, were outstanding.

Arsenal never gave up their fight to stay up with United in the League and the FA Cup (they lost to United in the semi-final), but Alex Ferguson had been stung by Arsenal's achievements of the previous season and was absolutely determined to see his team compensate. To some extent, he was helped by the fact that Arsenal's French contingent had begun the season so soon after the World Cup. There was an element of tiredness; also, possibly, a questioning of whether they had much else to achieve – the Double at home and a World Cup Final win over Brazil in France was enough to keep them in football's Hall of Fame for all time.

The matches of the season and the ones of lasting significance were the FA Cup semi-final clashes with United. The first meeting at Villa Park went to extra-time and remained goalless. Three days later came the replay in which David Beckham scored first and Bergkamp equalised after seventy minutes. Once the always influential Roy Keane had been sent off, United found themselves pressed further and further back. Yet Arsenal could not create the crucial opening. Then Phil Neville gave away a penalty. Bergkamp, bravely and riskily, took responsibility against the formidable Peter Schmeichel, who anticipated the side to which Bergkamp would aim and was right. It was the third penalty of the season that Bergkamp had missed. Extra-time. Arsenal still had the 'advantage' of the extra man, but how many times do we see the team with ten men put in outstanding effort or even appear to use the additional space to good effect?

In the final quarter of an hour Vieira, of all people, turned the ball across midfield without an Arsenal player as his target. Ryan Giggs moved in, collected the gift, ran on and sent a shot over the head of David Seaman, who, despite countless game-saving performances, did occasionally and famously seem vulnerable to just that sort of speculation. United were enormously lifted by their performance and remained unbeaten for the rest of the season.

Wenger did a good job of maintaining a forward-looking approach to Arsenal's own remaining matches. Indeed, the last few games still had them shadowing United. A 3-1 win at White Hart Lane certainly helped but points dropped at Leeds were damaging since they put United back in the driving position. United ended the season requiring a win over Spurs at White Hart Lane to take the title back to Old Trafford and did it. Then, after beating Newcastle in the FA Cup Final, they won 2-1 against Bayern Munich in the Final of the European Cup to achieve an extraordinary Triple. Not only that, they regained the high ground over Arsenal. That, amongst several other things, was another of the roots of the psychological battle between Ferguson and Wenger. Even so, only one point divided them in the Premiership.

As for Arsenal's FA Cup adventure of that season, it will long be remembered not for what it achieved but for the club's example of sportsmanship when in the fifth round in February at Highbury, they beat Sheffield United 2-1 but David Dein and Arsene Wenger's offer to have the game replayed was accepted*. Both would have taken into account the fact that, on the field, Arsenal had a poor reputation for discipline and that Alex Ferguson had aggravated the situation by saying: "The number of fights involving Arsenal is more than Wimbledon in their heyday". He later sent a letter of apology to Wenger in which he claimed that he had been "stitched up" by reporters (his suggestion being that what he said was off the record). One of the reporters present quickly responded, saying that what was written was verbatim. The controversy raged on with Wenger saying he had not received the letter ("if he sent it it must have been by horse"). It has to be said that if over the years Ferguson has seemed to have a persecution complex about his players either being falsely accused of being dirty, unsporting losers and victimised by referees, Wenger has often run him close.

*See page 247 for a more detailed account of the voluntarily replayed match

# CHAPTER 31
# A MOMENTOUS SIGNING

T HE RUEFUL EXPERIENCE OF THE EUROPEAN CHAMPIONS' League in 1998-99 emphasised to Wenger that he urgently needed to improve the club's playing resources. In the summer of 1999, he looked to use the considerable amount of money the club had gained from the sale of Anelka. His main target was Thierry Henry, who was with Juventus. First, though, he bought the Croatian international Davor Suker, who had been having a lean time at Real Madrid after a career that had blossomed at Sevilla, where he scored seventy-five goals in one hundred and forty five appearances, and was revived during the World Cup in France in 1998. In hindsight, Suker proved to be one of Wenger's few mistakes, starting his Arsenal career promisingly and scoring just enough spectacular goals to make the club and fans want more but not providing them. Unsurprisingly, he was later moved on to West Ham.

There is no doubt that Henry was a momentous signing – perhaps even the best by any Arsenal manager since Chapman bought Alex James. Henry had been taught his football at the French national school of excellence at Clairefontaine. In 1994, when only seventeen, he made his debut for Monaco. At the same time, Wenger was about to leave the club. When Jean Tigana took over, Henry was played as a winger and it was in that position that he was first noticed by British fans, who saw him linking with David Trezeguet when Monaco dismissed Manchester United at the quarter-final stage of the European Cup of 1998. Monaco went on to play Juventus in the semi-final and though the Italians won, they later signed both players. By the time Henry went to Italy he already had World Cup finals experience, having that summer helped France to win the title by scoring three goals yet not appearing in the final.

Henry's move to Juventus was fraught with problems. He was played in deep midfield and not given the freedom to attack from a wide position, which was what he wanted to do. Wenger had been monitoring the situation and, as soon as Juventus began talking about loaning Henry to Udinese, he pounced. He was delighted to spend £8.5 million of Arsenal's money to reclaim a player he had long recognised as a special talent.

The only problem for Henry was that he had no confidence that he could be an out-and-out striker, which was what Wenger insisted he should become. "I was surprised" Henry said. "The idea seemed a bit much to me". It was another example of Wenger knowing more about a player's potential than the player knew himself. Wenger wanted somebody who would prove to the fans that the club had a player who could be as good a finisher as Ian Wright. He had got the man, although it took some time and rough treatment on the training ground to get Henry ready for English football. Henry himself recalled that Martin Keown was particularly hard on him. Without such an introduction to what he was likely to face every week, he would probably have been unnerved as soon as he faced a typically bone-hard group of defenders from an opposing club.

There was always the feeling that Arsenal's rugged, familiar, loyal and still effective defenders would decline at the same time. Wenger knew that only too well and made attempts to insure against it happening by getting Dynamo Kiev's Oleg Luzhny, who was the captain of the Ukraine, which has produced many capable players. And Corinthians, of Brazil, were not happy about losing Silvinho, but they needed the money.

Charity Shield matches can never be trusted as safe indicators of a season ahead and the one against Manchester United at the opening of the 1999-2000 term was no exception. Arsenal were in trouble. Adams, Bergkamp, Overmars and Seaman were all unavailable. United dominated the early part of the game. Beckham hit a sweet free-kick that smacked the crossbar and, seemingly, went in. The referee said the ball had not crossed the line, so Dwight Yorke made sure it did. Wenger then decided to replace Silvinho with Boa Morte and move Ljungberg to the left side. There was an almost instant change in the balance of the game. The United defence came under pressure. The wily Irwin tried to pull down Vieira but this time the referee had a good view, awarding a penalty, which Kanu put away. Kanu, now raised in confidence, then played a match-winning pass to sturdy, reliable Parlour who scored the winner. In light of the Premiership season to follow, United were right not to take the outcome too seriously. Naturally, the post-match press-conference was more to do with Wenger's announcement that Anelka had been sold to Real Madrid than the game itself.

As a result of the early stages of the 1999-2000 European Champions' League being expanded, Arsenal got in. They were soon eliminated, though at least this allowed them to move into the UEFA Cup. That could have been interpreted as consolation, and certainly they took advantage of the opportunity by reaching the final, but their second successive failure to impress in the senior competition was far more important. In the first group stage, they came up against Sweden's AIK Stockholm, Italy's famous Fiorentina and Spain's eminent Barcelona. Unfortunately, they made a mess of things, although the clubs in the other groups would not have envied them their task.

Wenger had not rushed Henry into the first team. So the future king of the Arsenal attack was involved in the early European Cup games only as a substitute. Getting a goalless draw in Florence without the injured Petit was not a bad result yet it should have been better. Fiorentina's confidence had been eroded by an earlier injury to Batistuta (the player Wenger was so keen to sign before the start of the 2005-06 season). Kanu failed to score from the penalty spot in the final minutes. The stuttering team then made hard work of beating AIK at Wembley by 3-1, the last two goals coming from Henry and Suker as late as the 89th and 90th minutes. There was a lot of frustration, not least for Wenger. Increasingly, he was relying on the blossoming of Henry and the solidarity of the well-worn defence.

Then came a visit to the Nou Camp. Formidably, Barcelona included Rivaldo, Figo, and Cocu. Wenger fully appreciated that closing down Rivaldo was essential. Not surprisingly, in the early stages Arsenal struggled, could not get possession and went a goal down to Luis Enrique, Vieira making a hash of clearing. They had been taunted by the Barcelona players who made the antagonistic but plausible claim that their own level of skill was much superior. Annoyed by fouls against them, mainly carried out by the over-aggressive Suker, Barca began to lose the thread. Then, though, Grimandi was rightly sent off for elbowing. Yet, after 81 minutes, Kanu, who had an impressive match, managed to muscle into the edge of the crowded goal area and push in the equaliser. Even so, several of Arsenal's more experienced players had failed to prove that they could play with much confidence against the best in Europe.

Back at Wembley for the return visit of Barcelona, the mistake of moving European games away from Highbury was re-emphasised. Not only that, the run-up to the game was not helped by quotes in a Sunday paper from Overmars suggesting that he did not see his long-term future as an Arsenal player.

Whereas on their own home ground Arsenal might have been lifted to heights above the level of their individual skills, at the national stadium and in spite of a supportive crowd (the gate was 73,091), Barcelona swept them aside with a 4-2 win. The Spanish team's 2-0 lead after only sixteen minutes (including a penalty by Rivaldo after Cocu fooled the referee with a dive) made a comeback virtually impossible and Arsenal's organisation failed them. Even Adams was prone to mistakes. Once again, a Continental side showed the value of retaining possession and not charging around the field in energy-wasting pursuit of the impossible.

The result meant that, in theory, Arsenal could still get through provided they finished second by beating Fiorentina, who they met at Wembley at the end of October. Psychologically, Fiorentina should not have been at their best because their manager, Giovanni Trapattoni, had offered his resignation after the previous weekend's defeat by humble Piacenza whereas Arsenal had been to Stamford Bridge and beaten Chelsea with three goals from Kanu. That had been a remarkable game. Chelsea were in combative mood, having put five goals past Galatasaray away in the Champions' League. They were even more inspired when taking a two-goal lead on a rain-soaked pitch. But that surface did them no favours when Kanu slithered the ball in and added another. Then came a memorable winner as Suker moved in from a wide position, played the ball down the line to Kanu who almost lost it to Albert Ferrer but controlled it wonderfully almost on the goalline a yard inside the penalty area before curling in a tantalising shot. Ed de Goey, the Chelsea goalkeeper, was still stranded after his earlier headstrong run out to intercept Kanu, which was a fruitless, foolish task. Kanu's hat-trick ranked alongside Bergkamp's against Leicester in 1997.

Even in the opening minutes of the European game against Fiorentina, at Wembley, it was apparent that the visitors were in an angry mood, which could have played into Arsenal's hands. Instead, the 'home' side failed to capitalise on the opportunities they created and allowed their discipline to be shaken by some of the most ruthless tackling even their most experienced players had ever endured. But the pain was as much mental as physical. Arsenal had done well to squeeze out points away from home. In spite of the best efforts of the fans, playing at Wembley was sometimes like enduring some of the games in a vacuum. Wenger himself admitted it was a mistake that should have been accepted at the end of the previous season's campaign.

A goal by Batistuta after seventy-five minutes left Arsenal back in the European hinterland. Wenger's pre-match remark that they had to establish themselves as one of the top teams in the Champions' League because that was what was "historically missing" from the club's pedigree was a challenge that his players could not take on. Above all, they had failed to combat Batistuta, whose pace stunned Winterburn and allowed him to crash a shot past Seaman. Arsenal were again made to look inadequate.

At least they could now get back into European competition by virtue of the strange, improbable new rules that seemed nothing less than an attempt to offer reward for failure (it could almost have been invented by a British politically correct education minister). Sensibly, they decided that for their UEFA Cup ties, they would return home to Highbury. It would be an exaggeration to claim that going back was the main reason why they had home wins over Nantes (3-0, though actually an indifferent performance), La Coruna (5-1), Werder Bremen (2-0) and Lens (1-0). Certainly it helped but the standards of most of the visiting sides hardly compared with those the club had met in the European Cup itself. Also, they were fortunate to avoid the five Italian clubs.

The final, in Copenhagen, brought them up against Turkey's Galatasaray. No Turkish side had ever before reached a European summit but they had a skilful group of players. However, Arsenal were riding confidently on the back of a good run in the League. Wenger was keen to emphasise the importance of the return of Tony Adams, who confessed that earlier in the season he had come back too soon after a hernia operation and played too many matches before he had fully recovered. Many of the players were keen to praise Adams for the way he had overcome his drinking problems and now seemed a different, nicer man yet with the same intense determination. Adams was one of only three who had played in the side that had won the European Cup Winners' Cup in the same stadium back in 1994. The others were Seaman and Dixon.

It was curious that Adams, in whom Wenger had so much confidence, and Keown, who almost always seemed so reliable, both began the game looking far from comfortable. Bergkamp, who had travelled to the final by boat and road, had to make up for the fact that Petit looked the more jaded of the two. Parlour did manage to hit the post. Keown missed what looked like an open goal but Henry's centre was too quick for a natural defender to turn into an opponent's net. Wenger decided that Bergkamp should come off. Kanu came on but nothing changed. Extra-time. Hagi was sent off for a not very damaging punch on Adams' sturdy back, so Galatasaray decided the time was right to defend and hope for penalties.

Although Parlour sent over a centre directly on to the head of Henry, the experienced Taffarel managed to turn the ball away off the line and then pulled off a couple of crucial saves. The game remained scoreless, even through extra-time. Possibly, by then, Wenger was wondering whether it had been a wise decision to remove Bergkamp, a player who even when not playing to his highest standards could still do the unexpected. Arsenal finally lost 4-1 on penalties.

170

Even before the shoot-out had begun, their chairman, Peter Hill-Wood, shook hands with his Galatasaray counterpart and congratulated him on victory. Bemused, the Galatasaray chairman mentioned that his side had not yet won. "Oh, but you will" Hill-Wood was reported to have said, "we never win in penalty shoot-outs". No doubt he was not just thinking of Arsenal's experiences but England's as well. In addition, Seaman was no longer as imposing as he had been. The shoot-out turned to embarrassment. Ergun scored first (1-0); Suker hit the post (1-0); Hakan Sukur scored (2-0); Parlour scored (2-1); Umit scored (3-1); Vieira hit the bar (3-1) and it was left to a former Spurs player, Gica Popescu, to score the winner (4-1). Many of the Arsenal fans said afterwards that they had little appetite for the game after there had been riotous behaviour in the city preceding the match. They were subdued throughout. Even so, Galatasary well deserved their victory, mainly because they had identified Arsenal's strengths and countered them.

Looking back at that season in the League, the side had begun with a Bergkamp-Kanu strikeforce. Luis Bel Morte was sold to Southampton, not having scored a League goal. The rivalry with Manchester United continued and United again got the edge when the teams met in the first half of the season. Forcefully and familiarly led by Roy Keane, they won 2-1 at Highbury (the first defeat for Arsenal on their own ground for twenty months, though they had the excuse that neither Adams nor Petit were available and Wenger was experimenting with Ljungberg in the centre of midfield where the ball was too easily lost). In spite of that, Arsenal still got to the head of the table. Their advantage was then lost with unlikely defeats by Coventry and Bradford City. It was more acceptable, though no less frustrating, to go down 1-0 to Liverpool at Highbury. In his one hundred and fifty matches in charge, Wenger had won eighty-one but never beaten Liverpool. Significantly, though, that game saw Henry begin playing as a central striker in place of Kanu. A partnership with Bergkamp seemed ideal but when Bergkamp was injured that link was broken until mid-season.

Discipline had again become an issue. In a match against Spurs, David Elleray, a referee who always tried to find a balance between the letter of the law and the spirit of the game, sent off Ljungberg and Keown. Both players claimed that they were innocent and, in both cases, they could look back at the video evidence and feel justified in their protests. Nevertheless, the next day there were calls for Arsenal to be brought before the FA. Vieira was too often at the centre of disciplinary problems on the pitch, though, in many cases, it was obvious that he was being goaded by opponents. Everyone knew that Neil Ruddock was an expert in provocation. Vieira fell for it against West Ham and could hardly complain when given an eight-match suspension for spitting at his opponent.

At the club's annual general meeting, a shareholder made the point that the board had withdrawn an application to redevelop Highbury, which led him to believe, quite reasonably, that there was no intention to do so and that the real plan was to build a new stadium. He told Chairman Hill-Wood that the fans deserved to be told the truth of the matter. Hill-Wood said moving was the "preferred option" but added that it was not definite that they would. One of the most interesting remarks made at the meeting was by Wenger, who said that in the future he would like a team that was sixty per cent home grown and forty per cent imported players. It was surprising that, in future years, he would not be reminded of that ideal.

A visit to Old Trafford, towards the end of January, ended in a 1-1 draw, leaving the sides level on points. The difference was that Manchester United, who had been excused playing in the FA Cup because they had been asked to compete in the big-named but over-rated World Club Championship, now still had three games in hand.

Although between mid-March and early May, Arsenal had a run of eight victories, United romped away with the title with ninety-one points while Arsenal managed only seventy-three. It was a huge gap and a deep disappointment. United's squad was clearly the better and the club's financial resources considerably stronger. Not that their performance against Arsenal in January was anything less than a shambles. They were fortunate that Sheringham balanced out an earlier brave goal by Ljungberg, who moments earlier nearly had his head knocked off by Stam.

The FA Cup brought little in the way of consolation. Blackpool were outplayed and eventually beaten 3-1, though it was one of those games in which Arsenal seemed slow to capitalise on their superiority. Then came the old problem with penalty shoot-outs. There had been a goalless draw in the fourth round against Leicester City and no goals in the replay at Leicester. City won the shoot-out 6-5. Arsenal had been beaten by the same method in the fourth round of the Worthington Cup against Middlesbrough, although the comparatively weak team Wenger sent out on that occasion was a reflection of his view that it was not possible to give serious attention to the least important of the competitions.

Any analysis of Wenger's career at Highbury must accept his mistakes, though too few to regard them as doing more than taking the veneer off the deeper impression of a man who knows his own mind, is usually right and is meticulous in his homework. The decision to release Petit at the close of the 1999-2000 season was curious. Without the prompting of Petit and Vieira it is doubtful whether Anelka would have prospered in a way that, with good reason, many doubted would happen. Wenger felt that Petit was not really settled in England. Petit himself did not say that in so many words and later returned to England from Barcelona to play for Chelsea. On the other hand, many Arsenal fans had never been greatly impressed.

Much of the comparative disappointment of the 1999-2000 season stemmed from injuries to the strikers. The absence of Bergkamp for nine weeks and Overmars and Kanu for six each was clearly debilitating. However, it was becoming more and more obvious that several of the long-established players were showing their age while the bulk of the new ones did not seem ready for regular first team football. At least Henry had become a reliable goalscorer.

That United had the advantage could not have been more forcefully emphasised than in the 2000-2001 season. They made full use of their squad system while Arsenal did not have the depth of resources to do so in such an expansive way. However, their visit to Highbury in October resulted in a 1-0 defeat by way of a goal from Henry and despite the fact that Sir Alex Ferguson had tried to preserve his best players for this game by sending out a weakened team against PSV Eindhoven in midweek (they lost 3-1). But when the time came to host Arsenal at Old Trafford in February, they were keeping them at bay at the top and then humiliated them 6-1. There were excuses.

The most experienced of the Arsenal defenders were absent and the comparatively new signings were never going to cover for them in a match against such well-tried and determined opponents. Having Igor Stepanovs and Grimandi playing as the central defence was an accident waiting to happen. It was ironic, though, that one of the young defenders who was given the runaround by United was Ashley Cole, who in the not too distant future would become England's regular and best left-back. He was taken off when the score was 5-1. It would not be long, though, before he would also be the natural successor to the departed Nigel Winterburn, who had served the club so well for more than a decade. First, though, it was Silvinho who filled the breach outstandingly well.

To put an overview on the season, the departure of Petit and Overmars had given Wenger a handsome amount of money to buy new players. That led to a disruption in continuity. When Edu arrived in Britain from Brazil using a passport that the authorities refused to accept, his £6m transfer was put on hold. Wenger invested the same amount of money on Robert Pires, from Marseille, while Lauren came from Mallorca for £7.2m. The signing of Latvian defender Stepanovs (£1m) seemed an obscure decision. The last arrival before the UEFA closure date for playing in European games was Sylvain Wiltord, who had a lot of experience of playing in French football and twenty-nine caps for his country. Importantly, he had appeared with Vieira and Henry in the summer's European Championship. Indeed, he had scored the ninetieth minute goal that led to France winning in extra-time under the golden rule arrangement.

The return to Highbury for European Cup matches certainly paid off and needed to because a humiliating 3-0 away defeat by Shakhtjor Donetsk in the group games and a 4-1 thrashing by Spartak in Moscow in the second stage did a lot of harm to prestige (Bergkamp was sorely missed). Home wins over Shakhtjor Donetsk (3-2), Lazio (2-0 – thanks in large measure to a productive performance by Bergkamp who played wide on the right) and Sparta Prague (4-2) in the opening group games took them into the second stage which, as expected, proved much more difficult. Again, Highbury helped. At their real home, they drew with Bayern Munich (2-2). In that match, Cole took the place of Silvinho (a pointer to the future) and Henry ended a lean period in which he had been unable to find the net in League or European games. Henry scored in only the fourth minute and celebrated uncharacteristically joyously. Bayern went two down, then fooled the referee into a couple of poor decisions that allowed them back into the match, aided by a lack of concentration in Arsenal's defence and midfield.

Lyon were held (1-1) and Spartak Moscow beaten (1-0). Yet Arsenal were fortunate to stay in the competition because their survival was directly linked with the match between Spartak Moscow and Lyon. Lyon only needed to beat Spartak, who were already out, to force Arsenal into requiring victory in Munich to remain in. As it happened, Lyon failed to get the win, so Arsenal's poor 1-0 defeat in Germany was not the end, although it certainly showed up some flaws in their performance.

In the quarter-finals, they overcame Valencia (2-1) at home in a thrilling game that saw them go a goal down to Ayala and in danger of losing their European invincibility at Highbury. Henry then drove in an equaliser that was attractively built by Wiltord, Kanu and Pires. That brought the crowd to their feet. Less than two minutes later, on the hour, though, they almost leapt clean out of the stadium when Parlour scored arguably his most spectacular goal for the club, a twenty-five yarder. The whole team performance was a strong argument that they were at last capable of competing with the best sides in Europe, though only on their own terms. In other words, they had to dictate the pace and keep snapping away while being lifted by the Highbury crowd that on these occasions would make even a full house at Old Trafford seem like a whisper. On the other hand, they had conceded a home goal which was to prove their downfall.

The return match in Valencia was never going to be simple. Valencia looked happy that the game reached seventy-five minutes without a goal. After all, they had expected Arsenal to come at them with a powerful display. In the event, they had no difficulty in establishing containment and then John Carew headed a cross from Angloma strongly downwards. Seaman got a touch but not enough and Valencia went through thanks to their away goal, then beat Leeds in the semi-final round before losing to Bayern on penalties in the final. Again, the question was raised about Arsenal's real quality in European terms, especially away from Highbury. Curiously, in spite of the international nature of the side, too often at this level they performed like many an English side of the past. They failed to have patience when it was needed and became frustrated when their quick-passing game faltered or was broken down.

Taking into account the quality of the players that Arsenal had available, it seemed obvious that they should have done better. Wenger, more than anyone, was frustrated that even those who had been so impressive when playing for France failed to rise to the occasion in European club competition. It was a fault that would continue to haunt him and put further doubts in the mind over the long-term future both of himself and the club.

The main tactical question that the manager had faced that season was whether he could produce a goalscoring, strike partnership. Early League matches had emphasised that finding an ideal link could be a worry. In addition, the problem of discipline was again brought to the fore. Vieira was sent off in the opening game of the season at Sunderland and again at Highbury against Liverpool, though in neither case did he deserve the punishment. He stormed out of the dressing room and left the ground before the game against Liverpool had ended, later saying that he could no longer play in England. Wenger's only consolation was that, at last, Liverpool had been beaten (2-0).

Vieira soon calmed down and was given a lot of encouragement by the fans. In the third game of the season, he inspired his team to a 5-3 win over

Charlton. He had rarely played better and said: "I will never leave Arsenal". He almost certainly meant it ... at the time. Meanwhile, Wenger was accused by the FA of threatening behaviour after the Sunderland match.

The middle part of the season was particularly unsatisfactory, though with some highlights, notably a hat-trick by Ray Parlour in a 5-0 win over Newcastle United. Yet there was a substantial recovery with only three defeats in sixteen League games which brought about the runners-up spot behind United, although well adrift (ten points).

Arsenal were also runners-up in the FA Cup Final, 2-1 losers to Liverpool. By then Cole had recovered his confidence and joined Seaman, Dixon, Adams and Keown as the comparatively new boy in the long-established defence. Wiltord was getting more comfortable in the English game, though too slowly for the fans' liking. To his credit, he adopted the fierce, competitive spirit of the Cup, which is not by any means always the case with imported players. He had scored in all three early rounds, including two against Chelsea in the fifth.

The Final was at the new Millennium Stadium in Cardiff, which added extra miles to the journeys of the fans but was appreciated for its spectator comfort and atmosphere. Quite why so many people had put up with the appalling state of Wembley, who knows, except that the long-outdated national stadium reeked of nostalgia, not to mention overflowing loos.

In his starting line-up, Wenger chose to include Wiltord rather than Kanu, who had not reproduced his scoring form of the previous season. This was construed as a ploy by Wenger, who needed to show confidence in the player if he was to receive a good enough offer to let him go. He would like to have included Bergkamp, who had missed a lot of matches with injury and was not ready for a full game. He was named as a substitute

After negotiating the early minutes in a respectful way, Liverpool made some enterprising movements. Michael Owen was sprightly and cracked a few good shots that Keown and Adams blocked. Then Liverpool seemed to go cold on the idea of positive thinking. Cole tried counter-attacking and Ljungberg attempted to chip a goal. Sami Hyypia got in the way. Seventy-two minutes went by before Arsenal properly cut through Liverpool's' defensive hold. A shrewd pass from Pires swept through to where Ljungberg was running and he accepted it before slotting in a shot from less than ten yards. It was a splendid goal that showed the value of taking the opposition by surprise and not involving the always-marked Henry who was also having trouble avoiding Hyypia with his shots.

Wiltord was called off and replaced by Parlour – a strange decision since Arsenal needed Bergkamp's ingenuity and composure to build on their lead or simply deprive Liverpool of possession. It was not to be one of Parlour's better days. When he gave away a free-kick, Liverpool took full advantage. Gary McAllister lobbed it into the penalty area and Keown failed to make full contact with his header. Markus Babbel rose above Adams and headed down. Owen volleyed in the equaliser. There were seven minutes left. With only two remaining, Emile Heskey, rarely given much credit by neutral fans, was, nevertheless, always a weighty problem for any defender. He easily dismissed a challenge by substitute Kanu. His short pass found Patrik Berger who sent a much longer one to Owen who picked up speed like a real sprinter, beating Dixon and Adams before sending a shot beyond Seaman. It was another example of Arsenal losing concentration after taking the lead.

As for the future of Highbury, the annual general meeting of 2000 no longer had the board prevaricating about moving to a new stadium. Peter Hill-Wood said the Ashburton Grove project would cost about £200 million but the shareholders seemed more concerned about the fact that Wenger had yet to sign a new contract that would extend into the time when the club moved out of Highbury. Wenger himself made it fairly clear that agreement was not far off.

Behind the scenes that season, the players had to overcome shock and sadness when, in November, George ('Geordie') Armstrong, a valued coach and effective former winger for the club, collapsed and died at the training ground.

# CHAPTER 32
# SOME SCRAPPERS!

## 2001-02
## PREMIER LEAGUE CHAMPIONS AND FA CUP WINNERS

T HE QUESTION MOST FANS WERE ASKING during the approach to the 2001-02 season was whether Manchester United could win the League title for the fourth consecutive season and their sixth since 1996. To all intents and purposes, Arsenal had become second best. Wenger had to prove that although his squad did not have anything like United's reserves of strength, they were a smaller pool of top class players all of whom were gaining experience together and had exceptional potential.

Since 2000, he had brought in Campbell, Edu, Francis Jeffers, Lauren, Pires, Stepanovs, Toure, van Bronckhorst, Wiltord and Richard Wright, the highly praised Ipswich goalkeeper. The signing of twenty-year-old Jeffers from Everton was intended to give support to Henry as well as add a reliable goalscorer to the squad. Certainly Jeffers was quick. He was also known to be susceptible to injuries.

Predictably, the capturing of Sol Campbell from Spurs was hugely unpopular with the fans at White Hart Lane. They would never forgive him. Although Manchester United continued to buy, Wenger's squad was now deep enough for him to use a total of twenty-five players in this season and none played in every game. Vieira appeared in more than any other player (thirty-six) yet had begun the season by being reported in a newspaper article as saying that he wanted to leave because he did not believe that Arsenal would win a European competition. Wenger's feeling was that this was nothing more than a ploy by a third party to raise Vieira's wages. Not for the last time, the manager and Vieira needed to talk.

Wenger played the loyalty card, reminding Vieira that no player was bigger than the club and that a contract should mean a contract morally as well as in writing. He also knew that if Vieira did leave, others would almost certainly follow and his long-term plans would be in ruins. Vieira not only stayed but was appointed vice-captain or, in other words, deputy to Tony Adams. Once again, Wenger had proved a wily tactician in terms of persuasion.

Without doubt, Campbell was a crucial signing. Although not of the highest class on the international scale, he was a defender of stature who might restore the back line's former reliability. Being out of contract, under the Bosman ruling, he could be secured on a free transfer, though with considerable 'personal terms' for Arsenal to negotiate. It was reported that no other player in the League would be on a more lucrative contract. Technically, he had been under no obligation to stay with Spurs. Morally, so their fans would argue, loyalty demanded that he did not immediately set up camp with the enemy. Wenger had played the loyalty card when it meant loyalty to Arsenal, particularly in the case of Vieira. He was hardly likely to mention the word to Campbell ... that's football.

When Campbell first played against Spurs at White Hart Lane, many of his former fans observed a minute's silence as a way of showing their intense unhappiness. He was jeered throughout the game, before which thousands of balloons printed with the word "Judas" were released. The player himself seemed to ignore it all and performed outstandingly well in a 1-1 draw.

The opening few weeks of the League season gave few hints that this was to be so memorable. Although in their first match Arsenal overwhelmed Middlesbrough 4-0, with Henry, Pires and Bergkamp (two goals) acting the Three Musketeers, they lost to Leeds at Highbury, a result that was even more frustrating because they finished playing against nine men after Mills and Bowyer were sent off. Referee Jeff Winter issued eleven yellow cards.

Wenger was still experimenting tactically. He omitted Henry against Leicester and played Bergkamp as striker. Leicester were easily swept aside 4-0 but Vieira was sent off. Almost inevitably, so was Leicester's Dennis Wise. Word was spreading that Vieira could be provoked. Indeed, while everyone could see that the skills of the side were blossoming, any opponents finding themselves being outclassed could attempt to break Arsenal's concentration by playing on a few brittle temperaments. There was then a frustrating away draw with Chelsea. It was only when beating Manchester United 3-1 at Highbury at the end of November that real conviction began to gain a hold. Even so there had also been some worrying signs.

The question of discipline had been a lurking problem. Now it became the subject of nationwide debate. Parlour and Vieira missed the Chelsea match because they were already suspended. In the first of the season's European Champions' League games in Mallorca, Cole was sent off before a quarter of the game was over, meaning that an Arsenal player had been dismissed in all five early season matches. Cole's action allowed Mallorca to win through the ensuing penalty.

The old problem of Highbury not always being the most intimidating of grounds re-emerged when matches against lesser teams were drawn when they should have been won at a canter. As a result, that visit of Manchester United was, in anticipation, a possible make or break game as far as the psychology of the season was concerned. United themselves had made a comparatively slow start to their own but, in London, they began well enough, Scholes putting them ahead after fourteen minutes. That concentrated minds amongst the Arsenal players, who needed no telling that this game could point the way for the rest of the term.

Once Ljungberg had equalised, Henry became the dominant force. So much so that he seemed to cause United's unpredictable goalkeeper, Fabian Barthez, to freeze. Henry scored twice in the last ten minutes and the home crowd sensed that this could indeed be a memorable season.

That springboard brought about such a change in determination that, apart from a defeat by Newcastle at Highbury, in December, when Parlour was sent off, the team never looked back. Not that Parlour's dismissal and some play-acting by Cole that got Craig Bellamy sent off did anything to stem the tide of bad publicity over Arsenal's disciplinary record. Wenger was accused of never seeing the rogue tackles and other misdemeanours carried out by his players, which was exactly the reason why he retained their confidence.

Whether Wenger deliberately waited to see the outcome of the Manchester United game before deciding whether or not he would sign an extension to his contract, only he knows. But he did. In all probability, several things needed to be clear in his own mind before he made his decision. He wanted to bring the European Cup to Highbury and now felt he was close to having a squad capable of doing so. In the longer term, he needed to believe that the club would definitely move to a larger stadium.

His new contract would run until at least 2005. David Dein said of Wenger: "To me he is a miracle worker. He revolutionised the club". Dein also hinted that if, eventually, Wenger no longer wanted to be the club's active manager he would be welcome to stay as technical director. Wenger himself has rarely said much about the future, except to comment that one day he would like to return to work and live in Japan because he so much enjoyed the different culture.

With due respect to the positive achievements of George Graham, the club had successfully retained their most influential manager since Herbert Chapman and, earlier, persuaded Vieira, Wenger's right hand man on the field, to stay as well. Both could have made themselves considerably richer by leaving for Spain, and Vieira turned down at least two further offers.

Christmas could not have been happier at Highbury. As well as Wenger's decision to stay, after long deliberation, the Islington Council had at last given the go-ahead for the new stadium at Ashburton Grove. There had been times when it seemed that so many obstacles were being placed in the way of the club's future move that serious doubts were expressed at board level about continuing. There was then a 2-1 win over Chelsea, on Boxing Day, which had followed a 2-1, bruising victory at Anfield where van Bronckhorst fell in the penalty area and was sent off for feigning a trip, which he had not claimed. In a way, that wrong decision really brought defiance and spirit to a head. Parlour, taking responsibility in midfield for the suspended Vieira, was a tireless inspiration. Indeed, in some quarters, Vieira's value to the team was being questioned. On occasions, it seemed that his mind was again elsewhere.

Once leading the chase, Arsenal refused to be approached domestically and were unbeaten to the end of the season. Once again, the wider demand of European football was their bête noire. The unapproachable European Cup continued to be just that. No matter how well a team plays on home shores and irrespective of claims that it is harder to win the English League than the top European trophy, without the ultimate medal that can be obtained in club competition there is no deep respect from the top teams in Italy or Spain. In spite of Manchester United's European Cup victory in 1999, talk of the Premiership being the best league in Europe is difficult to justify. "Toughest" might be true. The early years of the new century stressed that the Premiership did not have the depth of skill seen in the Italian and Spanish leagues.

Too many players nearing the end of their careers and looking for a final pay-out came to the Premiership and, while, generally speaking, Arsenal could not be accused of buying many who were on the down slope of their active football lives, their failure to reach the summit in Europe was more evidence of this lack of distinction at the highest level.

So Europe was the only stumbling block in this otherwise remarkable span of performances. Although Arsenal were imposing at Highbury, beating Schalke, Panathinaikos and Mallorca, causing hopes to soar, those were opponents of no exceptional substance and all three extended Arsenal on their own grounds. As well as Mallorca's penalty win, Panathinaikos won 1-0 and Schalke 3-1. If Bergkamp was afraid to fly abroad, Arsenal now had the reputation for not flying when on foreign soil. In the second stage, they lost away to Deportivo La Coruna (2-0) when goalkeeper Richard Wright, who had an injured knee, had to be replaced by Stuart Taylor at half-time; only drew away to Leverkusen (1-1) and lost 1-0 to Juventus in Turin. Worse than that, they were beaten 2-0 at Highbury by Deportivo but they had two outstanding home performances, beating Juventus 3-1 and the surprise eventual finalists, Leverkusen, 4-1.

Juventus had looked menacing in their opening attacks but Cole stood firm, as did deputy goalkeeper Taylor. It took a powerful run from Vieira to alter the flow. His shot was fumbled by Juve's goalkeeper, Buffon, and Ljungberg gratefully knocked in the first goal. Henry then sent a dipping shot over Buffon. When Campbell attempted to clear off the line but struck Wright, causing the ball to rebound in, the fans wondered whether this was going to be one of those games in which an advantage would slip away. As it was, Bergkamp came on for Kanu and elegantly wrapped up the victory, notably with a splendid pass that allowed Ljungberg to move through and score. At last, Wenger had seen a fulfilling performance and win against one of Europe's historically most significant teams.

The defeat by Deportivo in mid-March seriously countered the elation that the team and the fans had experienced in the victory over Juventus, not only because it was the first home reversal in the competition since Wenger took over but it ended the club's hopes for another season. Deportivo's win had been made easy by a dismal Arsenal performance that came about despite the fact that they had been well prepared mentally by Wenger, who had said that Deportivo were, in his view, one of the outstanding teams in Europe. Arsenal knew that if they could win they would be through to the quarter-finals. Goals by Valeron and Naybet had them beaten before the second half had begun. In spite of that, they still had a chance to get through if they could beat Juventus in the last match. It was a curious situation in which they needed to at least equal Bayer Leverkusen's result in their own last game away to La Coruna.

Only UEFA (or perhaps FIFA) in their wisdom could organise a competition in which a team could lose and go forward or win and get knocked out. Yet again Arsenal's away form was not good enough and they lost to a second half goal by Zalayeta after Henry missed a penalty. It was a wretched showing in a near deserted stadium in Turin (Juventus were already out and did not include some of their best players) while Leverkusen won with ease, 3-1 against an apathetic Deportivo team including several fringe players.

Arsenal's standing in Europe was not made any better by the fact that, in the quarter-finals, Manchester United ejected Deportivo by 2-0 and 3-2. Wenger's defiant remark after Arsenal's dismissal that they would return to the European Cup the following season and win it was food for the sceptics on the Continent. The European baton as far as English club's were concerned was taken over by Manchester United and Liverpool, who were trailing Arsenal in the League. Both went through into the quarter-finals and United narrowly missed getting to the final.

In trying to assess why even in a season in which Arsenal would go on to achieve the Double at home they were not good enough to impose themselves in Europe, the question of squads rather than teams has to be taken into account. United's squad was then, and remained, the better able to make changes when injuries occurred and, simply, rest players when they were not at their best. That luxury was not in Wenger's bag. On the other hand, he was not always beyond criticism in the way he made changes at times when continuity was needed. Few managers have avoided that complaint but Alex Ferguson has usually avoided it better than most. He was also inspiring in his leadership when taking his team abroad, whereas Arsenal, metaphorically speaking, too often lost their sense of direction.

If the European scene proved too difficult, there was no such problem in the the FA Cup. Watford proved no match, suffering as Henry scored after only eight minutes, followed by Ljungberg two minutes later, then Kanu and Bergkamp. The fourth round was always going to be more testing because Liverpool were the visitors and they were on their way to finishing the season as runners-up in the League ahead of Manchester United. Bergkamp, who was in wonderful form, dismissed them with his first half goal before himself being dismissed by Mike Riley for an aggressive near miss on Carragher, who was then sent off for throwing a coin back into the crowd.

Poor Gillingham may have been a few badly needed pounds richer for their visit to Highbury in the Fifth Round but went down 5-2. As an indication of how easy that was, Parlour and Adams got on the scoring list. And that brought Arsenal up against the last team to beat them in domestic competition, Newcastle United.

A visit to the special atmosphere of St. James' Park is rarely enjoyable for any team and, sure enough, although Edu got a goal as early as the fourteenth minute, Robert equalised in the second half to force a replay at Highbury. Wenger had elected not to include Pires and Bergkamp in his starting line-up. The return was both satisfying and unfortunate in that although Pires, the incomparable Bergkamp (who had become the PFA Player of the Year) and Campbell took Arsenal though to a semi-final against Middlesbrough, it was at the cost of losing Pires for the remainder of the season with a cruciate ligament injury. Until that point he had accumulated thirteen goals. Nevertheless, the team continued to prosper. From the defeat by Newcastle on 18 December until the end of the League season they were unbeaten. Meanwhile they got through their semi-final after an own goal by Festa.

Chelsea had overcome their neighbours from Fulham in their semi-final and set up an all London final, again to be played far away at the Millennium Stadium in Cardiff. In the League, Arsenal needed just one more point from their remaining two League games away to Manchester United and at home to Everton. Because the climax to the season had been altered to assist preparations for the World Cup finals, both matches had to be played after the Cup Final.

Managers often make tough decisions that hurt the victims. Richard Wright had played in all but one of the preceding Cup games. However, for the Final, Seaman was now available and it was wise to use his experience of the big occasion. Wenger also chose to utilise Parlour's relentless running and strong tackling rather than name Edu in the starting side. Chelsea's Claudio Ranieri, an excellent and courteous Head Coach who was later to become so cruelly submerged in the Abramovich revolution at Stamford Bridge, did not need to burn the midnight oil to work out that if his team could stop Bergkamp's lines of communication, as the great *Times* Football Correspondent, Geoffrey Green, used to say, Arsenal would not be able to release the dangerous Henry. He wanted Frank Lampard to close down Vieira and stop his distribution. Lampard did a good job and the entire Chelsea defence began by pushing forward, keeping Arsenal well away from the danger zones. The nearest Arsenal came to scoring in the first half was from a header by Lauren that Le Saux headed away for a corner. Another header, this time from Bergkamp, drifted wide. Chelsea struck back with a fierce shot from Gudjohnsen that brought such an efficient save from Seaman that Wenger must have felt he was justified in returning him.

Chelsea approached the second half with a more positive outlook and, as a result, got caught out by a quick Arsenal counter that flowed from Cole, through the midfield via Vieira and Parlour before Wiltord beat Desailly and played Parlour back into possession. Parlour had not been having a particularly good season (he had been sent off on three occasions). He speculated on a twenty-yard shot and beat Cudicini, whom many considered to be the best goalkeeper in the Premiership.

Chelsea then fell under the spell of Ljungberg, who had been in storming form for many weeks. He seemed to take on the entire Chelsea defence, including men of formidable comparative size (not least substitute John Terry). With ten minutes left he bent a shot in to guarantee Arsenal's victory. All that bothered their fans on this beautiful afternoon was the drab performance of Vieira who, it was continually reported, had again shown an interest in moving on to Real Madrid.

In the past, Wenger had tended to be pessimistic about the chances of real success, at least in private. This season, when it got to March, he was prepared to believe that: "The championship is in our own hands". In the run-in, there were a few worried-looking performances but, generally, Bergkamp retained the momentum. With two games left, Arsenal had a five point lead over Manchester United, thanks largely to a superb display by Bergkamp at Bolton, who, despite struggling against relegation, could be a handful on their own ground.

The title was still in abeyance even after the FA Cup was safely back at Highbury. The opportunity to seal it against Manchester United at Old Trafford in the penultimate game of the season was a prospect that the Arsenal fans found almost too provocative to bear. Their nervousness was not helped by the fact that Adams was not available because of a knee injury. Wenger also decided to start with Kanu rather than Bergkamp and leave Henry on the bench because he too had a knee problem, though not as serious as the one Adams was suffering. The fact that a draw would be sufficient to secure the title and even a defeat would not be too damning because the final game was against Everton, who had won only three away League games all season, was not in the minds of the Arsenal fans. For them, it was less about points than proving a point against United.

Exactly as everyone expected, Roy Keane was not prepared to concede anything, let alone roll over and let Arsenal celebrate in his own back yard. It was always going to be a match full of fire and emotion. Keane was soon in the thick of the battle. Paul Durkin, the referee, probably wanted to take the charged atmosphere into account and allow some leeway but, as the tackles became ever more mean, he took the names of Scholes, Neville and finally Keane, who had taken on responsibility for ensuring that Vieira did not monopolise midfield. When Vieira managed to avoid being clattered by one of Keane's tackles, he then felt the force of the United captain's arm in his face.

Durkin sent off Keane and United were left without the impetus that had marked their early attacks. In the end, it was Wiltord who, just before the hour, brought the title and the Double to Arsenal, though it should be remembered that the ever-willing, ever-underestimated Parlour started the move by winning the ball off Silvestre. Wiltord took up the attack, moved the ball on to Ljungberg who blasted a shot that Barthez parried. The ball went back to Wiltord, who smacked it in. Wenger summed up: "What this team has achieved is tremendous and will remain in history. This is not only a team of good players, it is one of togetherness".

Alex Ferguson did not leap off the bench to congratulate Wenger. Rarely complimentary about any team that beats his own, on this occasion he was deeply hurt to finish third and remarked: "They are scrappers who rely on belligerence – we are the better team".

Put in purely statistical terms, Arsenal's pursuit of the League title involved an unbeaten away record and scoring in every single match. The unbeaten run since 18 December was remarkable. Some scrappers! More than anything, the season had shown that Wenger had successfully used the full depth of his growing squad, sometimes out of necessity when players were injured or suspended and, on other occasions, when he felt the need to adapt to specific challenges. In addition, he seemed to have got across the message that collecting cards was for children.

The excitement on the pitch that season possibly concealed the true importance of the club knowing that Wenger had committed his future to them. It was suggested that had he not done so Arsenal would not have made the decision to build the new stadium at Ashburton Grove. That is questionable, but it must have been a significant further incentive. Wenger himself had been waiting on Islington Council's decision whether or not to permit the building. Had they refused, it was conceivable that he would have left and taken up one of the many offers that had come his way – notably from Barcelona. When the decision came, he felt more confident about his commitment.

The Chairman, Peter Hill-Wood, said: "Arsene was important to the development of the new stadium". He explained that it was essential that everyone saw that the manager was properly under contact when the move was made.

## FA CUP FINAL
(4 May 2002, Millennium Stadium)

### Arsenal 2 (Parlour, Ljungberg) Chelsea 0

*Arsenal:* Seaman; Lauren, Adams, Campbell, Cole, Vieira, Wiltord (Keown), Parlour, Henry (Kanu), Bergkamp (Edu), Ljungberg.

*Chelsea:* Cudicini; Melchiot (Zenden), Babayaro (Terry), Petit, Gallas, Desailly, Gronkjaer, Lampard, Hasselbaink (Zola), Gudjohnsen, Le Saux.

*Referee:* M. Riley.

# CHAPTER 33
# THE CUP OF CONSOLATION

## 2002-03 FA CUP WINNERS

THE 2002-03 SEASON HAD A NEW BENCHMARK. The Double champions had won widespread respect. At the same time, Manchester United were stung and eager not to see the trend continue. Liverpool badly wanted and needed to be seen as, potentially, worthy inheritors of their own past glories and were not best pleased to be beaten in the season's opener, the Community Shield, in which Arsenal's new signing from Atletico Mineiro, Gilberto Silva, scored the only goal.

Because several of the old guard had gone, not least Tony Adams and Lee Dixon, both of whom had epitomised the Arsenal spirit of defiance against all odds, the season had to be one of transition. In future, there would be many times when the fans would cringe at the mistakes being made by the new defence and look at each other without even needing to ask whether Adams and Dixon would have been so generous. Nevertheless, a 5-2 home win over West Bromwich Albion in the third League game of the season emphasised the margin of difference between the champions and those who now regularly hovered between the Premier division and the First Division. No matter what pretentious name they call the old First Division (ie: the Championship), and, unless the American idea of spreading the leading players across the whole of the top division is employed (some hopes), this situation is likely to remain indefinitely.

There were no defeats until a visit to Everton in the middle of October. In fact, this was a period in which many fans were convinced that they had never seen their Arsenal play with so much imagination. It was significant that Vieira looked determined to win back their confidence. He played magnificently, powerfully and with a sense of leadership that was needed to fill the gap left by the loss of Adams. Bergkamp's experience was invaluable and Henry was virtually impossible to mark. But then Blackburn came to Highbury and won 2-1. The champions were clearly unsettled, although Kolo Toure, from the Ivory Coast, had a classy look about him. Against that, Vieira, who had gone to the World Cup, was now beginning to look leg-weary. His troubled frown made it difficult to believe the optimists who suggested that this would be the season in which Arsenal would surpass the previous one and achieve the Triple: League, FA Cup and European Cup, which would at last put them on the same footing as Manchester United, who had achieved that in 1999.

According to Alex Ferguson, Vieira had actually shown a lot of interest in leaving Arsenal for Old Trafford. He said: "There is no player in the country who would not want to play for Manchester United and Patrick Vieira would have loved to come here last season but they wouldn't let him". Vieira seemed taken by surprise. He replied: "I am just disappointed that someone like him is talking like that".

Along the trail of the early season matches, a landmark was achieved when Arsenal beat Chesterfield's seventy-two year old record for the greatest number of consecutive games in which a League team had not failed to score (forty-seven). The record came in a particularly imposing 4-1 win over Leeds at Elland Road, where Kanu scored twice.

After another exasperating loss at Old Trafford in early December, they played to the end of the season with only two more defeats (at Blackburn and at home to Leeds). Once more, however, the requirements of playing well in the Premier division and coping with the demands of Europe were not the same. The Champions' League, which was the club's prime target, held the promise, or threat, of a final that would be played on home soil, except that the pitch would be that of Old Trafford, where it would be difficult for any Arsenal side to feel that they held an advantage. In the event, yet again, they were unable to get that far. From the outset, the challenge was difficult. The French club Auxerre, who over the years had done amazingly well to maintain high European status in spite of coming from a town so much smaller than the huge cities from which emerged the more famous clubs, were in Arsenal's first group stage, along with Borussia Dortmund and PSV Eindhoven.

At first, there was high promise. Borussia lost at Highbury and there was a crushing 4-1 win away to Eindhoven. Auxerre lost 1-0 on their own ground but then won 2-1 in London. All in all, it became a mixed bag of results, furthered by a defeat by Borussia in Germany and a goalless draw at home to Eindhoven. Even so, Arsenal finished top of their group, as did United in their rather easier one. Would Arsenal be able to gain a place amongst the true champions of Europe? At the second hurdle, their enduring inability to reach peak form away from home again took hold.

Although they began with a promising 3-1 win over off-form Roma in Italy, in November, (Henry scored all three goals in his most devastating

European display), they failed to make the most of their home games. A 1-1 draw with an inexperienced young Ajax was particularly galling, adding as it did to the embarrassment of a home goalless draw with Valencia. Overcoming sides who came to Highbury with the sole intention of avoiding defeat was something that a team with such high quality players ought to have resolved. But there was still hope of progress.

Roma arrived at Highbury in March needing to win, which, in theory, made it quite likely that they would leave themselves exposed to a counter-attacking game. They did not help themselves when their captain, Totti, was sent off not long after Vieira had scored. Nevertheless, defensive errors were troubling Arsenal and one of them allowed Cassano to equalise. The days of the wall of red at the back seemed long gone. That was not a thought that appealed to Wenger who knew it only too well. His release of the maturing talent of Matthew Upson simply compounded the problem.

In spite of the doubts, there was still a chance of getting into the quarter-final stage. The last game was away to Valencia, who had not won a home match in the second group stage but had the encouraging memory of knocking Arsenal out of the competition two seasons before. Their away performances had given them a good chance of getting through this time and they had been rebuilding the squad with quiet efficiency.

Meanwhile, Arsenal's long mid-season run of undefeated League matches had come to an end and losing to Blackburn in the weekend before the crucial European match was troubling. On top of that, the news that Cole had a hernia problem was bad enough without Keown succumbing to a leg injury during the game against Rovers. And Vieira was struggling. Thirty-eight years old Seaman, whom many fans were reluctantly admitting no longer had safe hands, was out and Campbell a major doubt. Wenger, normally ultra-cautious when it comes to including players with even the slightest injury, decided that the target of a European Champions title was so important that against Valencia he would have to risk the irreplaceable Vieira and the stout central defender Campbell. Not only that, he went against his tactical belief and concluded that his depleted team would best be served not by a 4-4-2 formation but by having five players in midfield and only Henry up front. In spite of all the problems, Arsenal set out at pace and promisingly.

Gilberto's header was deflected up and on to the crossbar by Vicente. Then Valencia pulled themselves together. Aimar sent a pass through to John Carew. The Arsenal midfield slumbered. Carew beat the deputy goalkeeper, Stuart Taylor. Arsenal were still not without hope though, because a draw could put them through. An encouraging goal came when Pires found Henry and there was never any doubt that he would equalise. The problem was that Arsenal continually lost possession and that was why, late in the game, when Wiltord gave the ball away to Vicente he centred immediately for Carew to hit in the winner.

Even as the game finished, there was the outside hope that Roma would beat Ajax, which would have given Arsenal an escape. The result was a draw and, once more, Arsenal were strangers to the real demands of the European competition. Admittedly, the team had not been at full strength in that last game. Yet there was a strong feeling that the Arsenal of recent past would have been able to build attacks from the back and also defend any advantages that the men ahead of them achieved. And then there was always the problem of Bergkamp, the conductor, spending more time watching the games on his television than taking part.

With Manchester United narrowly defeated by Real Madrid at the quarter-final stage, the Old Trafford final was not what the British public had hoped to see (United v Arsenal), but an all-Italian affair, AC Milan beating Juventus 3-2 on penalties.

All through so many of Arsenal's difficulties in European competition there had been an enduring irritation. One of the men with the greatest experience on the international stage, Bergkamp, was not available for most of the away matches. Although he had occasionally travelled by boat and road, as he did to play against PSV, the club always had reservations, especially about the longer trips. Wenger never seemed able to grasp the nettle, even allowing him to travel far away then leaving him on the bench. The manager always had to face the conundrum of selecting a player to appear abroad but then almost certainly having to put him back on the bench for a return match at home because Bergkamp was available. It seemed unfair. It was also inevitable because Bergkamp was so valuable.

Whether Bergkamp would have made a massive difference to the club's European performances had he played in many more away games is not something that can be proved. Every indication is that he would. Suffice to say that in that tie against PSV, it was his pass out to Henry that led to Gilberto Silva scoring after only twenty seconds, a record in the Champions' League. Arsenal went on to one of their most comfortable European wins (4-0).

Bergkamp's hatred of flying stemmed from an experience when a foolish Dutch journalist instigated a bomb scare on the national team's aircraft during the 1994 World Cup finals. Without him, Arsenal's record in Europe showed that they were a much more vulnerable and less inventive team. Any analysis of the cost of his absences would have to remember that the first sign that away matches in the Champions' League would become a lasting problem had been seen back in November, 1998 when Dynamo Kiev outplayed them.

If the Bergkamp problem was like a dragging anchor on the team's ambition, of equal significance was the perception that for all of his abilities as a coach, Wenger was as fallible as the next manager when it came to identifying weaknesses and buying the right players to cover. The release of Upson at a time when Adams, Bould, Dixon, Keown and Winterburn were nearing the end of their careers at Highbury (or had already retired) was, as mentioned, a clear mistake since the young player later became a full England international. Admittedly, England caps had been devalued by the number of players used in international matches, but he left Highbury with unfulfilled potential. There was also the buying of players who were not up to the required standard, particularly Pascal Cygan, Igor Stepanovs and Giovanni van Bronckhorst (who did regain better form at a later stage).

Although Arsenal had at first established a substantial lead in the Premiership, once the quest for the European Cup had again been removed they fell behind Manchester United. Ambition had to be funnelled into retaining the FA Cup. Progress since the first week of January had been promising. Oxford United were swept away 2-0 at Highbury in the third round. The dread of being drawn against a non-League side on their own patch was overcome when a match against Farnborough was switched to Highbury, where Arsenal won 5-1, and then the draw came up with Manchester United at Old Trafford in the Fifth Round.

Here was the opportunity for United to get their own back after Arsenal had won the Championship title at Old Trafford. Before Christmas, they had gone some way towards that when beating Arsenal 2-0 in Manchester. That result had actually shaken up the Arsenal side who went on a twelve-match unbeaten run to regain top spot though, in the end, they finished five points behind United after a thrilling climax in which it was possible that the teams would finish equal on points. Arsenal's disappointing draw at Bolton after taking a two-goal lead and a 3-2 home defeat by Leeds put the Championship firmly into United's hands.

The Cup tie against Arsenal was the low point in United's otherwise satisfying season. So poor was their performance that Alex Ferguson went into one of his familiar teacup-throwing rages, except that this time it was a football boot that he kicked across the dressing room, accidentally (it has to be assumed!) cutting David Beckham's priceless eyebrow. The one who should have been a target of any missile, guided or misguided, was Ryan Giggs, ironically the player who, in the season before, had so frustrated Arsenal but, in this tie, missed an open goal which gave Arsenal the encouragement to feel that even luck was on their side. Goals from Edu and Wiltord sent Arsenal through to a semi-final with old Cup rivals Sheffield United. Meanwhile, Manchester United defied Wenger's philosophy that you can only harangue a team a couple of times a season. They took the manager's latest rant to heart. They went on to overhaul Arsenal in the League, though not before the teams had met again in April at Highbury where, in spite of a 2-2 outcome, the balance of the game seemed to go in United's favour.

First Ruud van Nistelrooy shot United into the lead. Then, midway through the first half, Vieira injured a knee, limped away and was unable to play again for the rest of the season. What happened after that had become a familiar story. Henry scored a slightly fortunate goal, a deflection, to give Arsenal the lead, but the defence failed to keep tight as United responded and Giggs equalised. Subsequently, Campbell got sent off for the second time in the season and was later suspended for four games – a sad reflection on the team's propensity for damaging themselves. He and Vieira were not only out of the remaining League games but the Cup Final as well.

In April, Arsenal had gone back to Old Trafford to face the United from Sheffield in a forgettable semi-final that was won by a single goal after thirty-four minutes by Ljungberg. Sheffield United made every effort to disrupt Arsenal from their attempts to play a flowing game, and who could blame them. When they attacked, Campbell and Keown repelled them, as did Seaman with one of the most spectacular saves of his whole career to deny Paul Peschisolido a seemingly certain equaliser and guarantee another visit to the Millennium Stadium for a Final against Southampton, who Arsenal had beaten 6-1 in a League match, Pires and Pennant scoring three each.

Gordon Strachan knew that he would have to tighten up his team defensively, which was why he decided to risk bringing in Chris Baird, a promising young full back who, nevertheless, had made only three first team appearances in the League. Up to a point it worked. The main reason why this was one of those quickly forgotten finals was because Arsenal played a tentative game that was forced upon them by a large casualty list.

Even on the morning of the match, there were fitness tests on Keown and Luzhny. As mentioned, they were without Campbell and Vieira and, after Pires scored the only goal in the thirty-eighth minute, there was none of the usual pressure to increase the lead and finish off the opposition.

After Brett Ormerod had slammed a volley that Seaman just about turned away, Arsenal played a possession game that almost backfired in added time, when Matt Oakley's corner was well met by the head of James Beattie. Cole was on the line and saved the game going into extra-time. Possibly the only player to come out of the Final with an enhanced reputation (if it was possible to improve anyway) was Bergkamp, who played as if on a different level to the rest. The Final represented Seaman's last game for the club

Although it was not a great Final, it came as a big relief to win a trophy in a season that had provided any number of exciting matches, not least because the team could no longer be sure of holding on to single goal leads.

## FA CUP FINAL
### (17 May 2003, Millennium Stadium)

### Arsenal 1 (Pires) Southampton 0

*Arsenal:* Seaman; Lauren, Keown, Silva, Cole, Luzhny, Parlour, Ljungberg, Bergkamp (Wiltord), Henry, Pires.

*Southampton:* Niemi (Jones); Baird (Fernandez), Bridge, Marsden, Lundekvam, M. Svensson, Telfer, Oakley, Beattie, Ormerod, A. Svensson (Tessem).

*Referee:* G. Barber.

# CHAPTER 34
# P 38 W 26 D 12 L 0

## 2003-04 PREMIER LEAGUE CHAMPIONS

IN SPITE OF MUTED CRITICISM for again failing to bring the European Cup back to Highbury, this season was astonishing. There had been many occasions on which people at the club had said that the most important thing year-on-year was not winning the elusive European trophy – the one that puts you up among the 'greats' internationally – but capturing the League title and retaining it. As far as many fans are concerned that may be true. As far as discovering whether or not a team have truly fulfilled their potential in terms of skill rather than endurance, the argument is less convincing. Yet to play through an entire League season in the exacting circumstances of British domestic football and not lose a single game is a feat that, as near as damn it, must rank alongside becoming the champions of Europe.

There were defeats in the European Champions' League, the FA Cup, the Carling Cup and the Community Shield. In the League, Arsenal were invincible. Players who, in previous seasons, had not reached their full potential came good. The defence steadied and Henry, who was the Football Writers' Association and Professional Players' Association Player of the Year, was at his peak (at least for his club; he was still unable to replicate his form on the international stage when playing for France in Euro 2004). His thirty League goals formed the basis of the success while Pires, who early in his time at Highbury was not totally convincing, now not only scored fourteen but was seen as a fine creative maker of goals for others. Wenger also made the typically shrewd purchase of Jose Antonio Reyes, from Sevilla, thus adding a quick, creative element to the attack, also a decoy to draw attention away from Henry.

Only one player, goalkeeper Jens Lehmann, who was in his first season for the club after being signed from Borussia Dortmund, appeared in all thirty-eight matches. There had been considerable doubts about the wisdom of buying a 'keeper who was known to live on a short fuse, but he did well to counter claims that he would never be as good as Seaman. In all, twenty-two members of the squad appeared in the first team.

There had never been a hotter day on which to play football in Britain than Sunday, 10 August at the Millennium Stadium, Cardiff, where, in the FA Community Shield, Arsenal opened their season by drawing 1-1 with Manchester United after normal time, then losing on penalties. Lehmann, known to be prone to making mistakes when riled, had a calm, satisfying debut, especially because he saved van Nistelrooy's penalty. In the end, however, his counterpart for United, Tim Howard, saved from Pires who, despite that, had a splendid match when he came on after half-time. It was a sign of performances to come. On the minus side, Francis Jeffers was sent off, which was the last straw as far as the club were concerned and they let him go back to Everton.

It was Everton who gave Arsenal a tough first League game of the season at Highbury where Campbell was sent off in the first half for tripping Gravesen, which put great pressure on the midfield players. Keown was brought on and Wiltord taken off. Up front, Henry was at his best and scored from the penalty spot. The disadvantage of playing a man short seemed no problem at all as Vieira dominated midfield and Pires beat the former Arsenal goalkeeper Richard Wright, who had competently beaten out shots from Henry and Vieira and was particularly keen to give a good account of himself. That forced Everton to keep driving forward and, eventually, Radzinski scored with a powerful shot from some twelve yards. All in all, it was a good test for the Arsenal side and it also contained early signs that Everton were reviving, especially with the help of the precocious young Wayne Rooney who was looking like a new version of Paul Gascoigne. The teenager obviously had a remarkable talent but already other comparisons with Gazza were being made. It was clear that he would need careful guidance to keep him off the road to self-destruction. A later move to Manchester United put him under the rigid wing of Sir Alex Ferguson.

Perhaps the earliest significant indication that this would be an exceptional season came in only the second match, away against Middlesbrough. Boro were simply overwhelmed as Arsenal took a three-goal lead within twenty-five minutes with goals from Henry, Gilberto Silva and Wiltord. Even Boro's wonderfully skilful Brazilian Juninho had few chances to show his wizardry. On the hour, Wiltord scored Arsenal's fourth.

Aston Villa, well organised by their manager, the former Arsenal defender David O'Leary, predictably made things a lot tougher when they came to Highbury at the end of the month. Arsenal were relieved when

Henry scored in the last minute after the team had clung on to Campbell's fifty-seventh minute goal for so long. Manchester City were similarly resilient at their new stadium but went down 2-1. And so the season continued with difficult games won and others being made to look extraordinarily comfortable. The improving form of KoloToure as a central defender was reassuring.

You would expect any team managed by Harry Redknapp to make life testing for opponents and he did when Portsmouth visited and went away with a 1-1 draw, which nevertheless still left Arsenal heading the table before the first European game of the season brought them down to earth as predictably as in most previous seasons. Ironically, in this term of such remarkable success on the domestic scene, they crumbled to their worst European home defeat, 3-0 in the Champions' League against an Internazionale side that swept them away in the first half with all three goals, two of them coming within a period of three minutes. Defenders glared at each other accusingly.

Arsenal wasted several opportunities. Even Henry, who missed a penalty, was unable to turn them into goals. Indeed, they were lucky to escape without conceding at least a couple more. Wenger thought his team had been naïve, which seemed a curious word to use since this was a side that contained players who were now supposed to be amongst the best in the world. The old Achilles heel of Europe had bruised them again.

Manchester United must have viewed that result with special pleasure because, four days later, they were to be hosts to Arsenal at Old Trafford. Arsenal tried to make sure that Giggs and Ronaldo were given little space. Despite that, Giggs hit the post with a free-kick. Chances for both sides came and went and United's goalkeeper, Tim Howard, did well to dive at the feet of Vieira. The tension eventually led to Vieira being sent off (Arsenal's fifty-second dismissal in seven years) after van Nistelrooy made it seem that Vieira had kicked him. In a bad-tempered final few minutes, Arsenal could easily have been beaten when Keown and Diego Forlan fell together. The referee was again persuaded that there was an offence but at least van Nistelrooy cracked the penalty against the crossbar. Goals remained absent but temperatures kept rising.

Keown, an intelligent and pleasant man off the field, certainly knows how to irritate his opponents and was one of those who then began to taunt the Dutch striker. As a result of a fracas after the players left the field, Arsenal were fined £175,000 and warned about future conduct. Lauren was suspended for four matches and fined £40,000, Keown three games and

£20,000, Vieira one (£20,000), Parlour one (£10,000), Cole (£10,000). Giggs and Cristiano Ronaldo were also fined for getting involved.

The Champions' League continued to bring dissatisfaction. Only one point was gained from a visit to Lokomotiv Moscow. There were some excuses in that, of course, Bergkamp was absent, so too were Vieira, Ljungberg and Campbell. At any time that Campbell was missing, the defence looked vulnerable (a situation that continued into the 2004-05 season when he was again injured). Lokomotiv's passing was both careful and positive and Arsenal had to play a disciplined game to keep them at bay. When counter-attacking, their own finishing was not of the best. In contrast, back in England victories kept on coming.

Liverpool were defeated in a demanding game at Anfield where Pires scored a superb winning goal with a long, curling shot. Newly-rich Chelsea, emerging as future Championship contenders, put up a commendable struggle at Highbury before losing 2-1 to goals from Edu and Henry that both took crucial deflections – the second after Cudicini had rushed out of goal to meet a centre only to lose his grip on the ball. Then, back into Europe and the old enigma. A 2-1 defeat by Dynamo, in Kiev, left them bottom of the group table. Admittedly, they hit the bar and post (Toure's shot hit the post in the last minute) and deserved to come home with a draw. However, sheer effort was not enough.

In a season that was already promising much domestically, it was understandable that, as in other ones, the Carling (League) Cup was not given prominence on the club's list of priorities. However, it gave Wenger the chance to involve some of the less experienced players and, at the end of October, a visit by Rotherham (who only lost 9-8 on penalties) marked the first appearance of Francesco Fabregas, who had come from Barcelona and was only sixteen years and one hundred and seventy seven days old. Thus he became the youngest player ever to represent the club at first team level, beating the record held by Jermaine Pennant, the Under-21 international whom Arsenal bought from Notts County in 1999. Sadly, Pennant's career was blighted by his own ill-discipline, culminating, in 2005, by his being jailed for three months for drink-driving.

Vieira was still injured yet there was a performance of the highest class against Leeds, who went down 4-1 mainly as a result of Henry's two early goals and the class of Bergkamp (re-emphasising what the team missed when he was not playing in away European games). When he appeared in a home Champions' League tie against Dynamo Kiev, he ran the midfield show and Arsenal won 1-0 after Cole dived to score two minutes from the end of an otherwise frustrating game of missed chances. It was the club's first European win in nine games and there was still hope of getting through the first stage.

The psychological boost of beating neighbours Tottenham 2-1 (which meant that Arsenal had become the only team in the four divisions to remain unbeaten) was hard won and Spurs were right to consider themselves unlucky losers. The effect was to keep Arsenal on the record track. By beating Birmingham 3-0 they regained top place above Manchester United, which was particularly sweet for Wenger who was celebrating his four hundredth game as the club's manager. Also on this day, the French connection continued to grow because Gael Clichy made his debut.

Bearing in mind the evidence of so much of the club's previous European Champions' League history, it seemed unlikely that they would suddenly show their full potential against foreign opposition. Nevertheless they did when visiting Milan to play Internazionale, who had not lost to a side from England for over forty years. Inter began well enough and were troubling Arsenal even after Henry scored from the edge of the penalty area in the twenty-fifth minute. Although Inter pulled a goal back from Vieri, it took a lucky rebound off Campbell and, shortly after half-time, Ljungberg took Arsenal back into the lead. In the last five minutes, Henry, after a breathtaking weaving long run, Edu and Pires added three more. That left Arsenal needing a home win over Lokomotiv to secure a place in the second stage.

As an indication of the positive way they were playing on their own soil, their draw with Fulham at Highbury at the end of November was the first goalless game seen there in forty-seven matches. Goals came back in time to beat Lokomotiv 2-0, taking Arsenal to the top of their group. Henry, who, with Zinedine Zidane and Ronaldo, had been nominated as World Player of the Year, was outstanding although it was Pires and Ljungberg who scored.

Although they had not suffered any defeats, Arsenal were finding it hard to shake off Chelsea and Manchester United in the pursuit of the title. Three draws in four games before Christmas cost them the chance to create a clear lead. In the FA Cup, however, they stormed past Leeds (4-1), with Henry and Pires again in formidable form and, soon afterwards, they regained top place in the League with a surprisingly easy 4-1 win over Middlesbrough, whose defence had been denying most teams space in which to work.

The value of Pires, or 'Le Bob' as he was nicknamed by the other players, to the modern Arsenal is not to be underestimated. After all, despite being a left winger who had always been happier playing the ball with his right, it was his ability to provide a cutting pass or take on and beat an opponent on the flank that so often led to crucial goals. Although it took time for him to prove himself to the fans, after a while he won them over. Fans of opposing clubs tended to remember him for other reasons. His reputation as a 'diver' was founded in 2003 when he was accused of doing that against Portsmouth. Of more importance was his ability to be a successful left winger despite being naturally right-footed. That made it difficult to understand why more players could not do the same – especially English ones.

When Manchester United lost to the bottom club, Wolves, Arsenal took advantage by beating Villa 2-0 at Villa Park and, at the same time, they created two points of daylight between them and United at the top. At about that time, the question was being raised as to whether it was possible to go through the whole season unbeaten in the three domestic competitions. Most people thought it unlikely and providence was tempted too much because in the next match, a Carling Cup semi-final first-leg against Middlesbrough, a less than full-strength side lost 1-0, so the unbeaten idea had to be altered to mean 'in the League'. Four days after that, Middlesbrough went to Highbury in the fourth round of the FA Cup and lost 4-1. Not surprisingly, Wenger wanted to field a stronger side than before but Kanu and Henry were with their international teams and Wiltord and Jeremie Aliadiere were injured. An experimental attacking partnership of Bergkamp and Ljungberg worked well and Pires was again outstanding.

February began with a wild, wet day at Highbury where Jose Antonio Reyes, who had spent all his previous career in the sunshine of Spain, came on in the seventieth minute against Manchester City to make his first appearance. It was immediately clear, even through the rain, that here was a special talent. Before that, Tarnat offered Arsenal an own goal with an attempted clearance that went wrong. Henry scored the winner. Anelka did manage a 89th minute goal against his old 'mates', who showed no friendship throughout (he and Cole were both given yellow cards).

The Carling Cup campaign ended with a 2-1 defeat at Middlesbrough, where Keown was sent off, but the younger members of the team showed promise and spirit. Back in the League, Henry achieved his century of Premiership goals with two against Southampton. If he was the undoubted star of the present, Reyes was making it known that he was the one for the future. His two goals against Chelsea eased Arsenal's passage into the sixth round of the FA Cup.

Chelsea, on the verge of becoming the team to chase in the 2004-05 season, had now been dismissed from the Cup by Arsenal for the fourth successive season. Only six days later, they were feeling even more depressed when Arsenal beat them 2-1 at Stamford Bridge where the home side had taken the lead through Gudjohsen in less than half a minute. Gudjohnsen later ruined his own good work by being sent off but Chelsea still battled well until the end.

Ever hovering in Wenger's mind was the need to reach the final of the European Cup. The trip to play Celta Vigo in the first phase of the knock-out round was a potential trap. Arsenal had never been successful in Spain. Not only that, Celta had not lost a European tie on their own ground for twenty-five matches and they defended that record with a passion as well as some eye-catching football.

Pires caught them out in the eighteenth minute when his free-kick found the head of Edu. The ball screwed away. Edu retrieved it to score. Another Edu (Luis) pulled one back for Celta, also after a free-kick, but Arsenal's Edu replied with a superbly struck bending shot. Although Ignacio brought Celta back to within a touch of winning, finally Vieira and Henry linked up their passes and Pires sent in a fifteen-yard shot. In celebration, they smashed five FA Cup goals past Portsmouth at Fratton Park, although Pompey were nowhere near as poor as the result seemed to indicate. That raised confidence for the return with Celta Vigo, who went down to two goals from Henry, who had been playing well enough without the bonus of getting goals as well.

All the way through this extraordinary season there were potential pitfalls. For instance, everyone had been impressed with the progress Bolton had been making under the guidance of Sam Allardyce, yet when they went to Highbury, although they gave a good account of themselves, they could not cope with the sweeping football Arsenal presented on another windswept afternoon. The 2-1 victory represented Arsenal's twenty-ninth unbeaten game, a record for the Premiership and the old First Division set by the Leeds team Don Revie built (1973-74).

Chelsea could not have been brimming with confidence when they faced Arsenal in the Champions' League quarter-final first leg at Stamford Bridge. They had not beaten their fellow Londoners in sixteen meetings. Notwithstanding, here they were certainly the better side in the middle stages and Gudjohnsen again gave them the lead. Frank Lampard was particularly dangerous and adventurous but Pires headed in from ten yards. When Marcel Desailly was sent off, Chelsea were forced to play out the rest of the game without taking risks and did so effectively enough.

Another significant draw was against Manchester United at Highbury. As always, this was a game full of tension and unrelenting physical challenges. And familiarly, Roy Keane was dynamic in his leadership for United. The first half contained a host of chances. Neither side could break through. Then Arsenal managed it with a beautifully crafted forty-ninth minute goal that was initiated by Reyes who played a neat pass to Henry. Still some thirty-yards out, Henry suddenly decided to have a shot. It completely beat Roy Carroll's reach. Although United were deprived of a penalty when Campbell tripped Giggs, at least Saha was able to head in an equaliser which slightly improved Alex Ferguson's demeanour. He had retribution in mind when the teams met again a few days later in the FA Cup semi-final at Villa Park.

If it was to be Arsenal's season, this was United's day. Of importance to the outcome was Wenger's decision not to start the match with Henry who, as with the rest of the regular team, would be facing a heavy programme of matches. Arsenal still had the power to press United back in the early stages and Carroll made an astonishing save from Toure's header. Ronaldo then got into his distinctive stride and ripped into the Arsenal defence. Pires missed with a header when no United defender could get near him. Eventually, Giggs played the ball across the goalmouth and Paul Scholes lodged a shot beyond Lehmann. Arsenal put United under huge pressure over the last few minutes without denying them their revenge.

There was only a three-day gap before the Champions' League quarter-final second leg against Chelsea had to be faced. Arsenal dominated the first half and led as a result of Henry heading across the Chelsea goal and Reyes knocking in a rebound from Ljungberg. Chelsea came out for the second half far more focussed. Lehmann did well to parry a twenty-five yard shot from Claude Makelele. The ball went directly to Lampard who had little trouble in beating the goalkeeper from much closer range. From then on there seemed no doubt that Chelsea were in the ascendancy. Wayne Bridge moved upfield to remove Arsenal from the European competition with a twelve-yard shot.

Small compensation came at Highbury by beating Liverpool 4-2, which stretched Arsenal's lead over Chelsea to a more comfortable seven points. Henry scored three, the second of which was magical as he swerved through the middle of the field, drifted past two tackles and easily beat Jerzy Dudek. Henry repeated his hat-trick against Leeds and added another goal for good measure. Wenger was asked whether there was a better striker in the world. A reasonable question? Only if those goals had been scored against some world-class defence, not one from a club struggling for their very existence.

The main questions now were whether an unbeaten League record would be achieved and when the Championship title would be won. There was still the north London derby against Spurs at White Hart Lane to face in the third week of April. By then, though, the title was comfortably within Arsenal's grasp. How ironic that it should be won on the home ground of their old rivals and neighbours. Only one point was needed but after Vieira ran some sixty yards to score in the third minute and Pires tapped in another in the thirty-fifth it seemed that all three would be obtained. Spurs then put up stout resistance with a sixty-second minute goal from Jamie Redknapp (a fine twenty-five yarder) and one in the very last minute by Robbie Keane from the penalty spot. One point for Arsenal was sufficient and they celebrated wildly while some of the Spurs fans who had not made a quick exit, stood and risked the wrath of the more bigoted ones by applauding.

In any other season there would have been good cause to start introducing fringe squad members to the team and take things easy. That was not an option as an undefeated season became a huge on-going challenge. Birmingham City were held to a dreary goalless draw at Highbury and there was a 1-1 result at Portsmouth, where Reyes scored his first League goal and the home side seriously worried the Champions. In the penultimate game, at Fulham, Reyes again scored, thanks to a howler by Edwin van der Sar in the Fulham goal. He failed to clear a back pass then tried to dribble the ball past Reyes, who took it under his control to score.

The last game ought to have been a gift: Leicester City at Highbury. City had already been relegated and all that was left was pride and the possibility of spoiling Arsenal's day. The sun was shining; the Arsenal fans were ready to party. The team played up to the occasion, tearing into Leicester from the kick-off. City knew that was coming. They had a five-man midfield and left Paul Dickov as the lone striker. Henry, Ljungberg and Gilberto all raided the City goal without penetrating. Arsenal's goal had not been threatened at all until, in the twenty-sixth minute, Vieira, of all people, was caught out by Frank Sinclair who went charging down the right side and put in a deep centre that somehow avoided the Arsenal defenders and allowed Dickov, not exactly a giant, to head in. That was not part of the dream.

Half-time was tense both in the home dressing room and amongst the fans. Bergkamp's experience, touch and feeling for what is needed at exactly the right moment became imperative. One minute into the second half, he sent a pass to the feet of Cole who had chased upfield and into the penalty area. He was brought to ground and the referee had no choice but to give a penalty which Henry put away to score his thirtieth goal of the season. It was entirely fitting that the last goal of the campaign and the one that absolutely confirmed that the team would remain unbeaten was sparked by Bergkamp who threaded a pass through the City defence to Vieira who strolled past Walker and brought a victory that meant that Arsenal had become the first club in well over an hundred years to go through a whole season without giving way to a single opponent in League competition.

The year of 2004 was also highly consequential for the club because, in February, it had finally been announced that the loans necessary to build the new 60,000 capacity stadium were in place. Six banks had agreed to provide Ashburton Properties with £260 million which would have to be repaid over a period of fourteen years.

# CHAPTER 35
# BYSTANDERS? IT FELT LIKE THAT

## 2004-05 FA CUP WINNERS

Q UESTIONS OVER THE NEED AND THE WISDOM OF MOVING to a highly expensive new stadium were made all the more relevant in the penultimate season before the move. The whole point about transferring to Ashburton Grove was to have a home large and grand enough to reflect and profit by the modern era of Wenger's Arsenal. Suddenly, though, things had changed. Chelsea had put spending into a new league. Not only that, they stormed through the 2004-05 season to became champions for the first time in fifty years, twelve points ahead of Arsenal and with only one defeat all season. They also reached the semi-final round of the European Champions' League, being beaten by Liverpool who went on to revive memories of their distant past by winning the trophy against AC Milan and the odds. It would be hard to say that having been Premiership runners-up, FA Cup winners and FA Community Shield winners Arsenal were mere bystanders, but it felt like that.

In the shadow of Chelsea's achievements, it was possible to under-value several of Arsenal's accomplishments. After all, they completed an amazing run of forty-nine unbeaten Premiership matches; Thierry Henry closed in on Ian Wright's club goalscoring record, and Francesco Fabregas became the club's youngest League scorer at the age of only seventeen years and one hundred and thirteen days. Yet, by the end of the season, there was much talk of difficult times ahead, the need to rebuild a team as well as complete the building of the new stadium, and concern that the Ashburton Grove project would mean that Wenger would not be able to compete at the highest level of football's players' market. In addition, the end of the season saw the club lose their most dominant player since Tony Adams when Patrick Vieira was transferred to Juventus. A long-running drama involving the future of Ashley Cole also did nothing for team spirit and there were persistent rumours of discontent within the squad.

The Vieira saga had been rumbling on for several seasons. Obviously, he was on the wanted list of most of Europe's top clubs, with Real Madrid often being linked. In fact, in the middle of the close season (18 July) Wenger decided to make a statement saying that he was sure the captain would stay. It must have taken a lot of negotiating to make that come about, although it turned out to be an agreement that lasted for only one more term. In August, Real claimed that a deal had been worked out and Vieira would be joining them for £23m. Vieira did not appear in the Community Shield against Manchester United but that was because of an injury.

Without him, Arsenal won 3-1 and the headline in the *Daily Telegraph* was "Arsenal show there is life beyond Vieira", which was jumping the gun but reassuring for the Arsenal fans. Fabregas, especially, caught the eye at the Millennium Stadium but Reyes was named Man of the Match. It had to be admitted that United, far from full strength, were a shadow of their potential. Afterwards, Wenger said that it was time for Vieira to make up his mind because he could not be "half with us and half with someone else".

A few days later, Vieira said he wanted to stay at Arsenal to the end of his career. "I have come to this decision with my heart". Wenger added that money had nothing to do with it. Really?!

At first, finding the net was not a problem as Arsenal embarked on what was to be a trying season. They were in pursuit of Nottingham Forest's unbeaten run of forty-two matches that had been achieved between November 1977 and December 1978. They opened with a 4-1 win over Everton at Goodison which, from their perspective, proved a misleading result since they went on to have an extraordinarily fine season, finishing fourth.

Wednesday, 25 August finally brought the run of unbeaten matches to forty-three. It was achieved in style with a Henry-dominated 3-0 win over Blackburn Rovers at Highbury. Henry not only scored the first goal but created the other two for Fabregas and Reyes. Fabregas, who was soon to sign a four-year contract, had thus become the club's youngest ever goalscorer. The whole team played exquisite football at a pace that, in the second half, Blackburn found impossible to control. Had it not been for the excellent goalkeeping of Brad Freidel, the score might have reached double figures.

Middlesbrough were beaten 5-3 at Highbury after Arsenal trailed 3-1. Steve McClaren, the Boro manager, said afterwards: "I have never seen a team with so many attacking options". Bergkamp was voted Man of the

Match because, in the words of Henry: "He played like a twenty-year-old not a man of thirty-five". Substantial victories continued: Norwich 4-1 and Fulham 3-0 (though that was a tougher win than the score suggested). Henry scored four goals in his first five games.

On the approach to the first Champions' league game of the season, against PSV Eindhoven, the former Arsenal striker Alan Smith commented that, although he felt it was difficult to name a more "potent force" anywhere in Europe than could be found at Highbury, he was worried that the succession of failures to succeed at the summit of club football had become a psychological battle. Self-belief, he said, rather than tactics might again prove the main hurdle. This was to be the club's seventh attempt to win the European Cup and twice they had been knocked out at the quarter-final stage. As well as PSV, this time their first group also contained Panathinaikos and Rosenborg ... hardly formidable if Arsenal could continue to play as well as they were in the Premiership. That had always been the crux of the matter.

The fluency, pace and style that had become so familiar at Highbury was missing against PSV and it took an own goal by Alex, the Brazilian centre half, to provide Arsenal with a win that was based more on hard work than eloquence. Then they again failed to kill off comparatively weak European opposition. Visiting Trondheim, they were held to a 1-1 draw. The performance emphasised what Alan Smith had been saying. They took the lead through Ljungberg but let Rosenborg back into the game. It was as if, psychologically, they felt that European competition had to be given disproportionate respect – even when the opponents, man-for-man, were much inferior, which was certainly the case against Rosenborg.

Inevitably, the slight dip in form led to speculation about unrest within the squad. There were even reports of a fight (Wenger called it a "minor incident" between Vieira and Lauren) but a 4-0 home win over Charlton in which Henry scored two glorious second half goals and came off to a standing ovation put Arsenal five points ahead of Chelsea at the top of the Premiership and quashed the rumours about disagreements. The Arsenal fans went away not talking about problems but an amazing goal by Henry just after half-time. He had turned his back away from a challenge by Jonathan Fortune, who was hustling him as best he could. Six yards out, Henry suddenly back-heeled the ball through Fortune's legs and beat goalkeeper Dean Kiely. "Only One Thierry Henry" ... unquestionably.

In the background, work had been going on to add more financial security to the club in the years after moving to the expensive new stadium. A fifteen-year £100m deal with Emirates, the Dubai-based airline, involved shirt sponsorship but, more importantly, as far as they were concerned, naming rights for Ashburton Grove. Controversially, it was announced that the new ground would be called the Emirates Stadium, which meant resisting nostalgic calls to have it named something like 'New Highbury' or perhaps the 'Herbert Chapman Stadium'.

Chairman Peter Hill-Wood said he appreciated that the traditionalists amongst the fans would not approve of the ground's title. He said: "I would be one of those supporters. I've been here a long time, a great many years, and if we named the new stadium after Herbert Chapman or even Arsene Wenger, it would roll off the tongue." However, he said times had changed "and this is a wonderful offer we have received – the biggest ever in English football. We must move on". Jubilantly, an Emirates spokesman later admitted that obtaining the naming rights clinched the deal because so few football grounds were named after their sponsors.

Many fans were outraged by the naming decision. Barry Baker, secretary of the official supporters' club, said: "The tradition has gone. We were all hoping it would be called Ashburton Grove, or maybe Emirates Highbury. We'll get over it but I can see many fans calling it Ashburton Grove rather than the Emirates Stadium".

On the field, the team sparkled in a 3-1 win over Aston Villa which seemed like good preparation for the Champions' League game against Panathinaikos, followed by a visit to Old Trafford, which, although it was still only mid-October, was being portrayed as the decisive game of the season, which ignored the fact that United were already eleven points behind Arsenal and that despite losing to Manchester City on the day Arsenal beat Villa, Chelsea were clearly the more serious title contenders.

The match against Manchester United was preceded by the now routine sniping between the two managers. Wenger had said United's era was over. Sir Alex Ferguson referred back to Arsenal's goading of Ruud van Nistelrooy in the previous season. The more important fact was that United knew that defeat would put them so far behind the leading clubs that the Championship would be all but out of reach.

An ankle injury to Vieira at Villa Park meant that against Panathinaikos in Athens he had to be replaced by Edu. With Bergkamp not available and Gilberto Silva suffering from a back injury, Wenger had selection problems. Arsenal failed to grasp a victory that was within their reach. They twice held the lead with goals by Henry and Ljungberg but only drew 2-2. But at least they were still in the competition.

In spite of their comparatively poor start to the season, United now had Wayne Rooney in their attack along with van Nistelrooy, Giggs and Ronaldo. Arsenal were still defending their unbeaten record, which stood at forty-nine. United, without Roy Keane, who had 'flu, were defending their pride. The bad-tempered meeting was decided by Rooney. Campbell had been controlling him for seventy-three minutes but eventually allowed him a small amount of free space. Giggs offered him a pass. Rooney made to sprint away. Campbell stretched out a leg. Rooney fell. Referee Mike Riley was convinced that there had been contact. None of the Arsenal players agreed, yelling their protests at Riley. Lehmann, in the Arsenal goal, had words with van Nistelrooy who waited to take the penalty. The Dutchman then beat the German with a surprisingly composed shot from the spot.

Arsenal were already angry because they thought Rio Ferdinand should have been sent off for bringing down Ljungberg, who had a clear goalscoring opportunity. Their mood was not made better by ragged challenges from the Neville brothers on Reyes and an unpunished foul by van Nistelrooy on Cole, who nevertheless was lucky not to concede a penalty when he brought down Ronaldo. Finally, Rooney hit in his first League goal for United in the ninetieth minute. Afterwards during a fracas in the tunnel, food was thrown over Ferguson, and Wenger accused the referee of having a record of favouring United and van Nistelrooy of cheating. In reality, Riley had a near-impossible task controlling a match so full of tension, speed and bad temper. But it was not one of his better days and several journalists reported that United should have finished the game with nine men. It was not known whether Heinze and Campbell were involved in the soup-throwing incident that followed the game!

Later, van Nistelrooy apologised for his rash tackle on Cole which had led to a three-match ban. Arsenal's vice-chairman, David Dein, went to Old Trafford for talks aimed at reducing the tension between the clubs. On the same day, Wenger signed a new contract binding him to Arsenal until May, 2008. Interestingly, he stressed how important it was for the club to build a strong academy of young players (on the same day twenty-one year old Robin van Persie scored his first goal in England during a Carling Cup win over Manchester City). Perhaps he was thinking that the cost of the new stadium might well reduce his spending power on established players. He said: "My intention has always been clear. I love this club and am very happy here. Signing a new contract just rubber stamps my desire to take this club forward and fulfil my ambitions". Peter Hill-Wood said Wenger had "revolutionised the club both on and off the pitch".

Possibly as a result of the disturbing features of the match against United, Arsenal then found themselves only joint leaders of the Premiership after drawing at home to Southampton while Chelsea smashed in four goals against West Bromwich. The pattern of the season had been set.

The return game against Panathinaikos at Highbury found Arsenal without Campbell, who had a calf injury that left Pascal Cygan in central defence. Campbell's absence was one of the unfortunate defining features of Arsenal's season. Cygan gave away an own goal against the team from Greece after Henry had scored a penalty. Failure in European games to profit by taking a lead had become almost a certainty. There was a real need to get at least a point against PSV in Holland.

The lead in the Premiership was lost to Chelsea after a 1-1 draw at Crystal Palace. Again, the absence of Campbell was important, although it was Palace's spirit that was crucial to the outcome. Spirits amongst the Arsenal players further deteriorated when the FA announced that they were charging Wenger with misconduct over events at Old Trafford and they asked that the clubs should settle their differences. It took an astonishing 5-4 win over Spurs at White Hart Lane, where defenders acted like novices, to bring back some smiles. Arsenal took a 5-3 lead and still looked in danger of being held to a draw over the last few minutes.

The return against PSV Eindhoven came after a frustrating league draw with West Bromwich that had Wenger troubled about poor defending and weak finishing. Campbell had been badly missed but returned in Eindhoven where Arsenal finished with only nine men after Vieira and Lauren were rightly sent off, costing them their places in the final group game against Rosenborg at Highbury. PSV got an early goal when even Campbell and Vieira failed to intercept Ooijer. Henry scored an equaliser after a splendid Arsenal build-up but, overall, the Arsenal performance was ruined by a lack of discipline.

A 2-1 defeat by Liverpool was only Arsenal's second in fifty-five Premiership games, but it represented a decline from high standards. Only six points had been gained out of a possible eighteen and the gap between them and Chelsea at the top was now five points. Freddie Ljungberg admitted that, at half-time at Anfield, the whole team got involved in a worried discussion about what was going wrong. "When you want to play the ball on the floor, and we do, we need to fight to get the ball". The fans pointed accusingly at Pires, whom they thought was not sufficiently involved when the chips were down.

In the early rounds of the Carling Cup, Wenger had insisted on letting the youngest members of the senior squad have their opportunities, and they had taken them with a healthy appetite. The quarter-final round brought Arsenal up against Manchester United at Old Trafford. Coming not long after the League battle, this was billed as another one waiting to happen. However, both Wenger and Ferguson clearly had more important competitions on their mind. Arsenal's team was again full of youngsters and they got caught out after less that twenty seconds by the swift-moving David Bellion. It was the only goal. Wenger and Ferguson exchanged a cold shaking of hands.

The real issues of mid-winter were concerned with keeping Chelsea within reach and the Champions' League. A 3-0 win over Birmingham was a confidence-building if uncharacteristically laboured performance. Wenger had sprung a surprise in dropping Lehmann and putting the Spaniard Manuel Almunia in goal. He decided to stick with him for the match against Rosenborg. Other changes were not voluntary. Vieira and Lauren were both suspended. Gilberto Silva, Edu, van Persie, Cygan and Aliadiere were all injured.

A win against Rosenborg, who had already been eliminated, and Arsenal would be through. In the event they not only went through but did so as leaders of the group with a 5-1 win that included three goals in the first half an hour and a 4-1 lead by half-time. Fabregas and Bergkamp linked superbly. Reyes and Henry were unstoppable. In the end, the crowd chanted "Bring on Chelsea". On the following Saturday, the visit of Chelsea to Highbury was previewed as the likely game of the season. It lived up to the publicity. Henry was magnificent and twice put Arsenal into the lead. Two of the youngest members of the side, Fabregas and Mathieu Flamini, were outstanding. Pires responded to criticism about his commitment by turning in one of his most determined performances.

Arsenal took the lead within two minutes. Henry made light of Chelsea's reputation for locking up the defence. Almunia was then beaten somewhat tamely by Terry. When Pires was nudged to the ground, Henry accepted the referee's invitation to take the free-kick quickly and scored. Chelsea responded in the second half in the manner of future champions. Gallas beat Cole to head to Gudjohnsen who, in turn, headed in the equaliser.

Wenger had been living with the knowledge that the FA were still looking into his conduct at the League match against Manchester United. Just before Christmas, he was presented with a record £15,000 fine and severely reprimanded after being found guilty of improper conduct. The FA had looked into his remarks accusing van Nistelrooy of being a cheat.

Around the turn of the year, performances were altogether smoother. After Chelsea had been held, there were wins over Portsmouth, Fulham, Newcastle and Charlton. But Chelsea were still five points ahead. And that became seven when Manchester City drew 1-1 at Highbury. Arsenal had been without Reyes, Campbell and Lauren but that was no excuse for a lazy-looking effort and missed chances. Wenger admitted that he thought Henry was looking tired and so rested him and several others for the third round of the FA Cup against Stoke City. A depleted side scraped through 2-1.

A long-term injury to Gilberto Silva had been a cause of defensive problems. Although the Brazilian had never won the full appreciation of the fans, he had been involved in only five defeats in sixty-seven League matches, which proved something.

The moment when Arsenal must have known that retaining the Championship title was beyond them came in mid-January when they went to Bolton and lost 1-0 while, at the same time, Chelsea were beating Spurs 2-0 at White Hart Lane. Although Henry was still offering wizardry there was a lack of confidence and communication. It was ironic that, two seasons earlier, Arsenal had more or less conceded their title hopes when giving up a two goal lead, also to Bolton.

Bad blood between Wenger and Ferguson continued to flow. The issue of the food-throwing incident kept returning. Wenger talked about Ferguson losing all sense of reality. Ferguson called Wenger a "disgrace" for not apologising over the incident. Finally, even the Sports Minister, Richard Caborn, implored them to stop their "pantomime" and admit that "enough is enough". Both managers agreed to end their sniping ahead of another League clash at Highbury.

In the meantime, a single goal defeat of Newcastle at Highbury, where Bergkamp scored a delightful goal and Vieira looked revived, had Wenger saying that the chase to catch Chelsea was not over. Wishful thinking. Most fans had already accepted that although their team were still involved in Europe, the FA Cup was the season's most likely target. Wolves gave them a tough challenge in the fourth round at Highbury.

There was obvious relief when Ljungberg made the finishing score 2-0 in the eighty-second minute. It was useful preparation for the visit of United in the League. Although this was the last match Arsenal would lose until the final one of the season (against Birmingham), it represented the low point. United were inspired by Roy Keane and boosted by the finishing of Cristiano Ronaldo.

Keane got stuck into Arsenal even before the match began. He and Vieira seemed about to come to blows. Keane shouted to Vieira; "See you out there", indicating to the pitch. Referee Graham Poll stepped in and told them to cool it. Poll had a busy night. United were up for combat. Arsenal were ready. Rooney was a target for abuse and severe tackles but equally ready to kick and swear back. Fortunately, there was also some eye-catching football. Vieira headed Arsenal into the lead. Giggs equalised thanks to a clever lay-off from Rooney. After thirty-five minutes, Arsenal again went ahead when Bergkamp sent a shot beneath Carroll. At half-time, Ferguson insisted that the Arsenal defence was reeling. He was right. Rooney thrived on being riled not only by the Arsenal players but their fans. He and Giggs provided the build-up that led to Ronaldo scoring. United took control. Giggs was unstoppable. He made another goal for Ronaldo and, even when Silvestre was sent off, John O'Shea lifted a shot over Almunia and Arsenal lost 4-2. Not only that, it was their first home defeat for twenty-one months. It also left them ten points behind Chelsea and two behind United.

Afterwards, Henry remarked: "Look at our bench on Tuesday; look at the United bench. We have great youngsters but it's difficult to rely on all of them in all competitions. For me, that is the key. I've been saying for a long time that we need a stronger bench to give you strength and competition". He was diplomatic enough not to mention that there was clearly a goalkeeping problem. That stung Peter Hill-Wood into denying that the burden of finding money for the new stadium had reduced the amount available for players. He said: "Arsene was offered money but said he wasn't going to buy for the sake of it. It is important to say that the new stadium finance does not impinge on him at all. The cash is totally separate".

Morale was not helped when rumours started to emerge that Chelsea wanted to buy Ashley Cole. That story ran and ran, with the rancorous undertone of alleged illegal approaches.

A match against Crystal Palace was easily won 5-1 but that was not the story that hit the headlines. Wenger had chosen a sixteen-man squad that did not contain a single English player. Not that the majority of fans really noticed or cared. They were in raptures about another superb performance by Henry after Palace began impressively. On the following day, the former Arsenal player Paul Merson called the selection a "disgrace". He explained: "For an eighteen or nineteen-year-old dreaming of playing in the big time and maybe representing his country, Arsenal's non-British sixteen was terrifying". Wenger commented: "I didn't know until I was told about it. I don't look at the passports of people; I look at their quality and their attitude". That was perfectly believable. The real concern was that the number of British-born players coming through at all Premiership clubs was pathetically small.

Meeting Sheffield United in the FA Cup had become familiar and, as always, curious. When they met at Highbury, Bergkamp was sent off. Pires gave the ten men the lead but Andy Gray equalised from the penalty spot in stoppage time. What really rankled was the fact that Wenger rested five first team players ahead of the mid-week Champions' League match against Bayern Munich in Germany. It seemed like another case of the FA Cup being devalued.

Bayern were not exceptional but still won 3-1. Kolo Toure's away goal late in the game brought Arsenal hope, though they hardly deserved it. The defence, without Campbell, had no central pillar of defiance. On the night, Oliver Kahn proved considerably the better of the two German international goalkeepers, though Lehmann was not exactly offered much cover by those in front of him. Wenger said it was Arsenal's worst performance in the Champions' League. Matters were not improved when it was announced that Reyes had been suspended for three games for violent conduct and Bergkamp also three. It got worse when van Persie was sent off in a draw with Southampton after recklessly charging into Graeme Le Saux.

Seriously depleted by injuries and suspensions, the team managed to beat Sheffield United 4-2 on penalties in their FA Cup replay. The brightest part of the performance was served up by the Dutch youngster Quincy Owusu Abeyie.

Another season of European aspirations collapsed at Highbury. After a 1-0 win over Bayern that meant a 3-2 defeat on aggregate, only Henry could look an Arsenal fan in the eye and say that he gave his all. Henry had given them hope with a second half goal but Bayern stood firm. Campbell was sorely missed but this was a performance that had the mark of a dispirited side without powerful leadership. There was talk that Vieira's mind was on yet more rumours of a move to Real Madrid. There was even more bad news when it was found that Henry had a calf strain that would keep him out for a while. For the first time, Wenger, who said the performance and the result had brought him close to tears, complained that the club had not been able to spend sufficient money on new players.

As far as the League season was concerned, the biggest frustration was that performances over the last third were generally impressive but, in terms of silverware there was only the FA Cup still available. In the quarter-finals, just three days after the dreadful show against Bayern, the team pulled themselves together. Once again they had to face the determination and physical strength of Bolton Wanderers. Referee Steve Bennett had a difficult job, taking the names of nine players and sending off Bolton's El-Hadji Diouf after only nine minutes. Even so, Arsenal, without the injured Henry, had to hang on grimly to a lead given by Ljunberg. The victory meant that they had reached their fifth successive FA Cup semi-final. Another positive aspect of the Bolton match was the performance of the twenty-year-old Swiss central defender Phillipe Senderos. The defence, without Campbell, had been struggling and, in early games, Senderos had won nothing more than the nickname "Ponderos". Now, he was beginning to show composure and authority.

Composure was not the keyword of the Cup semi-final against Blackburn at the Millennium Stadium. It was Rovers' clear intention to frustrate Arsenal at every turn. That culminated in the last minute with what looked like a deliberate elbow in the face of substitute van Persie by Andy Todd. Van Persie was magnanimous, saying later that he was unsure whether it was an accident or not. Todd said van Persie ran into his arm. Either way, by the time the incident occurred Arsenal were three up, van Persie himself scoring two in the final five minutes after Pires had scored shortly before half-time. In terms of entertainment, it was a match quickly to be forgotten, apart from a period in the second half when Arsenal strung together forty-five passes. It was highly unlikely that they would be able to repeat that against their opponents in the Final ... Manchester United.

Wenger more or less conceded the title when drawing with Chelsea at Stamford Bridge yet the performance itself was superb. Pires and Vieira were particularly effective and, despite all of the controversy surrounding him, Cole was magnificent. Wenger called Chelsea "worthy champions", even though there would be a few more days to go before the title actually crossed London. Meanwhile, Arsenal's younger players continued to impress and there were outstanding wins over Liverpool, the eventual European Cup winners, and Everton (7-0 including such a wonderful display by Bergkamp that the club's reluctance to extend his contract seemed churlish).

The Cup Final was between two teams who were only too aware that the losers would end the season without a meaningful trophy. For Arsenal defeat would also mean that they would be facing their last season at Highbury at a low ebb. Nevertheless, both teams had played some superb football. There had been a period in the middle of the season when Manchester United had taken thirty-five points out of thirty-nine, while, nearer the end, Arsenal had been the most exciting team in the division, even including champions Chelsea.

In anticipation, it seemed that the game could hinge on the fact that United had Wayne Rooney but Arsenal did not have the injured Henry. That apart, one of the crucial questions was whether Campbell's replacement in the Arsenal defence, Sendoros, would buckle under the weight of expectancy and United's attack. After all, Campbell had at last recovered from his Achilles injury and although he had since played only twice, he was available. Wenger considered him but thought Sendoros had done well enough over the final few weeks of the season to keep his place.

On the day, many of the United supporters wore black as a protest against the takeover by Malcolm Glazer. At the end of the game, the atmosphere amongst them was almost funereal. For the first time in the competition's long history, the Final was decided on penalties. Paul Scholes missed the crucial one but, in truth, United had ample chances to win the game before it reached that nerve-chilling finale.

The star of the day was undoubtedly Rooney. That he failed to score was not only surprising but unfair, since he put so much into his performance. Arsenal had little for which to be proud. Reyes seemed to have a grudge against any opponent who got near and was rightly sent off near the end. Wenger's strange choice of playing five in midfield and leaving Bergkamp as the lone permanent striker simply caused confusion. Indeed, Arsenal hardly had a shot on goal throughout the opening ninety minutes. Wenger had said that it was a day to ignore natural instinct and be cautious (strange how on other occasions he complained so much about opponents 'not wanting to play'). In the end though it was the efficient penalty-taking of Lauren, Ljungberg, van

Persie, Cole and Vieira (it proved to be his last kick for Arsenal) that won the trophy. Lehmann, who had earlier made a couple of fine saves from Rooney, added the final touch by denying Scholes.

Victory in the Final could not hide the fact that Arsenal needed to be rebuilt, and it was soon to be known that the task would have to be done without Vieira. Edu also left to join Valencia. Wenger insisted that the future was all about the highly promising young players. The fans were inclined to believe him if he was talking about a few years down the line, but the near future was of greater concern.

Although there had long been talk of Vieira leaving, and at one point he had more or less packed his bags, news that he had actually signed for Juventus before the start of the 2005-06 season still shocked supporters. He had not asked for a transfer and it was assumed that Arsenal would not be interested in releasing him, especially as the total Juventus were understood to have agreed (£6.9m rising to £13.7m over two years) was far less than the club's previous valuations. On the other hand, Wenger had something of a reputation for selling players when they still had plenty to offer, including Overmars, Anelka, and, to a lesser extent, Petit. He said: "I share the sadness with our supporters that Patrick has left but, on the other hand, I would say 'trust us and support us. We'll be strong next season. We will not disappoint you'". On his arrival in Italy, where, incidentally, he once said he would never return because of racism, Vieira expressed the opinion that by joining Juventus he would have a chance of winning the European Cup whereas at Arsenal he would not ... quite a challenge for Wenger. Henry was appointed club captain.

Wenger captured the Belarus international midfield player from Stuttgart Alexander Hleb, who began the last season at Highbury looking impressive, but he failed to sign Julio Baptista, who had scored thirty-eight goals in two seasons at Sevilla. Understandably, Arsenal fans were concerned that the squad had not been sufficiently strengthened to take on the new challenge of Chelsea and go to the new stadium with heads high.

How Chelsea had changed the transfer market, and how it reduced Arsenal's capabilities in that market, was emphasised by Wenger when he showed an interest in obtaining Shaun Wright-Phillips from Manchester City. He said: "I like Wright-Phillips very much but we are in a transfer market where you first have to let Chelsea make decisions and then come in when they have made that decision. That is because there is a price for Chelsea and a price for everybody else. It's very frustrating but it is a fact".

This was a time of dramatic changes both on and off the pitch and not even the shirts remained the same. It was decided that for the last season at Highbury, Arsenal would play home matches in the deep red colour that was worn during the very first season at Highbury (1913). A nice, nostalgic touch or a heartless ploy to extract more money from the fans, many of whom were of the opinion that the abandoning of Highbury would leave the club without a soul?

## FA CUP FINAL
### (21 May, 2005, Millennium Stadium)

### Arsenal 0 Manchester United 0 (aet)

(Arsenal won 5-4 on penalties: Van Nistelrooy scored, Lauren scored, Scholes saved, Ljungberg scored, Ronaldo scored, van Persie scored, Rooney scored, Cole scored, Keane scored, Vieira scored)

*Arsenal: Lehmann; Lauren, Toure, Sendoros, Cole, Fabregas (van Persie, 86), Vieira, Gilberto Silva, Reyes, Bergkamp (Ljungberg, 64), Pires (Edu, 104).*

*Manchester United: Carroll; Brown, Ferdinand, Silvestre, O'Shea (Fortune, 76), Fletcher (Giggs, 90), Keane, Scholes, Rooney, Van Nistelrooy, Ronaldo.*

*Referee: R Styles.*

# CHAPTER 36
## AU REVOIR

THE DEPARTURE OF A SINGLE PLAYER, even a special one, should not cause deep hurt to a major football club. But Patrick Vieira had been more than a special player for Arsenal who began their last season before the move out of Highbury with the look of a side relying on inexperienced youngsters who would have benefited from his leadership and experience. With Edu also gone (to Valencia), disproportionate responsibility was placed upon new captain Thierry Henry. Even when he did his mesmerising best, he could not depend on the defence, which had not been reinforced through the transfer market. Even so, many observers could still describe Arsenal, on their day, as the most attractive Premiership side in Britain. Writing in the *Daily Telegraph* David Miller, a discerning journalist who, unusually, also played at a high level, said their best moments were like 'cut glass'.

Losing to Chelsea in only the second game of the season was ominous, yet this was to be a term of contrasts and surprises. Only a few days later, they played beautifully to beat Fulham 4-1. Then, after a defeat by Middlesbrough, Ashley Cole said that without buying new players the club faced a difficult future. His was a worrying message. "We just have to do what we can with the squad we've got". His own season was to be curtailed by injury and although, at the time, his pessimism seemed justified, the young team's season became one of unforeseen quick progress.

In September, Sol Campbell came back after injury and Wenger admitted that, with Vieira, gone he was relying on the big defender's experience and inspiration. The manager was not to know that, within a few months, Campbell, who tends to be reclusive but had always been highly valued as a team-man on the pitch, would become a troubled soul. His two goals against Everton raised spirits all round but, in this strange season, optimism was a transient luxury. After six games, Arsenal were seventh, eleven points behind Chelsea. When Henry was injured the situation got worse, and a 2-1 defeat by West Bromwich Albion compounded the problems. The cut glass days were proving too few.

A 2-0 loss at Bolton, early in December, began an ominous decline, yet a 4-0 win over Portsmouth, at Highbury, at the end of the month contained much of the skill of earlier seasons. A goalless draw with Manchester

United at Highbury simply played into Chelsea's hands. However, in this season of such highs and lows, there was a superb performance in mid-January when Henry scored three times in a 7-0 win over Middlesbrough, managed by Steve McLaren, who was later to take over the England job. The third strike placed Henry on level terms with Cliff Bastin's all-time club record of 150 League goals. The difference was that Bastin had played three hundred and fifty games to reach his total whereas Henry had appeared in only two hundred and twenty.

The Carling Cup brought no satisfaction. Wenger put out an experienced team in the second leg of the semi-final against Wigan. Even so, the defence was exposed and Arsenal lost on away goals. In the same week, Bolton dismissed them from the FA Cup, though it took a late goal and the performance was surprisingly good in view of the fact that they did not have Henry to lead them. The 2000th game at Highbury brought a 3-2 defeat by West Ham in which Henry's beating of Bastin's League scoring record was overshadowed by unexpected drama. After several embarrassing errors, Campbell walked out of the ground at half-time. That was portrayed as a sign that all was far from well not only in the mind of Campbell but with the team as a whole.

Curiously, while many Premiership games in the first half of the season caused Arsenal more disappointment than joy, the Champions' League, which in the past had seen the occasional highlight and so many setbacks, now served as a broad hint that the young, emerging players were growing fast and might even do better in Europe than their established predecessors. Not that the veteran Bergkamp wanted to be left out. He was magical against Thun. Arsenal had to play out the game with ten men after van Persie was sent off. Bergkamp scored the winning goal (2-1) in added time. A second win came in Amsterdam against Ajax. Pires (penalty) and Ljungberg scored. Campbell was outstanding.

Henry returned after a six-week absence caused by a serious groin strain to score two against Sparta Prague and so beat Ian Wright's club record goals total of one hundred and eighty five in all competitions. Back in 1999, when Henry arrived at Highbury, the club's vice-chairman, David Dein, had given him a tape of Wright's goalscoring achievements and said: "That's what you have to do." Some challenge. Indeed, after he beat Wright's record Henry said: "I never thought I would do it".

Henry and van Persie then overwhelmed Sparta Prague at Highbury in a 3-0 win. At the same time, though, there was great concern amongst the Arsenal fans when rumours persisted that Henry might leave before the end of the season. Real Madrid and Barcelona both wanted him, as did many others.

The one hundred per cent record in the Champions' League was extended with an away win over Thun, thanks to a late penalty by Pires who, in a game against Manchester City earlier in the season, absurdly and embarrassingly tried to touch one to Henry but miskicked. A goalless draw with Ajax at Highbury should have been another victory. Henry missed a penalty. What felt particularly cruel in mid-winter was the fact that Tottenham were ahead of Arsenal in the League. When Chelsea won 2-0 at Highbury (Arsenal's first home defeat of the season) Wenger conceded "We are too far behind to challenge them now" (20 points). It was all very well having such promising players for the future as Mathieu Flamini and Cesc Fabregas but the present demanded qualification for next season's Champions' League.

None of the critics offered Arsenal much hope of defying erratic Premiership performances by beating Real Madrid in Spain in the first leg of the opening knock-out round. They had not taken into account the obvious fact that, in the Spanish League, Real were now a shadow of their past. Henry took advantage, scoring a glorious lone goal just before half-time, and so Arsenal became the first team from England to win in the Bernabeu.

The return at Highbury was one of those exciting and absorbing occasions that most American sports fans would fail to understand – a fantastic goalless draw. Goalkeeper Jens Lehmann was magnificent, and the now reliable Alexander Hleb governed midfield in partnership with Jose Antonio Reyes. Remarkably, they both upstaged Zinedine Zidane, the finest touch player of his generation. Henry was never controlled. For Real, David Beckham, ironically the only Englishman on the field, began well but faded. Afterwards, there was more criticism of Wenger for fielding an all-foreign team. Again, he said that it was not something he had considered. He remarked: "Did you mind whether Roberto Carlos was Spanish or not? You pay £50 to watch a football game – you want to see quality". It was the third time Arsenal had reached the quarter final round.

Henry said that overcoming Real was the inspiration that led to Arsenal taking their place in the final of the Champions' League. "Beating Real Madrid, the name, the place, the reputation did something in all our minds".

There was a resurgence in League form that could not have come at a better time. In the quarter-final of the Champions' League, they faced Juventus and, of course, Patrick Vieira. Before the home leg at Highbury, Wenger said he felt that Vieira would buckle under the pressure of returning to his former home. Vieira himself said he had no regrets about his move to Turin and that "the Arsenal page is over". The match itself had people saying that Arsenal had begun to write a new chapter in their own history. Fears that the club was relying too much on youngsters who would not mature until well after the move to the new stadium suddenly seemed like unnecessary foreboding.

Juventus and Vieira were humiliated. Teenager Fabregas, the boy whom many had suggested would take years to replicate the influence of Vieira at Highbury, showed a maturity far beyond his years, scoring once, virtually running the game and providing the pass that allowed Henry to score the second in a 2-0 win, which also meant that Arsenal had equalled AC Milan's European Champions' League record of achieving seven successive clean sheets. Kolo Toure organised the defence magnificently. Juventus lost their composure and finished with two players sent off. Even Robert Pires, not often a braveheart when it comes to tackling, slid in on Vieira and won the ball!

In the meantime, the club continued to be optimistic about the financial future. There was no lack of interest in the one hundred and fifty executive boxes at the new stadium, each costing at least £65,000 a season, and 45,000 season tickets were quickly spoken for. As for the future on the field, Wenger continued to search for youthful talent. Sixteen-year-old Theo Walcott was signed from Southampton for an initial £5m, possibly rising to £12m. Much as Walcott's potential was clearly worth the initial investment, it surprised everyone, including the young player himself, when he was later called into the England World Cup squad. By then, he was seventeen but he had not appeared in the Arsenal first team. The soon to depart England manager, Sven Goran Eriksson, had never seen him play a competitive match and included him on the basis of video evidence and watching him in training. Never before had Eriksson deviated from the predictable. At the time, his squad looked likely to be without Wayne Rooney, who had broken a bone in his foot, as had Michael Owen.

And so to Arsenal's return European tie against Juventus in Turin early in April. It was becoming clear that if they were to guarantee having European Champions' League football at the new stadium in the 2006-07 season it might well have to be as a result of winning that same competition this time round. Fourth place in the Premiership, which brought with it qualification, was not something they could be sure of achieving, especially as the reviving Spurs were determined to deprive them of that position. Juventus, nicknamed the 'Old Lady' of Italian football, proved to be frail in temperament and no match for the confident, exciting group of youngsters that Wenger let loose in an attempt to take Arsenal over a European hurdle the club had never previously crossed.

This was the night Arsenal began to feel confident about the future. The last thing they wanted was to leave Highbury without a final flourish. At last winning the European Cup was coming really close. After all, Liverpool had finished the previous season only fifth in the Premiership but won the ultimate European competition. Why not Arsenal? Well, there were several good reasons. By and large, this was a group of immature players supposedly taking the club through a period of transition; a collection without much experience of playing together; an assembly of emerging talents up against men Wenger warned would come at them like a hurricane. Would the new Arsenal come together as a team?

In fact, the forecasted hurricane was more of a breeze. Juventus, admittedly weakened by some absences, lost their way. Pavel Nedved, their best player, was sent off fourteen minutes from the end and, in a goalless draw, Lehmann, in the Arsenal goal, had probably his finest game for the club (one that established him as Germany's first choice for the summer's World Cup). He ensured that Arsenal achieved another clean sheet in the competition. The fans held up placards remembering Paul Vaessen, who had scored the winning goal, in Turin, twenty-six years earlier in a Cup Winners' Cup semi-final, but now they celebrated reaching the same point for the first time in a competition that really establishes a club's international status.

Tactically, Wenger got everything right, with Ljungberg replacing Pires, because of his ability to defend as well as attack, and Gilberto Silva totally reliable in front of the much improved Sonderos and the rest of the defence. Fabregas again showed that he was developing at a pace. The only downside was that Reyes received a yellow card that would keep him out of the first leg of the semi-final, which was to be against Villarreal, a Spanish club without long pedigree, though expensively assembled and not to be underestimated.

In spite of Real Madrid's decline, Spanish football was still formidably good. Even if they came from a comparatively small town and were virtually unknown to British fans, Villarreal had beaten Internazionale in the quarter-finals and had a number of quality players.

The semi-final first leg was the last European game Arsenal played at Highbury and the last floodlit game in any competition. Wenger said it would be an enormously emotional occasion. As the day of the special match and departure from the old stadium came closer, he spoke for everyone who loved Highbury. "I sensed that there was a special soul in the stadium because it is a little bit strange and you cannot have that feeling anywhere else. I feel that part of my own soul is there. When you first arrive at Highbury you do not expect it – you are saying 'where is the stadium, where is the stadium?' And then suddenly you are in front of it. It is in the middle of the City. It is something that I love about English football. A stadium that sits among the streets of houses."

If the fans were becoming more and more nostalgic about Highbury, they were increasingly worried about a future without Henry who had not committed himself to remain with the club when they moved to Ashburton Grove. Nonetheless, he too reflected on what the ground meant to him. "It's difficult for me to talk about Highbury because you have to go out there and play. My goalscoring record there makes it very special for me. The pitch is so small compared to others, and usually I need more space to run, but I find myself really happy there. I have some great memories. It's something special to play there. It's difficult to put into words. It's a feeling I have. People cannot say the word Arsenal without mentioning Highbury".

In the rebuilt team that Wenger had now taken to the verge of the European Champions' League final there were several comparative newcomers who had blossomed in a short space of time. Alexander Hleb was among the best. A native of Belarus, he had been invited to join Vfb Stuttgart but was persuaded to choose Arsenal because he liked their "passing style". He had always played in central midfield. Wenger wanted him to play wide right. As on so many previous occasions, the manager was right. Hleb's reliability allowed Emmanuel Eboue to settle into the team behind him.

Victory over Villarreal did not come in a great, fitting ending to Arsenal's years of European football at Highbury. It was not a match of huge drama and, in truth, Arsenal did not play particularly well. They won 1-0 … sounded familiar! The scorer, shortly before half-time, was central defender Toure, who symbolised the new faces, new spirit and fresh ambition. The goal was set up, almost inevitably, by Henry who did not have one of his more breathtaking games. He did what was needed at the right moment, providing Hleb with the pass that ended with a cross that provided Toure with the winner. The star of the last night was Gilberto who completely overwhelmed Juan Roman Riquelme, the Villarreal player Wenger feared could cause a whole lot of problems.

Wenger was still troubled, as were many people behind the scenes. For Arsenal to move to the new stadium without the promise of competing in the top European competition would be a massive moral and financial disappointment. As the domestic season moved towards its close, fourth place in the Premiership was held by Spurs, and had been for some time. Arsenal badly needed to displace them to rest assured of Champions' League football next season. The pressure was turning Wenger from a generally mild-mannered, comparatively undemonstrative manager to one looking nervous, worried and not talking in the rational, considered way that had set him apart from most others in the Premiership.

The last of all Highbury clashes with Spurs, who were four points ahead, came only a few days before the return European game with Villarreal. Wenger was torn between the importance of the two targets but said: "We must win or our chance may be gone. You can't plan to win the Champions' League". He had never lost at home to Spurs yet the pressure had never been as great. Ashley Cole, with a long-term injury, and Campbell (who had suffered a broken nose after returning to duty following his walk-out and ankle and toe injuries) were not in contention.

Arsenal's fame had been built on the dependability of their defences. Now one had been cobbled together. Against predictions, Toure, Senderos, Eboue and, most remarkably of all, the former midfield player appearing as a right-footed left back, Matthieu Flamini, were linking well. Flamini was not at his best against Spurs but, apart from that, he played a big part in changing Arsenal's season for the better. They were reliably supported in goal by Lehmann, whose experience made him the elder statesman, even if he still had the odd moment of juvenile behaviour. It was a group that almost overnight turned from a makeshift line to a semblance of the defence that George Graham had put together in the early 1990s, although, rightly, Nigel Winterburn suggested they should be judged over a period of ten years not half a season.

With the European game in mind, Wenger had Henry, Fabregas and Eboue on the bench. Bergkamp and Hleb were not even in the squad. He was gambling with the short and long-term future. Spurs controlled the first half. A 1-1 draw suited them more than Arsenal. Wenger was convinced, or so he said, that Tottenham's goal, by Robbie Keane, should not have been allowed because when two Arsenal players, Gilberto and substitute Eboue, collided and fell, he believed that Spurs should have kicked the ball out of play. The referee, the excellent Steve Bennett, looked back and saw that neither player had a serious injury. He allowed play to go on and it was a matter of whether Spurs had come to the same conclusion. Rather than kick the ball out of play, they elected to continue the attack from which Keane scored.

Wenger was furious. When the gentlemanly Tottenham manager, Martin Jol, claimed not to have seen the incident, Wenger accused him of being a liar, which was a bit rich for someone who himself had so often claimed not to have been watching when his own players transgressed. Either way, Henry then scored a fantastic, outside-of-the-foot equaliser. Spurs were reduced to ten men after the tetchy Edgar Davids was sent off.

The prospect of needing to win the European Cup rather than qualifying for the following season's competition through a League position may not have been turning Wenger into a nervous wreck but it was certainly wrecking the composure that, in earlier seasons, he had little difficulty in retaining (apart from when Arsenal were playing Manchester United).

The club had now achieved a European run of nine clean sheets. Villarreal had got to the semi-finals as the lowest scoring side ever reach this far, claiming only eight goals. And it may have seemed that there should be no problem in again stopping opponents from scoring, but the visit to the small industrial Spanish town, with its tight, atmospheric stadium, with only a one goal advantage was a far greater challenge than it appeared. Whether to go all out and score an away goal, which would have effectively knocked the spirit out of Villarreal, or sit tight on the single goal advantage taken at Highbury … that was the question. Were the young men of this emerging Arsenal capable of sitting tight in the manner of the old defence that Tony Adams had so often guided through tight situations?

The quandary was made worse by the fact that Senderos had been injured against Spurs. Wenger had to decide whether Campbell, who had missed three months of the season and only just recovered from an operation on his broken nose, was ready to pick up the fragments of his career and re-establish himself as a rock in central defence. The manager explained his gamble. "Don't forget Sol was in central defence when we had our forty-nine game unbeaten run. That's why we all have complete confidence in him. I agree that he has shown a weakness in his life on that day against West Ham. But the other players trust him". So Campbell played, not outstandingly well but this was a game in which only one player rose to great heights of personal achievement – Lehmann.

To be a German with an English club inevitably means listening to a lot of bad old jokes and comments that are not intended to be offensive yet must become tiresome. The story goes that in a League game against

Southampton Lehmann had deliberately antagonised several of their players, as he tends to do. As the referee walked alongside Vieira, he said: "They don't seem to like him, do they". Vieira is reported to have replied, tongue in cheek: "No, we don't like him either. He's German"

Ask any current generation Arsenal player about the way they like to take on their opponents and they will say: 'We like to play football', meaning that they would prefer not to mix it physically nor be ultra-defensive. On the other hand, there have been several important occasions on which Wenger has insisted on caution. That was clearly the instruction in Spain. He wanted no risk takers. The European Cup was no longer on the far horizon. It was over the next hill. This was not a time to seek compliments about how prettily they played and how many successive passes were strung together. The wow factor was not a priority.

The El Madrigal Stadium was intimidating. To defend a single goal lead and, at the same time, give Villarreal's best player, Juan Roman Riquelme, almost as much space as he wanted could have been an invitation to dismissal. Villarreal had twelve shots on goal; Arsenal two. Flamini left the contest early with a hamstring injury. In spite of the fact that Toure was outstanding in his determination to hold on to the lead achieved at Highbury, and Gilberto tackled with precision and venom, the Arsenal fans got more and more nervous. Fortunately, Villarreal's finishing was no better than had been expected and Lehmann safely coped with any real danger that came his way. More than that, when, with two minutes remaining, the referee wrongly decided that Gael Clichy, who was a bit ring rusty after being out of first team action since November, had brought down Guillermo Franco (who clearly fell without any real impact), he had to face a penalty.

If Lehmann failed to save, the game would almost certainly go into extra-time, and who knows what would have happened. He stood large and confident as the already frustrated Riquelme moved forward to take the kick. There is a vague precept in football that if the penalty taker is not absolutely convinced that the referee's decision was justified, he tends not to be wholehearted with his opportunity. Be that as it may, certainly Riquelme's shot was not the best that Lehmann had faced but he still had to anticipate its direction. He did so and drove the ball out. On the most demanding night in Arsenal's European history, he had answered the biggest demand of all. Throughout the match, he had put up with being bombarded by missiles from the home fans. He had returned their ire without saying a word. At the same time, he had justified Wenger's earlier decision to return him to the team after Manuel Almunia seemed to have established himself as first choice. And added to all that, he had overtaken the European Champions' League goalkeeping record of six hundred and sixty eight unbeaten minutes previously held by Edwin van der Sar.

Here in Spain was proof that Arsenal's loss of Vieira had been overcome. Febregas, Toure, Gilberto, Flamini, Eboue, Senderos and Hleb were now at the heart of the new Arsenal. Henry came to the conclusion that "we showed we are not just a team that can win by playing good football. We can also play badly and win". That has been a contributing fact in the success of many a successful team.

So now, at last, Arsenal had the opportunity to overcome the enduring blemish in their cv – failure to win the European Cup. The last barrier would be the greatest. Barcelona, generally considered to be the most talented club side in the world, had got through 1-0 on aggregate against AC Milan. For the uncommitted, it was not so much Barcelona v Arsenal but Ronaldhino v Henry. The best restaurants in Paris, where the final was to be played, could not serve up anything more appetising.

Steve Tongue, the *Independent on Sunday* Football Correspondent, summed up Arsenal's situation: "Given what was expected at the start of the season from a squad perceived to be on a downward curve, there can be no doubt that achieving so much in Europe has to count as a huge bonus ... For the young players to have gained so much valuable experience, and reacted so well to it was far more than anyone at Highbury had a right to expect last August."

Wenger said: "I am not shocked but pleasantly surprised by the progress of the team. Something we've missed since I started here was to do well in the Champions' League, and as long as you don't do it, people will always question that". Looking to the final, he said: "Now let's finish the job so there's a continuity. I don't feel it's the end. I feel it's the start of a new era because players like Fabregas, Sendoros, Flamini, Eboue and van Persie, if they have a Champions' League final at that age, it's a start for them".

The fear that Spurs would snatch the fourth qualifying place for the following season's Champions' League and put Arsenal under even greater pressure continued even until the last match of the season. Not that it showed on the pitch. In the run-up to the end, the new team played some scintillating football, with Henry scoring sensational goals. In fact, every time Henry conjured another the fans rejoiced but at the same time wondered whether he had simply made Barcelona more determined to prise him away. At least they could be sure that Wenger would be staying. It was reported that he had been the first to be approached by the Football Association to become the next England manager. Presumably, Arsenal's vice-chairman, David Dein, who was closely involved in discussions over the appointment, knew Wenger would turn them down and remain loyal to his club contract.

Wenger approached the last match at Highbury, against Wigan, in a black mood. The team had beaten relegated Sunderland 3-0 at the Stadium of Light, where Henry was again magical, but a badly mistimed tackle by Sunderland's Dan Smith left nineteen-year-old Abou Diaby with a broken ankle. Wenger later talked about possible legal repercussions. On the positive side, Ashley Cole returned for the first time since January and played well as a substitute midfielder.

UEFA put Spurs under pressure by saying that there would be no place for them in the following season's Champions' League if Arsenal won the Cup in Paris and they finished fourth in the Premiership. The build-up to Highbury's final curtain fall was getting more and more tense. Beating Manchester City 3-1 away meant that, on the following Sunday, if West Ham, who were looking forward to appearing in the FA Cup Final, were still sufficiently determined and focused to at least hold Spurs to a draw, Arsenal would take a Champions' League place – provided they beat Wigan.

The day itself brought an extraordinary combination of emotion, drama and a strange twist. Spurs' manager, Martin Jol, liked to have his team stay in an hotel before away matches, even if they were playing in London. So there was nothing unusual about doing that on the night before meeting West Ham at Upton Park. According to newspaper reports, he was woken by the club doctor at 5am and told that a number of the players he had selected for the match were suffering from food poisoning. For several hours it seemed that the game might have to be called off. In the end, Premier League officials decided that the club ought to have a sufficient number of players available to go ahead.

Irrespective of what was happening elsewhere, there was a feeling that this would eventually be Arsenal's day. How could the planned Highbury party after the game against Wigan be pooped either by the opposition or Spurs at Upton Park? How could Henry fail to seize this moment in history and score a winning goal? As it happened, he scored three, but what an afternoon of tension before he could finally sit back with his Highbury memories while at the same time perhaps mulling over whether he was ready to commit himself to the club for another season, or more.

Wigan, resolute, well organised and able to play constructive football, were not ready to let Arsenal celebrate without one last challenge. That said a lot about them and the team honesty of English club football (individual honesty when it comes to trying to cheat referees is another matter). Equally, West Ham, who had good reason to hold back in readiness for the Cup Final, were determined not to give Spurs an easy time, whether or not they were a sickly bunch.

At Highbury, which was bursting with emotional sound, there were three goals in the opening ten minutes. Pires took Arsenal into the lead with a second stab at the ball after Mike Pollitt had saved his first attempt. If the home crowd welcomed that high on the decibel scale, they increased the volume when hearing that West Ham had taken the lead at Upton Park. Then Arsenal gave away a weak goal when failing to beat out David Thompson's free-kick. Paul Scharner was able to equalise when the ball went loose. Wigan consolidated, playing the ball around neatly and, as far as Arsenal and their fans were concerned, annoyingly.

Reyes made claims for a penalty when he fell as Chimbonda slid the ball away from him. The referee, Uriah Rennie, would have none of it. However, Rennie was lenient when Campbell, still not back to full alertness, took down Jason Roberts. That hardly mattered because, in the thirty-third minute, Wigan took the lead. Thompson hit a free-kick from a distance. He had little hope of success but Lehmann had been demanding more players in the wall. He was right. The ball went through a gap. Even so, he was unusually slow to react and the ball flew past him. To be fair, he had played well enough all season (not least at Villarreal) to be excused that error.

Henry, we need you, was the thought that must have been dominating the minds of thousands of Arsenal fans at the game and watching on television. The telepathy worked. Pires offered him a delightful through pass and he ran on to score a goal that for some would have been easy physically and yet too difficult mentally. There is no such thing as an open goal if the mind gets in the way.

Suddenly elation at Highbury turned to deflation. The fans heard that Jermain Defoe had scored for Spurs. Although that still meant Arsenal were holding fourth place, the nerves were painfully stretched. But Teddy Sheringham later missed a penalty for the Hammers (bringing the usual unsupported conspiracy theories, since he was a former Spur) and Henry was soon in centre stage at Highbury, as he had been so often before.

First he intercepted a poor Wigan back pass and dribbled round Pollitt to score. Then he was more or less offered his hat-trick. Wigan's Andreas

Johansson and Arsenal's Freddie Ljungberg had only just arrived as substitutes when Johansson fouled the Swede in the penalty area and was sent off without having touched the ball. For the penalty, Pollitt dived one way and Henry placed the ball the other, thus achieving his seventh hat-trick for the club. He dropped to his knees and kissed what he had said was always the best pitch in England. By appropriate coincidence, the first hat-trick ever scored at Highbury had occurred ninety-two years previously and was achieved by another Henry, Henry King, who was playing against Grimsby. What the fans needed to know was whether Henry's kiss was his own farewell to Highbury and the club itself.

Wenger had not been swayed by the emotion of the day. It was not until he was confident that his team would win that he sent on Bergkamp for his last competitive performance for the club (he did not come off the bench in the Champions' League final). The fans responded with massive appreciation, and so they should because this was a player who, more than any other, had been the jewel around which the Wenger era had been built.

This final victory was Arsenal's 2,010$^{th}$ and, in it, Henry's third goal was the 4,038$^{th}$. Meanwhile, West Ham held on at Upton Park for a 2-1 win and Arsenal were released to enjoy the rest of the evening, which was described as a party. More accurately, it should have been called a 'wake' to the memory of Highbury. Tottenham felt particularly hard done by and later challenged the Premier League officials over the decision that their game had to go ahead. The appeal was rejected.

As the final minutes of Highbury's life ebbed away, more than eighty players from many eras paraded on the pitch. Among them was Alf Fields, who had been playing for the club sixty years earlier; and Arthur Milton, one of those men from a generation in which it had been possible to play football and cricket at international level. Obviously, Ian Wright got the greatest ovation and enjoyed the day in his usual extravagant fashion. At the end of the evening, a television shot of Ashley Cole, Robert Pires and Thierry Henry sitting on the podium in the middle of the pitch after most of the fans had gone left a confusing impression. Were they savouring not only the final moments of Highbury but their last as Arsenal players?

Among those who believed that Henry was saying farewell was Gary Lineker who said he had a strong feeling that Henry would be at Barcelona in the following season. His theory was that if Henry had made up his mind to stay he must have been aware that to say so would have given the whole team a lift before the Champions' League final. As a former Barcelona player himself, he said he knew that of all the clubs in the world, Barcelona and

Real Madrid were the two to which great players truly aspired.

Noticeably, during the emotional evening there were lots of references to the move to "Ashburton Grove" but few to the "Emirates Stadium".

The preamble to the Champions' League final brought a welter of predictions, opinions and player interviews. Ljungberg was a popular subject for the interviews. After all, only Bergkamp had served the team longer in European competition. He made an interesting observation about the team's progress to the final whereas in the Premiership a lot had gone wrong. "In the League we struggled a bit when we played physical teams. Perhaps in the Champions' League you're not allowed to play as physical and that has suited us". Also, he suggested that because of their League position they had been treated as underdogs in Europe, which may have helped. "In the past a lot of teams tried to stop us from playing football and didn't play their own way. This year they think 'we'll beat Arsenal, we'll play our own game' and that suited us. The way we pass and play we've been able to go at them".

The final had one special magnetic appeal and it was, of course, whether Henry, returning to his home city of Paris, could upstage Barcelona's Ronaldinho, the best player in the world. The point about Ronaldinho was that while other players could be clever with the ball, they usually did so in safe areas and only occasionally delivered the final damaging pass or shot. Ronaldhino could entertain the fans and deliver at the same time. While Henry would have a smile on his face only when the job was done, Ronaldinho even seemed happy to smile in the face of adversity.

A Spanish journalist, Angel Alonso, explained Ronaldinho's influence at Barcelona. "He arrived when Barca were mired in desperation and became a miracle-maker, lifting the club back on to the big stage. But more than that, he brought humour back to the fans; the self-esteem; the good football; the pleasure of the beautiful game. He is the best present Barca ever had".

Wenger had been immensely relieved to know that come what may in Paris, Arsenal were in the next season's Champions' League. He explained: "There will be one hundred per cent less pressure. The biggest pressure you always face in football is the question of what happens if you fail". He had the feeling that once his players knew they had no chance of winning the Premiership, they were determined to concentrate to the full on the Champions' League. On the eve of the final, he said he was convinced that the result would depend more on the way Arsenal attacked than the way they stopped Barcelona. "We don't man-mark", he said. Even so, a huge responsibility seemed likely to fall upon Eboue's young shoulders. As right back, he was the one with the perceived task of frustrating Ronaldinho. However, Arsenal's fear was that Barcelona were far from a team with only one match winner. Danger could come from a spread of sources.

On the day before the final, thousands of Arsenal fans arrived in Paris and spent the evening enjoying themselves along the Champs Elysees. That was probably why, on the afternoon of the game, most of them were still in their hotels, while Barcelona supporters gathered beneath and around the Eiffel Tower and outside the stadium where ticket touts were anticipating that prices shortly before kick-off would reach £2,000.

Neither Wenger nor Barcelona's manager, Frank Rijkaard, planned to announce their teams until as late as possible. Would Arsenal attempt to control their illustrious opponents by having five in midfield? Would Pires come in for Reyes, who had started eleven of the twelve Champions' League matches but was not a 'holding' player?

Arsenal seemed in no hurry to get to the Stade de France. They arrived just as some officials were looking uneasy, wearing "where are they"? expressions. When Wenger handed in his team sheet, the only doubt was cleared up. Pires was in from the start. It would be five in midfield.

The bonhomie between the players as they took to the pitch was remarkable. Henry, the boy from an impoverished area, just outside the city, and Ronaldinho, brought up in similarly unpromising surroundings in Porto Alegre, hugged. Wenger, back in the land of his birth and football education, looked nervous and proud.

The final was billed as the most enticing in decades. Nobody could have predicted that the thoughtlessness of two men would all but ruin it as a true test of ability and devalue it as a spectacle. Not that there was any lack of drama. First there was a tactical surprise from Barcelona. After the kick-off, Ronaldinho immediately moved to the middle of the pitch, foregoing his preference to sweep in from the left. Sammuel Eto'o, leading scorer in the Spanish League, took up a left side attacking position. Eboue was probably not unhappy to see that his huge task of subduing the genius of Ronaldinho was not going to happen, at least until Rijkaard later realised that his tactics were not working and changed to the normal system.

Arsenal began positively; Barcelona apprehensively. Henry quickly caught the eye by making several crafty runs that, nevertheless, had no positive ending. In one moment that had the Arsenal fans believing anything was possible, he controlled a firmly struck pass from Eboue and moved in to face Victor Valdes in the Barcelona goal. However, his shot crashed against Valdes' legs. All the while Gilberto stood firm and determined against his fellow countryman, Ronaldinho, who was not to have one of those performances that catch the breath and bring comparisons with the best players of all time.

Deco became the one Arsenal really had to watch. Lehmann reliably stopped him but then, in a moment of match-changing mental carelessness, both goalkeeper and referee, Terje Hauge, a Norwegian, turned the ascending intensity and anticipation of a memorable engagement of skills into a battle of attrition unrelated to what might have been.

Lehmann moved out as Eto'o moved in towards the penalty area. Lehmann tackled low with his feet but was beaten. Rashly and damagingly, he took a grab at Eto'o's foot. Eto'o, clearly unbalanced and not acting, fell. Contact had been made just outside the penalty area. Barcelona were not about to stand and appeal. Instead, Ludovic Giuly swept the ball away and into the net, but the referee had already blown for the free-kick, absurdly not waiting to see whether Barcelona would score anyway. Lehmann knew what was coming. Eto'o had been on clear path to goal. The referee applied the letter of the law and brought out the red card to make Lehmann the first player ever to be sent off in a European Cup final.

Hauge was widely criticised by impartial commentators and Arsenal fans alike for failing to use his commonsense, though the same could be said of Lehmann. The day after the final, the referee admitted that he had made a mistake by not letting the game continue after the foul. Had he done so the goal would have been given and Lehmann's punishment only a yellow card.

So now we had a different match. For the remaining seventy-two minutes, it would be ten men, some really only boys, against the most majestic of all club sides. Manuel Almunia took Lehmann's place (he had not played a first team game for four months). Pires, who wanted so much to impress in his native France and in what was rumoured to be his last match for Arsenal, was called off, sobbing with frustration.

After all of this, and to Arsenal's massive relief, Ronaldinho hit the free-kick wide. Suddenly there was a completely different atmosphere. Bonhomie was forgotten. Tackles got tougher. Eboue received a yellow card for felling former Arsenal man Giovanni van Bronckhorst, and all the time Henry was being bruised by tackles from behind that the referee either did not see or chose to ignore. Yet if Arsenal were aggrieved about the sending off, they were enormously fortunate in the thirty-seventh minute when Eboue fell without being touched by Carless Puyol. The referee was taken in (he really did have a stinker). Henry sent over the free-kick. Campbell had risked leaving his own defensive lines and climbed high above Barcelona's comparatively small defenders to head in a goal that in an instant erased memories of the disturbing, mind troubled, body damaged days of his personal season.

If there had ever been a script for this game, it had already gone through the shredder. Naturally, Barcelona now became an armada. Henry had to be left even more isolated upfield as the Arsenal defence, with Toure commanding, battled to hold the slender lead. When Henry did get possession, understandably he often seemed to wilt under the pressure of the situation. Whereas on other days, against lesser opposition, he would have skipped past a moderate goalkeeper like Valdes and slide a shot confidently into the net, here there was no final flourish.

And so Barcelona eventually got the victory that perhaps, even if the match had not been deformed by the sending off, they would have achieved anyway. Who knows? As the rain poured down and thunder rumbled, Ronaldinho, who produced an occasional cameo of his skills, looked bedraggled and tentative. Barcelona had always maintained that they were not a one-man team. Unquestionably that was so. Substitute HenrikLarsson came on and took his place in the spotlight. After seventy-six minutes, he accepted Eto'o's pass and slipped the ball past Almunia who, four minutes later, suffered the indignity of having a shot from another substitute, Juliano Belletti, go between his legs. Larsson had been the deft provider. Belletti had never previously scored for Barcelona. Almunia could be excused because, earlier, he had made some fine saves and an exceptional one from Eto'o.

By the end, Arsenal had given the last drop of energy simply denying Barcelona what could have been a comfortable victory. Thoughts of a grand entry into their new stadium holding the European Cup had gone. Anger, fatigue, disappointment all welled up in the minds of players and fans alike and, uncharitably, burst out in a torrent of despairing vitriol from Henry who criticised the referee, said Ronaldinho and Eto'o were virtually absent from the game and that he had been fouled unmercifully. "They kicked me all over the place but I was the one who got a yellow card. No disrespect to Barcelona, but we were the better team when it was eleven v eleven". They were hardly the comments of a player talking about possible future colleagues.

On arriving back in England, most Arsenal fans did not want to look back at the events in Paris and were more concerned with waiting upon Henry's decision whether to stay with the club. A few who travelled with the team heard him speak on the plane's public announcement system. To their relief, he said "we" would come back stronger next season. It was the biggest hint he had given that he intended to stay. The following day, it was announced that, having signed a new four-year contract worth a reported £130,000 a week, he intended to lead the team out for the first Premiership match at the multi-million pound Ashburton Grove. In today's football, investing in the future is frighteningly expensive.

## CHAMPIONS' LEAGUE FINAL
(17 May, 2006, Stade de France)

### Arsenal 1 (Campbell) Barcelona 2 (Eto'o, Belletti)

*Arsenal: Lehmann; Eboue, Toure, Campbell, Cole, Hleb (Reyes), Gilberto Silva, Fabregas (Flamini), Ljungberg, Pires (Almunia – in goal), Henry. Substitutes not used: Bergkamp, van Persie, Sendoros, Clichy.*

*Barcelona: Valdes; Oleguer (Belletti), Puyol, Marquez, Van Bronckhorst, Edmilson (Iniesta), Van Brommel (Larsson), Deco, Giuly, Eto'o, Ronaldinho. Substitutes not used: Jorquera, Motta, Xavi, Silvinho.*

*Referee: T. Hauge (Norway).*

# CHAPTER 37
## ARSENE WENGER – THE BEST?

WHEN ARSENE WENGER BECAME ARSENAL'S MANAGER in September, 1996, it was forgivable for the fans to ask "Arsene Who"? Five hundred and more matches later, there was no longer any question that Arsenal had appointed a man of exceptional ability. The proof was in the record book: three Premiership titles, four FA Cups, four Charity (Community) Shields and a season without a League defeat. His teams had also finished runners-up in the Premiership five times and reached the finals of another FA Cup, also the European Champions' League and the UEFA Cup, but were beaten. In his first full season in charge, Arsenal achieved the Double and they repeated it in 2001-02. They also beat Nottingham Forest's record-breaking run of forty-two unbeaten League games and extended it to forty-nine. None of this seemed remotely possible to the fans who in 1996 had anticipated that Bruce Rioch's replacement would be one of the most famous names in football. Among those that had been mentioned in the Press was Johan Cruyff, but the media had not taken sufficient notice of the fact that Patrick Vieira and Remi Garde had already agreed to join Arsenal. Both had said that they were keen to work with one Arsene Wenger, even though, as far as the fans were concerned, he was not even in the running.

The success that Wenger has brought to Arsenal has been the result of a complete revolution in the way the players play, the way they live, the way they train and the way they have been brought together by his dealings in the transfer market. In spite of having less money to spend than the managers of Manchester United, or, more recently, Chelsea, he has generally bought and sold well. His signing of Nicolas Anelka cost a mere £500,000 but Arsenal received £23m when the troublesome but wonderfully talented goalscorer went to Real Madrid. With some of that money, he bought Thierry Henry but, before that, he had ensured that Arsenal put in a successful bid for Vieira, who was going nowhere with AC Milan but took Arsenal more or less everywhere except to a European Cup final.

With such an illustrious record, Wenger has often attracted comparison with Herbert Chapman. Realistically, taking into account the vastly different eras, the way football has changed, the pressures of the modern game as a result of television, and so on, making that judgement is almost impossible. Suffice to say, the only negatives in Wenger's career at Highbury are his prolonged inability to replicate domestic excellence in European competition (which was not something Chapman had to face); his slow reaction to the need to replace the tightest defence in the League, and his petty, unbecoming spat with Sir Alex Ferguson. That last weakness, which both managers probably saw as nothing more than a psychological battle that would be well received by the players, harmed their reputations and added ammunition to the critics of football who, with justification, interpreted it as further evidence that the game's leading figures were setting poor examples to Britain's young people.

On the positive side, which was substantial, perhaps his value to Arsenal and the whole game in Britain was best summarised in 2005 by the former Liverpool manager Gerard Houllier, who himself had done so much to raise the standards of French football. Although Houllier and Wenger are close friends, the tribute is no less acceptable. He said: "Arsene is a clever, modern coach whose record speaks for itself. When he came to England in 1996, Continental coaches were a rarity. Since arriving at Highbury, Arsene has managed to finish in the top two of the Premiership in every complete season, and adding more silverware with his successes in the FA Cup.

"When you look at his achievements I would say that he is somebody with great vision, somebody who has the right philosophy and enormous dedication to his work. I can see attributes in Arsene that you see in Sir Alex Ferguson and Jose Mourinho. They are three different characters but have many similarities in how they fulfil their ambitions. He looks quite English. He is made for the English mentality and the English game. At times, I see him as the archetypal British gentleman. As a manager, he fulfils what is required for the job. I regard him as somebody who quickly puts things into perspective and somebody who is very loyal to those around him".

Those making a more cautious analysis of Wenger might point out that his determined loyalty to the players was also the reason why he became known as the manager who always happened to be looking elsewhere when those same players acted injudiciously on the field. In that respect, he was not alone ... far from it. He will be remembered for turning Arsenal into a truly cosmopolitan organisation that extracted some of the world's best players and, in most cases, imbued them with loyalty to what, for them, was a 'foreign' club. Occasionally that has been questioned, especially in the case of Vieira who, because of his talent, was pursued by just about every major club in Europe. Had it not been for Wenger, he would not have stayed for as long as he did.

As for the criticism that followed a match in the 2004-05 season in which, for the first time, Wenger announced an all-foreign team, that was the consequence of his search for the best available players on the day. To suggest that he was snubbing British players was absurd. But why was the home-produced talent not available? That is the pertinent question. Was it because rich clubs do not have the inclination to search out and raise British-born players? Is there a great lack of young, promising players anyway? The answer encompasses both. And the situation is certainly not helped when young, useful players who, with proper guidance, could become older, exceptional ones are disillusioned by seeing foreign imports of questionable ability and intent brought in to create a barrier to their progress. That particularly applies to the less well-off clubs who scour the world for ready-made players with experience but, as often as not, find that they have an imminent sell-by date. The manager is at the sharp end and, although he may have influence over the whole of the club's affairs, his primary responsibility is to provide the club and the fans with the best team he can name.

An interesting assessment of Wenger has come from Professor John Williams, of the Sir Norman Chester Centre of Research on Football, who said that the Arsenal coach was as much concerned with the mental approach of the players to the game as the physical and that they could be trained to make their own decisions. Nevertheless, Wenger did not set out to bring a bunch of intellectuals to Highbury. Simply, he brought in players who believed that they could adapt their special talents to the particular demands of British football and were keen to prove it.

As for the English players he inherited, almost all say that they changed their ways because of his influence. After he left Highbury for Middlesbrough, Ray Parlour recalled the early days of Wenger's management. "When he became manager I turned over a new leaf. He said: 'If you change, I'll stay loyal'. English football culture used to be all about going out with the boys and, with me, drinking became a routine. It's a chapter in my life I wouldn't alter because we had great times but I just decided that if I wanted to stay in the game I needed to change. Arsene handles big players well. He gets great individuals playing as a team. He knows their strong and weak points and does a lot of work on ironing them out. I've only seen him angry once but we were 5-1 down. He never shouted; he'd never criticise until he had been through the video and assessed everything properly."

Tactically, Wenger is not unlike Herbert Chapman in that he believes that opponents are at their most vulnerable when they are attacking. At the slightest chance of an interception, he expects his midfield men or defenders to make instant decisions that form the starting point of counter-attacks. The square pass is not a tactic he favours, unless the receiving player can quickly turn it into something more positive. In domestic competition, that philosophy has often been devastating. Against the highest quality of foreign opponents, it was often less successful.

It has to be remembered that, throughout his time with Arsenal, Wenger has not been deprived of money but the purse has never been as deep as that into which Sir Alex Ferguson has been able to dip. In those circumstances, it would have been satisfying to say that he was able to strengthen his first team squad with home produced players. Unfortunately, only Ashley Cole came through the system to secure a regular place.

# CHAPTER 38
# IT HAPPENED AT HIGHBURY

## THE OFFSIDE RULE

IN THE FIRST QUARTER OF THE TWENTIETH CENTURY, Newcastle United's Bill McCracken and his full back partner Frank Hudspeth caught attacking players offside with worrying regularity. The Football Association talked of doing something to restore the balance between defenders and forwards. The law in those days insisted that an attacker could not be offside if three players were nearer to their own goal-line when the ball was last played. The game often became trapped in an area of the pitch not more than twenty yards either side of the halfway line. Its appeal to the public was threatened, yet it was not until 25 January 1925 that the FA accepted that they actually had to do something positive to resolve the problem.

On that Saturday, several of the leading clubs were facing an afternoon without matches. Arsenal and Chelsea had both been knocked out of the FA Cup, so the FA arranged a friendly at Highbury and carried out several experiments. During the first half, a line was drawn forty yards from each goal. Players could not be called offside if they were within that area. During the second half the referee, Mr Todman, declared that an attacking player could not be offside if only two players were nearer to the goal-line. By both methods, the number of offsides fell considerably short of the average. Mr Todman was asked by FA officials which system he preferred. He went for the two-man idea and, within the year, the new law was approved by the international federation. In the following two seasons, the number of goals scored rose by almost a third.

## BROADCASTING BEGINS

A live football commentary was first heard on the radio on 22 January 1927. The match was Arsenal against Sheffield United at Highbury but football was not the first sport to be relayed to radio listeners. A week earlier the BBC had taken their new equipment to Twickenham for a rugby international between England and Wales and the broadcast was a success. Encouraged by that, they decided to follow it up with Arsenal's next home game. The newspapers on the day of the game announced: "2.30: Community singing and Arsenal v Sheffield United Association Football Match (relayed from the Arsenal ground, Highbury)."

The commentator was Mr H.B.T. Wakelam with additional information provided by Mr C.A. Lewis. The *Radio Times* published a diagram of the pitch divided into eight squares. Mr Lewis called the number of the square as the ball moved around the pitch and Mr Wakelam described the action (this may have been the first reference to the saying "back to square one").

The experiment was another success and that season's Cup Final between Arsenal and Cardiff was also broadcast live nationally with George Allison and Derek McCulloch commentating. McCulloch was to become better known as 'Uncle Mac' on 'Children's Hour' while, of course, Allison became manager of Arsenal.

## FLOODLIT FOOTBALL

The first experiment with floodlit football took place as long ago as October, 1878, when some 20,000 people went to Bramall Lane and watched a match between two Sheffield representative teams. Although there were many more experiments at various grounds around the country, the idea was not seriously pursued because power failures in wet weather too often meant that matches had to be abandoned.

In 1930, the FA decided that floodlit football was not to be encouraged. Herbert Chapman was not alone in thinking that they were 'in the dark' to the potential. He had paid a visit to Belgium, where he saw an advanced example of lights being angled so that they covered the whole of the pitch without the shadows that had been a problem in earlier experiments in Britain.

Not put off by the FA, Chapman arranged for lights to be put up at Arsenal's training pitch adjoining the stadium and also in the stadium itself, for training purposes. Sadly, the FA refused to accept Chapman's premise that, on dark winter evenings, football grounds could become illuminated theatres of sport. It was not until 1951, long after Chapman had died, that, at Highbury, lights were first used, apart for training. Other clubs had done the same but it was at Highbury that the real potential of night football became obvious. An exhibition match between Boxers and Jockeys drew an amazing forty-thousand people.

The then Arsenal manager, Tom Whittaker, had enthusiastically pursued the possibilities of floodlit games after a visit to Brazil where it had become enormously popular. Later in the year, a friendly against Hapoel, of Tel Aviv, attracted forty-four thousand to Highbury. The drama of football under lights did indeed create a feeling of theatre. The grass looked that much greener and the white ball seemed to travel more slowly and was like a star against the night sky. The lights had been installed by the club's own electrician, Ron Franklin, who was probably the proudest man at the game. Arsenal beat Hapoel 6-1, but the result was far less relevant than the establishment of a new form of football entertainment. The *Daily Mail*'s Roy Peskett wrote:

> *The darker it became, the more you could see last night at Highbury where Arsenal staged the complete Soccer Show in colour, featuring the League side against Hapoel-Tel Aviv from Israel.*
>
> *Under the massed banks of eighty-four 1,500-watt lamps, stage manager Tom Whittaker turned producer. A few minutes before kick-off time he ordered the electricians to put on the lights at half power. The switch-on was greeted with the 'oohs' you get at a firework display.*
>
> *But, with perfect timing, he waited until the two teams were entering the field before switching on full power.*
>
> *I am certain that this moment and the spectacle which then unfolded before 44,000 people will attract many new customers to Highbury while it also opened up visions of night football played in the perfect setting.*
>
> *It was all there. The bright emerald pitch, the table-tennis white of the ball, Arsenal in their red and white and the Israel side in the light blue, the flashlights from the cameras, and the cigarette smoke vanishing into the sky above the many lights which, although bright enough to give a daylight glow, never dazzled.*
>
> *I am glad there were many high officials of the Football Association and the Football League to see this extraordinarily attractive spectacle. Perhaps floodlit League football is not very far off.*

Later that year, Arsenal played their annual friendly against Rangers under lights and the attendance was over sixty thousand, thus proving the fascination with something that, if Chapman had been supported, could have come about more than twenty years earlier. Yet it was still another five years before the FA officials finally saw the great commercial advantages of floodlit football and gave it their approval so that League games could, at last, be played after dark. By then, Wolves had played their unforgettable matches against Honved, Moscow Spartak and Moscow Dynamo under lights.

Unlike other grounds, Highbury always benefited from having all of its lights positioned facing each other along the lengths of the two main stands that ran along the length of the pitch. As a result there were no shadows.

Arsenal were in the forefront of another electrical revolution in football. Hard winters had long caused matches to be postponed. So, in the early 1950s Arsenal decided to invest in undersoil heating. It was another experiment that needed time to be perfected but, in the end, became commonplace, although the problem of clearing snow and ice from the open terraces that were still in use in those days often caused postponements when the pitch was in almost perfect condition.

## THE FIRST TELEVISED FOOTBALL

On Thursday, 16 September, 1937 live television cameras, rather than just film cameras, first appeared at a football ground. Highbury was chosen because it was close to the BBC headquarters at Alexandra Palace. The match, itself, was specially arranged between the Arsenal first team and the reserves. Since very few people actually had television sets in those days, the number who saw the extracts must have been very small. *The Times* reported: "Football at The Arsenal. A demonstration by the members of the Arsenal team at the Arsenal Stadium". It was introduced by George Allison who was not only the manager but an experienced radio broadcaster

Readers of the *Daily Herald* had already been told by their reporter Douglas Walters, who had sneaked inside the studios to watch the preparations, that televised football was about to become a reality. Yet the transmission itself went almost unnoticed and it was not until 30 April, 1938, that a whole match was televised live – the Preston v Huddersfield FA Cup Final. It was estimated that the television audience was no more than ten thousand. Regular televised football did not come about until the early 1950s.

## NOT THAT HENRY ... OUR ENRY

Highbury has occasionally been the venue for events unrelated to football. The one that stands out was held on Saturday, 21 May, 1966 when Henry Cooper took on the world boxing champion, Muhammed Ali, for the second time. When they had first faced each other at Wembley, in 1963, Cassius Clay, as he was then known, was nowhere near as famous. The 1960 Olympic light-heavyweight champion had not previously met a serious opponent. The only big name he had beaten was Archie Moore, who was forty-nine.

For their first bout, Cooper thought that Clay, then twenty-one, would be quick and dangerous but would lack experience. He was certainly not put off by the American's publicity minded antics ("I am the prettiest. I am the greatest" and so on). He was right to respect Clay's talent. In the first round, Cooper had come to the conclusion that he was facing the fastest heavyweight of all time, but he did well and it was expected that sooner or later he would land with his famous hammer blow left hook. But, in the third round, he was cut over the eye.

He had to try to finish the fight quickly and so let loose with that famous, huge left hook while Clay had his back to the ropes. The punch saw Clay slide down those ropes, but it was near the end of the round and he wobbled back to his corner where it was "discovered" that he had a split glove. There was a delay long enough to bring Clay back to his senses. He immediately went for Cooper's injured eye, opened the wound and the fight had to be stopped. Cooper had to wait nearly three years for his opportunity for revenge at Highbury.

Ali, remembering how close he had come to defeat at Wembley, prepared for a difficult fight. So hard, in fact, that he arrived in London lighter than ever before in his professional career. On the night, Cooper was allocated the home (Arsenal) dressing room. The crowd kept building up. It included Cooper's wife, Albina, who, curiously, had never before seen him fight.

As the bout started, the ring stood out, spotlit in an otherwise nearly dark stadium. Ali had insisted on a large ring. Cooper said it seemed like ten minutes before he got to the centre of it. In their first clinch, Ali showed that this time he was not going to allow himself to be caught by a sudden left hook. He held Cooper like a vice. After they broke, Cooper forced Ali back. Both jabbed, neither felt a damaging punch. That pattern continued into the second and third rounds but Cooper was well aware that, unlike when they fought before, this time Ali was much better at dealing with the inside work.

The fourth round saw Cooper flash several left hooks that missed Ali by less than an inch. The fifth round was even. The sixth brought despair for Cooper. Ali threw a right hand just as Cooper was moving forward. The blow was so heavy that he thought there had been a clash of heads. Not so. As Ali's right hand came in, Cooper also threw a punch but Ali evaded it and crashed his own on the brow of Cooper's eye. Blood spewed everywhere. Cooper knew it was bad. "You don't feel pain, you just feel the warm blood on your chest and shoulders." It began to blind him. Although the referee took a look and decided to let him go on, several more punches tore into the cut and there was no choice but to stop the fight. Cooper remained convinced that, but for weak skin tissue around the eyes, he would have won. His many fans would agree. After all, he had tested Ali who was in his prime and, arguably, was what he claimed – the "greatest".

## THE FAMILY CONNECTION

Arsenal and the Hill-Wood family go back a long way. Sir Samuel, who died in 1949, joined the club in 1919 and later became a Chairman in the old style. He allowed his managers to manage and gave advice when asked. Nevertheless, he was deeply knowledgeable about the game both on and off the field and had attended a vast number of Arsenal matches before the Second World War. He was the son of a cotton mill owner in Derbyshire and gave financial support to the Glossop team that held a place in the First Division for seventeen years. When the cotton industry failed, the Hill-Wood family moved to the south. Denis Hill-Wood, Sir Samuel's stockbroker son and all-round sportsman, succeeded him and, in turn, he was followed in the early 1980s by his son Peter, whose experience working for Hambros Bank stood him in good stead in the modern highly commercial world of football. He had become a director in 1962 when he was not thirty. Although he once spoke of his work with Arsenal as a "hobby", it has always been more than that. His famous slip of the tongue that allowed everyone to know that Arsene Wenger would be the new manager brought not criticism but a greater feeling that he was a real fan who could not wait to tell everyone the good news. His devotion to the club, and good humour, has won great respect.

## A MURDER MYSTERY

In 1939, Highbury took centre stage for a film staring Greta Gynt, Leslie Banks and Esmond Knight. Called 'The Arsenal Stadium Mystery', it was adapted from a novel by Leonard Gribble and featured Arsenal's last First Division match before the Second World War which was against Brentford who, for the purposes of the film, became the Trojans.

It was a murder mystery in which Banks, acting a detective in the extravagant style of Sherlock Holmes, had to find out who murdered an Arsenal player. Among those who appeared was the manager, George Allison, who had a short speaking part. The author, Graham Greene, gave the film great praise when he said it was as good as the enormously popular *Third Man* films, which he wrote. Others were less complimentary.

# A VICTORY REFUSED

Perhaps the strangest event in all of the years of Highbury's football history occurred on 13 February 1999. Arsenal were playing Sheffield United in the fifth round of the FA Cup. Vieira had headed Arsenal into the lead in the first half but Mercelo had equalised, giving United some hope of a draw and a replay back at Bramall Lane. But, in the last quarter of an hour several of the players found themselves bothered by tiring muscles. United's Lee Morris collapsed in the Arsenal penalty area with cramp. Arsenal cleared the ball upfield directly to United's goalkeeper Alan Kelly who immediately drew attention to Morris's problems by kicking the ball out of play over the touchline to his left. Morris's injury was obviously not exaggerated and he required several minutes' treatment. When, finally, he got up it was only to make his way off, allowing substitute Bobby Ford to come on. Only then could Arsenal take the long awaited throw-in.

Ray Parlour directed his throw not to one of his own team but in the general direction of the United goal, as is the tradition. But Nwankwo Kanu, making his first appearance for Arsenal, took it under his control and centred. The United defence hesitated in surprise. Marc Overmars received the ball and scored. Technically nothing untoward had happened. The referee, Peter Jones, was trapped in a situation out of which he had only one option. It had to be a goal. Understandably, the United players were horrified and made their feelings known to the unfortunate referee. Meanwhile, United's manager, Steve Bruce, was of a mind to call his players off the field in protest. It took six minutes for the game to be re-started. The game ended ungraciously but without further goals.

Arsene Wenger and Arsenal's Vice-Chairman, David Dein, were both deeply troubled by the outcome and the possibility of it reflecting badly on the integrity of the club. Dein quickly left his seat in the Directors' Box and went to Wenger. Dein said he felt they should offer to have the game replayed. Wenger agreed. On two previous occasions, Arsenal themselves had been the victims of similar situations when they had conceded goals to Spurs, in 1996, and Blackburn the following year, though neither incident was quite as blatant. Wenger spoke to various officials and the referee before coming to the Press Room to say: "I have offered to replay the game here at Highbury. It is the only thing I can do. I am trying to repair an accident. Kanu and all of us are very, very sad."

The FA made one of their rare, quick decisions and agreed to the offer, although that quickly raised a debate about whether a precedent would be set because the referee had been in the right and none of the Laws broken. FIFA had to be informed but finally agreed, telling both clubs to sign a statement saying that the winner of the re-match or any subsequent replay would go through to the next round. They ordered that part of the proceeds of the re-match should go to charity. Arsenal won the re-match by the same score, 2-1.

## HIGHBURY ... THE FUTURE

Unlike many famous old football grounds that in recent years have been demolished, at least parts of Highbury will be saved. Because the East and West stands are listed buildings, they cannot be destroyed but will be redeveloped as apartment blocks, with the pitch landscaped as a communal garden under which there will be a health spa and car park. In a way, all of this will only heighten the feeling of sadness that a once vibrant theatre of sport will be like a great ship destined to spend the rest of its days in some dry dock.

Arsenal decided to keep control of the redevelopment themselves, saying that they wanted to ensure that it was done with respect for the club's heritage. Some three thousand people, many of them fans and shareholders, registered as prospective buyers.

The marble hall, the entrance gates, boardroom, street lamps, iron letterbox and the whole of the East Stand's façade are all Grade II listed. So future generations will not be deprived of seeing some of the original Highbury. Some may even live there, but they will never know what it was like when it was the home of Arsenal.

# APPENDIX

# HONOURS BOARD

**First division champions**
1930-31
1932-33
1933-34
1934-35
1937-38
1947-48
1952-53
1970-71
1988-89
1990-91

**Premier League champions**
1997-98
2001-02
2003-04

**FA Cup winners**
1930
1936
1950
1971
1979
1993
1998
2002
2003
2005

**Football League Cup winners**
1987
1993

**The Managers**

| 1894-97 | Sam Hollis |
| 1897-98 | Tom Mitchell |
| 1898-99 | George Elcoat |
| 1899-1904 | Harry Bradshaw |
| 1904-08 | Phil Kelso |
| 1908-15 | George Morrell |
| 1919-25 | Leslie Knighton |
| 1925-34 | Herbert Chapman |
| 1934-47 | George Allison |
| 1947-56 | Tom Whittaker |
| 1956-58 | Jack Crayston |
| 1958-62 | George Swindin |
| 1962-66 | Billy Wright |
| 1966-76 | Bertie Mee |
| 1976-83 | Terry Neill |
| 1984-86 | Don Howe |
| 1986-95 | George Graham |
| 1995-96 | Bruce Rioch |
| 1996- | Arsene Wenger |

**Record Highbury attendance**
73,295 (v Sunderland, 9 March 1935)

**Fairs' Cup winners**
1970

**European Cup Winners' Cup winners**
1994

**Charity (Community) Shield winners**
1930, 1931, 1933, 1934, 1938, 1948, 1953,
1991, 1998, 1999, 2002, 2004.

# INDEX

250

253